The Furious Others

Ashley Baker

Genius
Book Publishing

Published by:
Genius Book Publishing
PO Box 250380
Milwaukee Wisconsin 53225 USA
GeniusBookPublishing.com

ISBN: 978-1-958727-45-4

241012 Trade

Contents

"When the dead are done with the living, the living can go on to other things," Franny said.

"What about the dead?" I asked. "Where do we go?"

— Alice Sebold, *The Lovely Bones*

"There are certain crimes that are simply too cruel, too sadistic, too hideous to be forgiven."

— John E. Douglas, *Journey Into Darkness*

Preface

This novel began from a naïve place, before I was touched with the stain of grief, an insidious, permanent tattoo that's now carved on my bones. For sufferers and victims, there's always a distinct before and after. This one is mine.

Shortly after completing my third novel, my younger brother was arrested for allegedly grievously injuring both of our parents on a cold night in January of 2023. He's charged with malice murder for the death of our father, and aggravated assault for seriously wounding our mother. He is currently awaiting trial in our small Georgia town, and the lengthy court preparations have begun. I'm told it will be years until some sort of resolution can be reached.

My nightmare included articles on national social media and a deluge of both curious and kind people's questions. I became the girl who lived through patricide, my name now associated with a label I didn't choose and never wanted. In the midst of my sadness, I thought of the words I'd written here, of the simple truth contained in these pages.

The central theme of The Furious Others *is that victims are forgotten in favor of murder and mayhem. That script, a horribly predictable story, became true for me, too. Exclusively, people asked about my brother, at the funeral, at the neighborhood pool, at the grocery store, both loudly and in whispers, with no respite found.*

They investigated his motives, his mental state, his awareness of his actions, and his weapon of choice. Arraignments were re-scheduled, and court dates found dockets, but still the focus remained on my sibling. The legal case continues to pore over his sentence, his thoughts, and his feelings.

And waiting in the wings, overlooked and half-forgotten, lies my innocent father, a career pathologist, who deserved better. As a writer, I yearned to create a better ending for my dad, a sweet and airy oblivion, quick as a blink, to send a hardworking man off into the heavens.

But life is not fiction, though in this case, my life inadvertently mirrored this novel. And so I consider it crucial that this book be published, to be read by those who've lost a loved one to violence.

My father joins the ranks of numerous casualties, their names and lives ignored in favor of the sensationalism of violence. But I choose to remember my father rather than focus on the details of what my brother allegedly did and why.

For me, this book helps to cement my father's memory, to show that I will never forget the dad I lost and continue to mourn.

Dedicated to

John Garland Boswell (1957-2023)

&

To all the survivors and mourners of those taken by violence.
May we never forget their names and their stories.

Also for my Kentucky girls: Hayley, Katie, and Mackenzie, who held
me close and kept me whole during the crisis and beyond.

Chapter 1
Jason LeDown
Date: December 2nd, 2027, location unknown

A tidal wave of fright ping-ponged in his belly, the cold creating craggy goose bumps on his skin, a shiver of something amiss. Jason rarely felt the swirl of emotions, and when he did, anger took center stage, not fear. Still, the fist of nausea in his stomach was difficult to ignore, as was the hairball of worry jammed down his throat, threatening a coup.

His short-term memory was long erased, his last recollection a question-mark half formed and just out of reach. A swift hit to his head shook nothing loose, no memories laid bare for his review. He was dressed casually in a stranger's clothes, his heartbeat two drumbeats too loud.

A mist enveloped him, smoothing out his surroundings, the same effect as a whiteout, the most serious of all snowstorms. It created a slimy sensation on his skin, of algae or glue not yet dried. *Mystical*, he thought, and chided himself, for he was a man of reason, a chemist, with a heart made for textbooks, not folklore.

But there were limits to logic, evident in this hazy space, with its spongy iridescent floor and ubiquitous florescent light, his body crouched in a space too bright. He tilted his head and saw only wispy clouds, miles of white cumulus, threatening to blind him with their radiance.

Jason closed his eyes, reaching to stroke his hair, an unconscious habit meant to steady himself. His hands found smooth skin, too slick for comfort. His black hair, once supple, was removed completely. Jason thought of Mr. Clean, with his cueball scalp and gold earring, the very picture of '80s glory, and he gagged. He wiped his hands on his pleated khaki pants, feeling contaminated by his baldness and the thick slice of vomit blooming in his throat.

Jason tested his feet, a wobbling baby giraffe. There was nothing to hold on to, and his balance wavered, but he regained his posture. Standing up straight secured his control, his size-thirteen shoes anchoring him to the ground.

To his left was a sign, tacked to nothing, suspended completely in the air. The writing was ornate, reminiscent of Old English, the script cursive and heavy-handed. He wanted to investigate how the proclamation hung by itself, to hypothesize and follow the scientific method until he understood it in full. But he assumed that time was limited in a place like this, with its magic and its nonsense, the rules dictated by fairytales. He was now hairless and quivering, so all bets were off in a place where parchment floated. His eyes drifted to the words, which he mouthed out loud, an old habit.

<u>Rules And Regulations:</u>
Welcome to Purgatory.
Yes, it is real, and you are in it.
Are you dead? Yes.
Is this the afterlife? No.
Please wait for your attendant to arrive.
Standby.

A sound, like a dog shaking off water, reverberated around him, causing the floor to vibrate. Jason fell to his knees, cowering, distaste sloshing in his belly. He was in the same bowing position as every lacky in the Old Testament right before they saw an angel. He shook his head, disappointed in his kneeling servant's pose, allergic to the deference it portrayed.

The sound shut off, and in its place was *not* an archangel.

First, Jason saw a clipboard, the muted brown familiar, then registered low, sturdy heels, suitable for lengthy walks down scuffed hallways. His eyes moved upward, onto a schoolmarm frown, her face meant for whacking knuckles with crisp wooden rulers, the self-satisfied smack alighting her every neuron.

The stranger was a petite woman, with the air of a strict librarian, sporting a silver eyewear retainer chain around her neck in lieu of pearls. Her body type was typical grandmother, thick in the waist and sturdy, except she was also floating three inches off the floor, her stance flagpole rigid. Her suit was well ironed and starched, not a crease misplaced, monochromatic save the flash of gold cinching her waist.

Jason peeked up at her through his eyelashes, awaiting instructions but remaining capitulated. She squinted at him, pulling her wire frames to her nose. She wore no jewelry, no rings to indicate possession or preference. Her glasses fogged, and she cleaned them with a monogrammed handkerchief. He couldn't make out the letters, just the glint of embroidery reflected in her lenses.

"Get up. Now," she ordered, her voice school-principal stern, no megaphone needed.

Jason stood, though he wasn't a natural rule follower, his eyes tracing invisible zigzag patterns on the illuminated floor. She cleared her throat, a soft command of respect. He decided to play along until the rules were explained. Chin to chest, he listened, broadcasting sufficient deference.

"Did you read the sign?" she queried, her voice a sneer, the stink of sarcasm dripping through each inflection.

"Yes." Brevity was enjoyed by those in command, but he added, "I mean, yes, ma'am," for good measure, to cover his bases.

His reward was a nod and a lightning crack that lit up the sky, the force of it knocking his knees together.

No rain came. A rush of wind whistled through his clothes, then disappeared, an impromptu tornado completed in thirty seconds.

Show off, Jason thought but didn't say.

"There are rules and regulations in Purgatory," she began. "I'll summarize. I'm not your spirit guide or a specter that's going to lead you down the path of your life. My name is not Ebenezer, nor is that our purpose." She smiled a predatory grin, exposing pointed canines, a wolf in a cashmere cardigan.

"I'm here to explain the rules to you, and then I will monitor you in silence. I suggest that you pay attention to what I say. It's very important, and I won't repeat it, Jason LeDown."

She was crisp, which he appreciated. Jason nodded his consent but silenced future queries. This wasn't a question-and-answer format, and she was the type who liked to lecture.

"Very well. As you read, you are dead. This is a holding zone. Essentially, it is a waiting room where everyone gathers before their afterlife begins. Depending on how things go here, next steps are formulated."

He ate his words. She wouldn't tolerate an interruption; she made that clear, with her sensible shoes and stoicism. She was meant for boarding schools, her gray bouffant a hill of tight hairspray, not a whisp out of place. He tried not to mourn his lost locks, replaced with the vulnerable glossy skin where his hair should be. Involuntarily, Jason shivered, recalling his dewy head and the grease of sweat on his palm.

"Are you with me so far? Are you paying attention?"

He waited a beat, not wanting to seem eager. Jason glanced up, then away, a show of respect found in his lack of eye contact. He was the stray dog, and he'd play his part well, as long as it suited him.

"Yes. I'm in Purgatory, a holding space to listen and learn," he parroted, monotone and military.

"Good. Now, onto the purpose of why you're here. This isn't a judgment zone. There are no pearly gates to be found here. Whatever you've done in your life has already happened, and there's no changing that script. However, this is a place where we review your life to decide your fate."

"So, Heaven and Hell and all that jazz?" Jason couldn't believe his future had been whittled into something so simplistic, so common. A smirk crept into his voice, a whiff of mockery tapdancing in his skull.

She grinned, but it was not kind. No crinkles reached her eyes; no dimple crossed her lips. Bitterness crawled out of her, her gestures a sea of cockroaches and malice, tailored for a storybook villain.

"For you? Ha! No, not for you, Mr. LeDown. Again, I urge you to save your comments for the end of this discussion. It's in your best interest to pay attention." Her voice dipped, a threat hissing through clenched teeth.

Jason acquiesced.

"The purpose of Purgatory is to evaluate your life and your relation to other people, those you hurt, and those you impacted. A variety of individuals are allowed to speak their peace, and we include all who volunteer. You are allowed to view a summation of your life that was curated in advance. Then, at the end, a decision is made surrounding your future. This is based on a formula we've developed here that has prevailed for centuries." She cleared her throat and continued.

"You are not to speak, interrupt, or intervene in any way. You aren't a witness in a court case, and you won't be called upon to give an opinion or an account. Instead, you are a bystander, and a silent one at that. Any attempt to react, explain, or interrupt the voices on the screen will be met with serious and immediate punishment."

From behind her back, she brandished a fireplace poker, its hook bright orange and smoking. She angled it closer, allowing Jason to survey the weapon, the burning tip not far from his right foot. She twirled it, then passed it, ninja-like, from hand to hand. Her motions were fluid, a majorette of one, expertly choreographed. She circled him, the movements hypnotizing, while she balanced the handle on her middle finger. She bared her teeth, pleased as punch.

"I'm cleared to use whatever means necessary to encourage full compliance, and I have an assortment of unpleasant ways to do so. I don't enjoy torture, but I am well trained. Do you understand?"

· He shied away from her stoker, scooting backward. This part was self-explanatory, and he replied with a shaky, untested voice.

"Yes. I watch whatever narrative you've compiled, and I don't flinch, or else you'll use your fire iron to make me regret it." *What a fucked-up afterlife*, he thought, but at least it was creative. Jason was sure even the most devout hadn't predicted a violent granny trained in special ops.

With a snap of her fingers, her weapon disappeared, gone but not forgotten.

"Correct," she clarified. "The final decision surrounding your future is based on the recommendations of a specific jury of your peers."

He looked up at her quizzically. So Heaven mimicked the American justice system? Those courts were soaked in injustice and greed, the opposite of spirituality and grace. A chuckle arose, swooping down his synapses. Jason clamped his lips together once, and again for reinforcement. No sound escaped, his humor pushed far away, for now.

"So, to recap, Jason LeDown. In purgatory, your task is to

listen to the stories of those on Earth you affected, without intervention, and to view our curated documentary in full. You must not react, emotionally or otherwise, or else subsequent intense and unrelenting consequences will be rendered." She tapped her clipboard twice, the echo jet-engine loud.

"Upon the conclusion of the post-Purgatory narratives, you'll be judged on the summation of your life, a verdict rendered for all eternity. No chance for an appeal, of course, because here all judgments are final."

She paused, her rehearsed speech complete.

"I don't need your consent. However, as a courtesy, I will ask. Do you have any questions?"

She eyed him, not a drop of warmth in her voice. Her expression held no empathy, just hurry-up eyes and quick sighs.

"Yes. I understand all of what you said, but... What's the point of all this?"

"Well, it's certainly not to change the outcome for you, Jason," she stated, her gaze an incision, laser-focused upon his forehead.

He considered his options, knowing the gist of how his life played out, except for the final act. It wasn't regret that he felt, no gnashing of teeth or tearing of robes. Maybe it was curiosity, the pinprick of wonder wading across his mind. There was something else, too, a low hum of excitement, reverberating down his spine and making him tingle. The opportunity to watch his life in real time was a precious thing, not a punishment, but a gift.

Jason caught a smile and wiped it off quick. He assumed no one enjoyed this process, even though he would. Plus, if the sample of jury members was truly random, maybe one would see things his way, a hereafter get-out-of-jail-free card, the equivalent of a divine mulligan.

"I understand and accept the terms you've discussed. I won't speak or intervene. If I need to sign something to make it official, I will." He glanced around to see if a covenant would descend, a document akin to Ursula trapping the Little Mermaid. No additional scrolls dangled in the air, no bone-white pens appeared, or blood-red ink.

"No, that will do," she uttered laconically, all formalities completed. "Soon, a projector will descend from above, and the taped segments will begin, starting with the most recent account onward."

Jason steadied himself, ready for the show to begin.

She turned, but there was no door. A wooden chair appeared in the corner. Before she sat down, she faced him, her thick eyebrows arching skyward.

"Oh, there's one last thing." Her voice was too saccharine to be real. "The jury of your peers, well, it's a mixture of people from these interviews. Your fate rests in their hands. And they have the opportunity for a sneaky little caveat." Her eyes zeroed in on him, and he saw that they were green, same as his. Then she winked, and it was cruel.

"You see, for the worst people imaginable, we have curated a very special level of Hell, nicknamed Tier 4. Not a popular option, but still, it exists, for those who earned it. Whatever monsters reside there, I can only speculate. No one is allowed beyond those doors, though their screams often convey enough."

She smiled jovially, her mouth so at odds with the seriousness of her words. A last note of cheer, as jubilant as a Christmas carol, hung suspended in the air, festive and misplaced.

"In your case, your victims control your future. A sort of judgment quid pro quo or tit for tat. Quite creative, no? Our team pieces the statements together, and all decision-making capabilities are given to those most aggrieved. In your case, that means the women control your sentence. You know the ones I mean."

A titter escaped her lips, then an exposed lascivious throat, long and lean. A laugh bolted through, more cackle than giggle, triumphant and self-assured, reverberating into every lonesome corner.

"Jason, you'll hear from many familiar people. But the jury is made up of your victims, and they're the ones who'll determine your fate."

He scanned the room, desperate for an escape hatch. The only sound was his breath, circling in and out, and her amused laughter, witch-like and thunderous. She'd morphed, from headmistress to miscreant, a character fit for black cauldrons and sour stews made of putrid green bubbles and severed fingers.

"Now, now, Jason. Here, sit, and *watch*." A chair appeared, and he was locked into it, his arms restrained, his feet bound, the holy equivalent of an electric chair. He couldn't move, and his neck was secured against the headrest with a steel bolt. His eyes faced the large projector screen that descended from the sky, the display stretched wide for high-definition viewing.

His auditor sat behind him, humming to herself, waiting for his demise to commence. Jason could barely wiggle his head, and his eyes were glued to the sloping screen, all free choice removed.

He couldn't blink his eyes or control his toes, his body frozen while panic raced through his veins.

"You're in for it now, Jason LeDown," she warned as his life flashed before his eyes, much different than his previous imagination. He tensed, her whispered threat tickling his ear. "For once, you'll understand what it's like to be bound and tied up and forced to endure whatever comes next."

Her laugh echoed, ricocheting around his brain, as he winced, and he watched.

Chapter 2
Officer John Green
Date: November 10th, 2007, 4:30 AM

A cheer reverberated through the late shift, an impulsive reaction to the killer's capture, before the stony silence descended, like a thick fog after a heavy rain. Any show of levity seemed inappropriate with a serial killer on the loose. Now that he'd been arrested, the worry remained, not easily displaced with Miranda Rights and legal formalities.

I appraised the sea of black uniforms, and I thought about the wails. For a police officer, it was a piss-poor initiation to a club whose membership nobody wanted. In my line of work, there were those who heard grief and those who hadn't. The sound in question wasn't a scream or brief like a yell. It was nothing from the normal world, where people borrowed library books and reserved summer vacation homes. Instead, this noise reverberated with unadulterated suffering, pure and potent, with no end in sight.

It was the sound parents made when their children died.

Somewhere, on this Saturday night, a mother was howling sick with it, the cause of her torment a first and last name.

Jason LeDown: serial killer, chemistry student, and murderer-at-large.

At least we'd added "apprehended" to his list of descriptors, though that was only a minor victory. I'd hoped to avoid another round of shrieks, would even exchange vomit or tears over those kinds of sobs. It was enough nightmare fuel to keep me awake for a week, sometimes even longer, because the survivors made that sound unconsciously. When they became cognizant of it, they still couldn't stop.

When the call came that a man fitting LeDown's description was sighted off Route 27, our station got jittery, until the official phone call confirmed his arrest. The chants died down further when we learned that three female bodies were recovered near the J & J gas station, all fatally wounded, the last one a young nurse, her balmy body located face down in a roadside ditch.

He'd killed again, and this time, the victims were local. Hell, the bodies could be last year's prom queen, or my favorite bank teller Lisa, who cashed my paycheck on Fridays with a wink, her pink lipstick bleeding onto bleached-white teeth. The not-knowing created a churn of concern, releasing a riptide onto my stomach lining, and a subsequent cramp that kept me from standing up straight. My brain blared an inappropriate rhyme, *three in a row, tic tac toe,* LeDown's actions reminiscent of Ted Bundy in the Chi Omega sorority house. It was bound to be bloody, the manic carnage of the last killing spree, the limbic system in overdrive and shoving logic out the door.

A veil of sorrow kept us silent, the station a graveyard, and twice as still. Then the buzz of details began, bowed heads swirling and trading information like baseball cards, under the guise of keeping us informed.

The established detectives promised it got easier, adjusting to the macabre, but they lied. I still went home nauseous, eating Tums like they were Skittles, my stomach knotted no matter what. The nightly traumas of law enforcement whittled my bones, keeping sleep away, filling my nights with crime scenes, perps, and fingerprint whorls.

I curbed the nagging feelings of fear with another sip of my Mountain Dew, but it didn't help. The sickly-sweet swish tasted like rotten mouthwash, too hot and rancid to enjoy.

Night shift had impacted my waistline, pushing the limits of my belt with extra caffeine and vending machine Combos, the snacks quick and caloric. I tried to limit myself to one purchase per night, but the extra hours required to catch a murderer had wreaked havoc on my diet. The top button of my khakis cut into my stomach, marking my skin with an angry welt. Soon I'd have to go up a size and admit defeat.

I wondered if that was another thing to blame on Jason LeDown and if he could be charged with it. I thought about making a joke, offering up some dark humor to keep things light. My partner Benny was typically the go-to comedian, but lately he'd been annoyed, trading his shtick for huffs and puffs, a troll-under-the-bridge routine. Perhaps the jovial clown baton had been passed to me, and with it an opportunity to turn sadness into entertainment.

I smoothed out my features, noting that Benny shot me a judgmental glance, his eyes resting on the Combos I'd ingested.

His gaze ran up to my waistline, and I tried to laugh but gagged, the food caught in my windpipe. I heaved a bit, and he rushed over to help.

Benny jostled my back harder than necessary to dislodge the stuck snack, but he's good people. I'd won the partner lottery, being paired with Benny, quick as he was to provide backup or keep me from choking.

"Take it easy, John," he murmured, awarding me another side-eye. I'd been paired with Benny long enough to read his nonverbals. His nerves were clanking sky high, with LeDown headed to our precinct after a statewide manhunt. All the Southern states had issued an APB after his bungle in Chapel Hill. After the campus slayings and months of lingering terror, reports circulated that the Co-Ed Killer had attempted another break-in. But this time, the perp was identified as graduate student Jason LeDown before he disappeared.

How he landed in small-town Ohio was anyone's guess. The weight of his crimes was solemn, more appropriate for undertakers than cops. Even the whoosh of my wrapper in the trash can caused swiveled heads and flickering eyes, the station a hive mind on red alert.

I felt claustrophobic already, anticipating the barrage of news that would descend upon our rural town. Jason was accused of killing multiple female college students after breaking in and binding them, a knockoff BTK. His methods were notable because his victims were close to his own demographic, the equivalent of shitting where he ate. For him, killing wasn't a midlife crisis; it was a taste he'd developed early on, his need for carnage initiated before he could legally purchase a six-pack of Budweiser.

Detectives now linked him to the early millennium killings at North Carolina Central University, noting the similarities in Jason's handiwork, his victim type petite and college aged. He'd continued his streak from 2006 to present, earning the moniker "The Co-Ed Killer" slashing his way through UNC Chapel Hill and beyond.

They'd briefed us on his backstory. Before he was a villain, Jason was pursuing his master's degree in science with a specialty in chemical engineering at the University of North Carolina Chapel Hill. His suspect profile showed a somber student barely able to grow a mustache. The additional pictures on television revealed a bespectacled, long-haired lab rat so at odds with his list of legal charges. Jason's pale, unlined face looked appropriate for a library, not a federal prison. His skin was almost translucent, his posture slightly hunched, typecasted as the forgettable nerd in a lily-white coat. I would've discarded him outright, labeling him an honors student in need of some serious vitamin D and a gym card. Just goes to show what lingered under the surface of a person, his blood variegated with ill intent.

I tried to suppress a shudder, imagining him here, evil a foot away, introducing himself, breathing a hello. Superstitious goose bumps sprouted on my skin, making my terror tangible, and I vowed to keep my distance.

Benny was less able to keep his emotions contained. His infant Tessa had taken ownership of his heart and changed his outlook overnight. She'd barreled into his life full speed, and each time he said her name, it came out like a prayer. He informed me that love weighed exactly seven pounds, two ounces, and he grinned so much it felt indecent. Benny admitted that he'd traded his nightly brew for a whiff of his daughter's hair, his open face mirroring the transition from husband to parent. Pairing that new life with a man who allegedly murdered eight women, well, it was surreal, and Benny's flashfire emotions reflected the disparity.

Benny flexed his bicep muscles and stewed, pacing back and forth, his restless energy set to a high boil. The chief had just lectured that this arrest had to follow the rulebook to the letter. Dissatisfaction flowed like a wave down the uniformed line, with officers eager to rough him up a bit before he was behind bars.

"The eyes of the world are on us now, in Oxford, Ohio. No mistakes. No heroes," Chief enunciated, his face radiating concern. He was the coach making the locker room speech, and we all dipped our heads in respect, though Benny marched his frustration out in heel-to-toe strides.

"We're under a boatload of scrutiny, and I need you to remember that. It's an order. If we make errors, it's my head that rolls on this one, and I sure as shit don't wanna fall flat on my face at a national level. So look alive, team, and keep it legit." Serious nods made their way through the force, a silent agreement to remain lawful.

It looked like Benny needed to vent, since he was staring holes in the worse-for-wear wallpaper like he wanted to rip it apart.

"Remember what the boss said," I whispered, not wanting to draw attention to Benny's anger.

"I heard what he said, and I'll abide. Doesn't mean I agree with it, though." His voice sputtered, teeming with angry pauses.

"Most of us feel the same way." He wasn't alone in his hate. In fact, the disgust was contagious, an airborne infection of scorn and distaste, and we'd already been infected.

"Well, for parents, this one's personal. It's the difference between a soft slap and a gut punch."

I thought about lecturing Benny. Having a newborn didn't award him extra grievances. We all had women in our lives that meant something to us, faces that flashed when LeDown racked up body counts on the news.

But I figured the less fuss made the better, especially since the suspect was scheduled to arrive at 0500 hours. I chugged the rest of the Mountain Dew, wincing at the taste, while keeping an eye on Benny and the clock. I'd make sure to keep him in line. He could thank me later when his good sense caught up to him and cooler heads prevailed.

I owed Benny a debt, and that balance was never far from my mind. I was new to the force, and it showed, with a backdrop of muffled reminders, and a notepad brimming with chicken-scratch instructions. My hands felt too big, my feet too clumsy, and I had at least three good reasons why I shouldn't have made it out of the academy.

But Benny was patient with me, covering the basics like logging evidence and counting bullets, and he remained within earshot on our first domestic call. He stayed close, talked protocol, and calmed my nerves, until minor drug busts felt like trips to Publix grocery store. They called the police force a brotherhood, and with Benny, our connection was all family. But that's why I remained alert, because LeDown's ability to unnerve Benny was unique.

Typically, Benny was an optimist, humming off-key along to Kicks Country 92.9 on the radio. He crooned Kenny Chesney classics and rapped his fingers on the steering wheel, shimmying his shoulders to the beat. Being his partner also meant accompanying him to Kroger on Fridays to pick up daisies for his wife, Missy. Then Benny would suggest closing out the week with a draft beer pitcher at McClarty's. "My treat," he'd insist, signaling another round with the quick flash of his Visa card. Seeing him rattled was enough to make me stir-crazy, with feet that tap-danced under the nicked conference room table.

Whether he realized it or not, Benny needed me to smooth out his anger. I registered his tense jawline, all heated muscle memory, the attitude of a boxer itching for a fight.

The front doors swung open, and a chorus of black uniforms made their way inside. The mass of officers kept the prisoner flanked, as they half-carried, half-dragged him forward. Jason LeDown's head sunk low, his chin tucked, his eyes skimming the floor. They gripped his forearms, and slowed down, allowing us a station version of a frog march. Everyone got a good look at the most notorious criminal the station had ever seen.

His hair was so greasy it looked wet, and it hung in tangled curtains, grazing his gaunt shoulder blades. He resembled a '90s grunge rocker, in need of a shower and down on his luck. His eyes stayed trained on the tile floor, no flashes of defiance found.

LeDown complied with the officers, keeping his tall body loose, his jeans beltless and in danger of falling. He didn't struggle, and our force brimmed with the confidence that comes with outnumbering a predator.

Benny stiffened beside me, then charged into the mix with an abrupt jerky movement. I shoved my arm out, and shook my head, fast as a motor tic. Benny stopped but clenched his jaw.

As I watched the procession, a piece of me felt disappointed.

Jason LeDown looked every inch a regular man. I'd expected to see obvious signs of insanity, like jagged teeth, or feral wolf snarls. Instead, he looked deflated, his spine curved, with wet leaves stuck to his dark parka. He didn't resist, and several officers frowned, their hands clenching holsters, looking for a reason to punish him.

Ten officers scooted the prisoner into the nearest holding cell. Our base was overloaded with nighttime staff, collecting overtime with voyeuristic intent until the FBI arrived. The closest officers secured him in the cell next to the warden's desk, mere inches from where the night shift completed our daily logs. If Jason squinted, he could see his personal data, scribbled in the margins of a legal pad, confirmed by federal agents moments before his arrest.

The collective eyes of the police force burned into him, a seething, volcanic powder keg. There wasn't a brass in the place that'd look elsewhere. Every officer stood at attention, rigid and waiting for the next move, with shoulders back and stomachs clenched. Some clutched their weapons, others licked their lips, a mob in need of a proverbial match.

We all ached to beat him to a pulp. It swirled around us, the stench of testosterone and locker rooms, of bloodied knuckles and an unfair fight. We salivated for justified violence, but still we held our ground, the chief's words rumbling in our minds.

No one made any announcements. The whole of our precinct paused, observing every flick of his hair, every heave of his chest. LeDown was deposited gently into the cell and instructed to remove his clothes. He complied, and they were bagged for evidence, exchanged swiftly for baby blue prisoner scrubs.

Before, there might have been wolf whistles, designed to catch him off guard and make him blush. Instead, our eyes lingered, but no one said a damn thing.

The silence was worse than the heckles, all of us locked into his solo performance. The grime on his body dirtied up his new clothes instantly, staining them with the rusty color of still-wet blood. A circular spot of it grew on his chest, fanning outward, the effect a leaking gunshot wound, though the injuries weren't his own. He continued to wear his victims on his body, their DNA mixed with his curly brown chest hair, spattered upon his new blue shirt.

I felt vomit rise from my belly, my prior snack burning against the back of my throat. I swallowed it, the acidity keeping me from gagging audibly.

"That outfit should be orange," Benny emitted beside me, not bothering to conceal his disgust. The officers responded with rambunctious clamor, the wide room humid with hate. The chief chose that moment to make his speech, and not a second too soon.

"All right, men. The Feds will arrive in two hours. Until then, let me remind you, no funny business. This prisoner gets treated like any other, and you know my stance on this. Anything less than that and it's an immediate dismissal. Everyone will know about Oxford, Ohio, tonight and we won't disappoint them."

We refrained from applause, but handshakes rippled throughout the room, bursting with a job well done. The crowd dispersed into small clusters, eager for coffee and conversation, breaking into trios and quartets of gossips. The nervous energy rebounded, while we pretended to ignore the prisoner, our eyes everywhere but on LeDown.

Our boss settled into his leather desk chair, both overstuffed and overused, content with the long wait. He turned on the overhead television to ABC Nightly News, his countenance unreadable. In our jail, the five initial holding cells were assembled in one long row, with the lone television secured above, reflecting against the black metal bars.

The chatter of the television gave me a chance to study the inmate's dirty fingernails, his face ruddy with superficial scratches on his cheek. LeDown wasn't used to handcuffs, you could tell, since he kept touching them behind his back, tracing the outline with his thumb. That will rub his wrists raw; its best to sit still.

But I hoped the cuffs worked hard on him, like we longed to do. I wanted his skin splintered with deep, jagged cuts, his suffering acute and unyielding. Hell, I wished I could fast-forward to when he's only bones and unfurled guts, the snake of his intestines ripe for the viewing. With a man like that, the only acceptable justice was an ivory-white skeleton. His outcome was already slated for the needle or the electric chair. The method was just details, long as it was fatal.

My eyebrows creased, watching him try to find comfort. The strength of my distaste for LeDown rose higher, threatening to overtake me. I envisioned rattling his cage, letting spittle drip down his chin that he couldn't wipe away.

Benny continued to glare at Jason, his face bullish and tomato red. I stepped closer to my partner, our shoulders locking together. I hoped my presence reminded him of our duty, that it created a barrier between his outrage and that holding cell. Benny, with his squinty eyes and forehead sweat, was a whisp away from doing somethin' stupid.

The chief turned up the volume on the breaking news story, distracting Benny from executing LeDown with his eyes. The intro music stole our attention, a symphony of heads slanted in unison.

The first thing I noticed was that the reporters looked nervous. My momma used to say, "The devil works hard but evening reporters work harder." She was a nightly news aficionado and stayed up late, even on double-shift nights, so she could summarize the events for me and my brother over breakfast. She narrated while we gulped down Cheerios, her stories focused on local crimes and petty theft, sharing the headlines in that sweet Southern tilt. She knew it was important to keep us informed before we skirted off to another boring school day.

I never told her how grateful I was that she educated us. But missing her was my default setting; I had to work not to do it, even though she's been gone five years.

In some ways, though, it's good Momma didn't have to live through this wickedness. She'd spent her whole life fiddling with her gold cross necklace, commanding us to believe that the world was full of good people and bad luck. I became a cop at her urging; her belief in my aptitude for the job never wavered.

"John, you're a good man, but more than that, you're kind." Her words made me feel confident, like she'd been given a premonition, from her lips to God's ear. "Policework don't need more violence, but it does require your compassion."

She'd never understand Jason LeDown, whose presence ruined everything good, curdling purity and spoiling dignity with a look.

The italicized ticker below the program flashed blurbs in capital letters, the bold text so underlined that even the visually impaired could read it. Journalists in dark suits shuffled their papers, their faces blurred with worry.

ALLEGED SERIAL KILLER JASON LEDOWN CAPTURED

A roar rose through the crowd that Chief quickly squashed.

"Quiet, quiet *now*," he yelled. "We won't get to hear what they say about us!"

The room silenced, a choir of held-in breaths.

The reporter pulled her face into one of concern. No smiles were found, not even a hint. Her face was meant for crematoriums, set to deliver bad news.

"As always, every hour, at the top of the hour, we're here to provide you with the latest breaking news story. Tonight, we've received word that alleged serial killer, Jason LeDown, has been captured in the town of Oxford, Ohio, about forty miles from Cincinnati. Our sources say he was taken alive, sustaining no significant injuries."

We stifled another cheer, though some hoots peppered through.

"Jason LeDown, age twenty-five, a native of Hickory, North Carolina, has been arrested after a nationwide manhunt and a multi-day coordinated search. Law enforcement across several states were on high alert, as he was considered armed and dangerous. Evidence has surfaced surrounding new slayings within Butler County, attributed to the Co-Ed Killer. Reports confirm that three female bodies have been discovered, pending formal identification, all fatally wounded from numerous stab wounds within the Oxford, Ohio community. Sources indicate the murder weapon was discovered at the scene of the crime."

She took a breath, and I wondered what it cost her to say that. Her voice wavered, but she continued, covering up her reaction with a professional flatness.

"Mr. LeDown was studying chemical engineering as a master's degree student at the University of North Carolina at Chapel Hill before his capture. He is alleged to have killed multiple young women on campus in a brutal rampage that ravaged the university, sparking national outcry. Authorities now believe LeDown is the primary suspect for the multiple breaking-and-entering deaths on the UNC Chapel Hill campus from 2006 and 2007."

She looked down at the paper, gathering her thoughts, allowing her voice to settle.

"Jason LeDown is also believed to be behind the college slayings at North Carolina Central University in 2003 and 2004, with prior cases reopened and of interest to law enforcement personnel. As always, the tip line, shown at the bottom of the screen, remains open for anyone with pertinent information surrounding these alleged crimes."

The reporter puffed her cheeks, eyes wide, her frozen stare conveying the urgency of the accusations.

"We will continue to keep you updated as further news develops. For now, Jason LeDown remains in police custody, which will continue until his arraignment. Reports indicate that he will be extradited back to North Carolina as soon as possible."

My colleagues' eyes tracked the television, waiting for droplets related to our department, each yearning for five minutes of fame. I turned to observe how LeDown reacted to the broadcast.

He was watching the news like it was sacred, the screen a sermon, his expression one of reverence. His whole body was oriented toward the television, his eyes stagnant and non-blinking. He leaned in, his nose darting through the metal bars, like he could hold the reporter's words in his greedy fingers.

"ABC News will continue to report on the LeDown case and his alleged eight victims, which include the three most recent slayings in Ohio. Victim details remain unknown at this time as this in an active investigation. Anyone with relevant case information is again encouraged to call the toll-free number at the bottom of our screen. We will continue to provide hourly updates as we receive them about the apprehension of Jason LeDown. Now, onto our nightly entertainment update with Robert, and his projected winners for the 35th American Music Awards. Don't miss his interview with finalist, and country music superstar, Carrie Underwood, after the break."

When the reporter had widened her mouth to say eight, I saw a ghost of a smirk on Jason's face.

"Ten," he murmured, in a tone so low it was almost imperceptible. He closed his eyes, bowed his head in veneration. Statue still, he stayed in that position, before popping his eyes open, a Cheshire-Cat grin jammed upon his mouth, triumphant and topsy-turvy. His light pink tongue caressed his lips, the movements seductive and showy, a vaudeville act lobbied in my direction. He continued to smack his lips together, the pop of an air kiss slicing through his cell.

LeDown dipped his head back, opening his mouth wide, showcasing all his molars. He stalled, courting his rapt audience.

Then a laugh escaped, girlish and bubbly, paired with shimmying shoulders.

Everyone turned to watch, the jail a makeshift theater.

The sound reverberated off the walls. His laugh was high-pitched, much different than a chortle or a chuckle. It poisoned the room, sucking out all the oxygen and recirculating it with sorrow. He continued to laugh wildly at nothing, or at everything, his voice a deranged carnival clown.

"Stop it!" Benny screamed. "Stop it, *right now.*"

Unanimous agreement flowed through the police force, while some officers acted, banging on his jail bars with fingers curled around gun grips.

The chief stalled, unsure of how to control the situation.

Jason ignored all of us and continued with his laughter, shaking with it, his body writhing, gyrating on the floor of the cell. He fell to the ground and began humping the floor, his laughs paired with swirling hip movements. He continued his sexual hysterics and the high-pitched cackle, both designed to enrage us.

"Hold up," the chief bellowed, his voice a bullhorn. "Stand down!"

While the rest stared, I jotted down a note. He said ten; that meant two bodies were still unrecovered.

That made our work much harder. A duo of undiscovered souls, in addition to the other reported victims, their names a bullet point of heartache. We were the designated bloodhounds, designed to uncover a trail of bodies left to rot, discarded in the wake of this mediocre man.

Benny wasn't wrong. A man like Jason deserved the worst. The stink of regret should follow him all his days spent in squalor and boredom. He didn't deserve a drop of our empathy because his soul was decayed, a shriveled kidney bean not worth saving.

But that's why I loved being a police officer. Integrity started once we got him in cuffs, shackled and contained. We'd find and detail his worst crimes, and we'd make Jason bear the weight of all he took. We'd let all his sins rest on his sagging shoulders. By acknowledging his victims, we'd sink him, even deeper than six feet under.

The boys in blue dealt with the worst of humanity, and Jason was the apex predator, the top of the most wanted list. He would pay for his inequities, even the ones we didn't yet know.

I'd make sure of it, and I'd have backup, so fierce and fast he'd never stand a chance.

Laugh now, bellow even, I thought, *get it all out, Jason. Because the whole police force will come for you, and we were made for this. We were created to take you down, trained for it, practiced and furious, full of righteous rage, laser pointed at your ugly face. Every giggle, every drop of levity will be brought to justice. You'll be locked away for good, the rest of your life spent in a six-by-nine cage of your own making. Or you'll laugh while the executioner readies your arm on the gurney, the needle prick cold in your vein, the audience packed with bated breaths behind the one-way mirror, ready for your demise.*

I stared him down, then I picked up my pencil, ready to begin connecting the dots before the sun rose in the east, providing the light necessary for a new day.

Let the good work begin.

Chapter 3
Ashley Parker
Date: November 10th, 2007, 2:45 a.m.

By the time he came for me, everyone knew his name. Mine became an adjunct, a tacked-on reference to the latest breaking news. My name and story were a footnote, the last of the LeDown serial killer victims, three lives stolen in quick succession before he was caught.

Ashley Parker, nurse, age twenty-four, the sum of me shorter than a paragraph, my epitaph a blurb online sandwiched in between Coke commercials and previews for *National Treasure 2*.

They flashed a picture of me, but it was an afterthought image swiped from my Myspace page. My face could be anyone's, all washed-out skin and shoulder-length dirty-blond hair. The photo didn't include my typical messy bun, an afterthought hairstyle necessary for moving patients and preventing bedsores. Despite the male fantasies, most nurses aren't there for client enjoyment. The work I completed was physical.

The media doppelganger of me wore bright-pink lipstick, but

at work I kept my face bare, my cheeks pink with exertion, not blush. I'd rush through the hospital double doors, a second before my shift started, with my badges tangled around my neck, and my forgotten lunch resting in my car. I'd been warned about tardiness, so I had neither the time nor inclination to impress ER overdoses and gunshot victims.

But now the whole of me was reduced to a driver's license snippet; five foot four, one hundred twenty pounds, blue eyes, full of wrong place, wrong time. I was a cautionary public warning, my surname a code red reminder to never walk home alone.

On some TV stations I was only a location, a simple latitude and longitude, my final resting place marked off Route 27 in Oxford, Ohio. My makeshift grave was a trench of standing water and gnats, not big enough to create a temporary memorial. As the facts splashed across computer screens, people grimaced, their sadness for me lasting the length of an internet scroll.

I wouldn't even receive the roadside white cross, or the pink gas station teddy bears, to mark my last location. Those sweet reminisces were reserved for car crashes and accidents, not for mass murder victims. My death was too brutal for innocent trinkets, the harshness of it inappropriate for the daylight.

The morbid armchair detectives recorded my deathly details, labeling slash marks, lacerations, and writing hasty scribbles on ruled notebook paper. Having lived it, there's no way to write brutality and spin it pretty. Not even Rumpelstiltskin could make murder sweet. Call it what you want, but I was gutted, gashed, and split apart. The cruelty and quickness of the violence surprised me, because once I registered what had happened, the final act was half over.

I was walking home from the late shift at the hospital, trying to ensure that my scrubs didn't drag the sidewalk. I only had two pairs, and I didn't want to spring for extras, since that would negate my overtime cash flow. I was saving up for a long weekend away, and I didn't have the luxury of wasting my hard-earned cash on another uniform. The rain had stopped, but I had to concentrate to avoid the puddles, the slick pavement a worthy adversary against my shoes' traction. I'd already skidded once, so I took it slow, one footstep at a time.

I was halfway to my townhome, almost to the J & J gas station, one block away from the first of the fancy house mailboxes that resembled brick ovens. It made my commute go faster naming the landmarks I passed. I'd cleared the bus stop, and the hospital lights could no longer be seen; that's how close I was to making it home. That's another caveat I became, one of the thirty percent of people who died within a mile of their house.

I'd completed the same nightly routine every day that week, the structure of it set in stone. I'd pause at the slight turn in the road and wave to the gas station attendant, Debbie. It felt right to commiserate with another late nighter, my greeting an acknowledgment of our schedule reversal. Sometimes I'd go inside, and she'd share a weary smile and access to her employee discount. But I only stopped occasionally, not wanting to take advantage of down-on-her-luck Debbie, with her threadbare cardigan and red-rimmed eyes. That kind of hangdog sadness, combined with the chaotic ER pace, made it seem like Satan was skating on my coattails, doling out an ollie of pessimism, a quick kickflip of doubt.

Most nights I'd stick to giving Debbie a brief acknowledgment, then I'd jog past the three streetlights, and there was my front porch, the gaslit lanterns providing a welcoming glow. The cold breeze kept me from dawdling, while the air nipped at my hands, making me wish I'd remembered mittens.

The overhead lights of the gas station gleamed a blurry beacon as I sidestepped the gutter. The slight curve was up ahead, and I trudged on, my thoughts circling to my mom.

She'd warned me not to walk home in the late night or early morning hours, but I told her that was the point in living close to work. She'd cautioned me about some NBC story regarding a young man on the loose, targeting single women and tying them up.

I'd heard that version of a bogeyman my whole life, and it'd lost its luster years ago, along with urban legends and haunted houses. I'd prefer saving on gas and getting some fresh air, rather than worrying about some lunatic with a hook for a hand and a belly full of bad intentions.

Save that shit for Halloween, I mused, though I dialed down the sarcasm with Mom. Better to assuage her, and I was too tired to fight.

"Yes, Mom, no worries, I'll be careful. Love you." I'd rushed off the call, citing a busy workday, my eyes rolling skyward, my fingers closing my Blackberry.

My family didn't understand that walking home eased the staccato pace of the emergency room. By the time my feet found my front porch, I'd already be primed for sleep, the roadside jaunt a wall between me and work. I needed that separation because it kept my dreams far from beeping codes and crash carts.

I stepped gingerly on the pavement, avoiding a tributary of water. The night air was crisp, and I stretched my arms up high, my neck tight from my shift. I moved in a circular motion to release the muscle kinks. I noticed a green Jeep, the interior lights blinding, the doors left wide open despite the chilly night.

Something was wrong. The car was empty, but the engine still purred. The door-ajar beeps disrupted the night's solitude with their high-pitched warble, certain to burn down the battery or worse.

Before I could investigate, a cloud of movement barreled from the J & J in my direction, the jingle jangle of the gas station door-bells dinging a faint warning. The rush of wind was paired with the squeaking sound of a shoe on pavement, then another. I glanced up, confused, when a man in a black parka sped into me. My head remained halfcocked, the force of the tackle knocking me breathless. I winced, and my palms pounded on the pavement, the tops of my kneecaps skinned against the blacktop.

A robbery gone wrong, I assumed, until his sinewy arms flung me into the roadside ditch, my weight no match for his muscles. I landed hard on my stomach, the force of his assault stealing air from my lungs. The attacker jumped beside me, panting from the strained effort of knocking me down. His knobby knees crushed into my back, grinding deep into my spine. I was pinned completely, while the stranger made a symphony of moans and grunts above me. I tried to buck him off, but his grip held firm, his knees twin pillars keeping me confined.

The runoff tore at my cheek, infusing my mouth with dust and dirt. I locked my lips to keep the grime out, but the sludge surged on, coating the tip of my tongue with wet leaves. Spit pooled, choking me, the gutter water flowing through my nose, the same sensation as swallowing chlorinated pool water.

I gagged, and my throat felt constricted, though his hands were far from my neck. I struggled to move any body part, my hands upturned, searching frantically for a weapon but finding only air and mud.

I smelled blood, the copper aroma clogging my nose, though I wasn't wounded. I'd worked at the hospital long enough to recognize the taste of rust and pennies, of water merged with iron. There was enough of it that I squirmed, the amount butcher shop heavy and much too fresh, making my head woozy.

He'd hurt someone else. That was the only explanation for why he was drenched with blood, enough to coat my clothes, the moisture soaking the back of my scrubs. I looked ahead at the gas station sign and screamed.

"No. God, no! Debbie!" I panicked, trading air for another gulp of drainage that tasted like refuse. I felt his erection graze my back, the stiffness ramming against my vertebrae.

He grunted animalistic, the sounds from his mouth a language of lust, wedging himself on top of me.

"Shut up!" he yelled, his voice a shrill pant. "She's gone now, and you're next."

He seized my hands behind my back, the strength of his legs crushing me, until I could no longer distinguish my body from the cold ground.

I twisted, praying he'd lose his grip, but the rigor of plastic cut into my wrists. He'd zip tied me, the makeshift handcuffs carving into my flimsy skin, creating a sting of pain. I strained to move, but that only pushed his erection closer to my bottom. I stopped, not wanting to excite him, when I felt the pinprick of a blade, cool against my backbone.

"Help!" I tried again, but my words were muffled, barely a whimper in the quiet night. The crickets chirped to one another, their sounds distorted into one long music note. My eyes filled with tears, listening for the sound of an engine, the squeal of tire tread. An owl hooted a response, the chorus of nocturnal animals my only witnesses. The cicadas hummed, and I prepared for the worst. I was alone, and no one was coming to save me.

The knife tore through my skin, that first flush of hurt zapping away my energy. Air caught in my throat and my lungs blared an SOS, my muscles removed of all free will. A stab connected with my shoulder blade, ripping the deltoid away from the bone. He removed the blade, and my wound poured blood, causing my vision sway. He granted a brief reprieve, allowing me to register my injuries, to let the pain pile up.

Then he plunged the knife so deep into my back that it severed my abdominal wall. I looked down, expecting to see the glint of silver puncturing my insides. It stung electric, the torture threatening to take me into the black space, where women surrendered, and death held court.

My eyesight was fuzzy, the sounds of the street no longer recognizable. The only sound was the sick swish of the blade and the wail of my bewilderment. It came out pitiful, a baby-calf whine that my synapses rejected since they were screaming, crying out danger in every known language. Crinkled leaves cradled my head, the foliage creating a crimson pillow of my own making.

He flipped me over, my head swimming with bursts of light. My consciousness teetered, but then my vision cleared. It hurt to be touched, and I winced in the dark. His face zoomed above me, no joy found in his features. He muttered, his face streaked with lines of blood, his mouth a full-on sneer.

Alarm swept through my body. I took a silent inventory, moving my body parts one by one. My legs obeyed, much too slowly, lifting only an inch off the ground. It took too much energy to budge, to think, to fight. My feet felt numb, and then I knew. Blood pressure drops before death. My eyes widened, realizing the harbingers of death now applied to me. I'd studied them after all, passed all my tests, and chose to get well acquainted with death in the ER.

My breath kept erratic time, and a phrase from nursing school sprang into my mind. Cheyne-Stokes breathing, another doom prodrome. I forced myself to inhale properly but it was difficult to find a rhythm.

"Look at me," he grunted, his gloves sandpaper against my chin. He pressed his fingers down hard on my collarbone, creating a bruise that'd be investigated later. His covered hands were wet, and he flicked residue across my face, Jackson Pollock style but with my own DNA.

Don't lick it, I thought, determined to separate myself from his filthy fingers. I couldn't see the sky, and the whole of my surroundings were pixelated, his words running together like a monastery chant. My arms burned, a train-track of fire scorching my veins, searing every vessel found.

My vision swam, but I felt his nose rub against mine, his hot breath fragrant with granola and chocolate. His features were a funhouse mirror, improbable, complete with a half-smile on a wide moon face. Nothing made sense, with a world partitioned into jigsaw pieces.

I was better than that last scene, my life more meaningful than a girl in a gutter. My girlfriend Gretchen and I were in the thick of knock-you-naked love, immersed in the honeymoon phase where everything was new and passionate. She was Lip Smacker sweet, the quick swirl of a soft-pink tongue. She tasted like Cherry Blow Pops because she allowed herself one sucker per day, swearing she'd replaced cigarettes with sugar for good. We'd danced in my kitchen, her head grazing my shoulder, the nearness of her intoxicating. Her hair smelled like Pantene and lemons, the scent tickling my nose, before I took a hit of it and kissed her. I loved waking up to her smile and the teasing smooches on my collarbone that turned serious. It was difficult to leave that bed, wrapped up tight with legs intertwined, her arm slung across my bare chest. I felt safe linked together, our shadows combined on the closet door. I could've stayed in that room with her and let the rest of my days pass without fanfare, drunk on happiness and Gretchen's hip bones.

I loved dinner plate Dahlias, and the way flowers taught me patience, to wait for their coveted merlot blooms. I collected decorative vases the way boys treasured baseball cards, the prettiest ones awarded with the best fresh-cut flowers from my ever-expanding garden.

I had a sarcastic brother, and a new niece I'd never meet, her name something unknown and perfect. Diminutive and pure, due in May, her nursery painted a dainty rose hue, her welcome gift wrapped in my coatrack closet.

My purple carrots had survived the frost, the black nebulas crowning and ready for harvest, bursting with rare antioxidants. I would never find out if they were savory or sweet or if the sun had ripened them into the perfect salad adornment.

There were so many questions left unanswered, a tight coil of responses unknown and timelines unfinished.

I had an obese cat named Felix, who was more fat than fur. I'd just bought diet food to implement feline Weight Watchers. He'd resist, and rightly so, since diet cat food probably tasted like chalk, same as the human variety. I planned to sell it to him hard, even though cats were short on logic. But I needed him to live a long life, content with catnip dreams and lazy Sundays. His meow was my favorite alarm clock, paired with claws tapping a buckshot rhythm on the honeycombed kitchen tiles while I brewed my morning coffee. Felix was waiting for me, mewing to himself about his mom who'd never make it home.

I was many things, but Jason reduced me to one word. Victim. And what was murder except a claim that his wants and needs were greater than my life?

He took not only my existence, but my narrative. Might as well have joint names listed on my gravestone, his and mine, make it official. I ceased to exist except in reference to him. He made me his and stole every opportunity for me to be anything else.

As I struggled to exhale, my eyes bulging into basketballs, I tried to convey my disdain, one final look of resistance to channel all I'd lost.

My bowels released, the steamy liquid filling my underwear, coating my upper thighs. The putrid smell sickened the air, the final scent of horror and discharge. I could no longer close my eyes or my mouth, and my tongue fell to the side. I'd lost control of that too.

But I was Ashley Parker, sister, lover, kind caregiver, would-be aunt, and an excellent bowler.

A headache seared through my brain while his knife carved into my scapula, creating gashes to my rotator cuff.

I was a green-thumb gardener and a lover of '90s hip-hop.

My heart ticked slow, once, twice, savoring the last bits of precious oxygen.

I was a gentle kisser, a rainbow-wearing, croc-buying, badass nurse who could find a good vein faster than anyone in my ward.

But my memory was cut short, relegated to a dot on a map, and the number ten, the very last victim of Jason LeDown.

Chapter 4
Debbie Smith
Date: November 10th, 2007, 1:53 a.m.

My late-night shift had just ended, the fatigue of it making my bones creak and crack. The J & J gas station closed at two a.m., later than most, and the weariness of the work made my eyes wilt, droopier than my age allowed.

I heard a yelp outside, coming from the tree line across the highway, the squeal of a mouse caught in a trap. The cold kept me from investigating. It might be Sammy, Oxford's lone homeless person, known to take refuge nearby when the weather dipped. He snuggled up in his sleeping bag on the metal bench, protected from the cold in his bus-stop cocoon. Sometimes I'd bring him a treasure trove of broken snacks, too damaged to sell, since his temporary housing was right outside the gas station. He'd show such gratitude that it made me blush, like I'd given him filet mignon instead of squashed Tostito chips. He would give me a blessing, complete with prayer hands, before whispering a goodbye. I hoped a full belly helped him sleep, his head dry under the transportation schedule and route guide.

But I remembered I'd seen Sammy and his trash bag suitcase before my shift, his hunchbacked shadow forgoing the bus stop in favor of the Baptist church. So he couldn't be the owner of the nighttime squeal. His absence was notable, because Sammy's overnight choices were our town's equivalent of the groundhog seeing its shadow, his vacancy meaning the temperatures were sure to drop.

The earlier downpour of rain had stopped, but the wind chill whipped across my face as I huddled close to the shop door. The icy blast could freeze my eyelashes in a flash, and bitter cold warned me to hurry the heck up.

It brought to mind winters in Nebraska as a child. My best friend Bonnie and I would pretend to smoke, letting the frigid air waft around our pressed-together fingers. We probably looked like an odd pair, her so gangly, me thick and awkward, unsure of myself even then. She swore her older cousin had taught her to blow smoke rings, but I never saw her make even a cylinder shape.

I smiled, recalling Bonnie and her propensity to tell big whoppers. She once told me that she'd stopped the clock with her mind in PE class, proof of latent superpowers she'd conjure at will.

When had I lost touch with her? I tried to track our last contact but failed. I'd skipped our twenty-fifth high school reunion because I needed the extra shifts and overtime pay. Bonnie and the rest of the class of 1982 partied like Marty in *Back to the Future* while I was stuck behind the gas station counter waiting to punch out.

The reunion was another sacrifice in my long lifetime of

responsibility, my timeline full of good intentions that I regretted later. Maybe it was first child syndrome, or maybe I was a martyr. Probably not the latter, since I wore my resentments like a cloak, complaining too much to be a saint. I followed the rules, but with less gumption and more grumbles, quick to let others know exactly what I'd forfeited.

My daughter Pam was a newly minted mother and barely out of high school herself, making me a grandmother before I was ready. Baby Grayson was a sickly little thing. First RSV, then croup, with Pam drilling a well-worn path around the kitchen table until she gave in to my outstretched arms. I pretended to hem and haw, but I liked feeling needed. *It keeps you young*, they say.

Not that I feel particularly spry, with the extra shifts wreaking havoc on my sleep schedule. But I needed the work so I could save up for Grayson's asthma medicine and his special formula that smelled like cow piss and dirt. Nutramigen, hard to pronounce, and even harder to afford. But Grayson had reflux and could hardly keep anything down, and their state Medicaid could barely be called health insurance. Pam needed advice, she needed the help, but most of all, she needed the cash.

I was a mother, so I provided. Now as a grandmother, I continued. No rest for the weary, and less in the 401k, but it's not all taxes and timesheets.

Last Tuesday was my first day off in forever, and I spent it with baby Grayson and Pam at the park in downtown Oxford. It was a clear autumn day, warm enough to keep winter's icy fingers at bay. We couldn't stay long, both of us afraid of exposing the baby to too much direct sunlight. Pam fussed over Grayson, covering his carrier with a light blanket, a brief veil of protection for his curt face and cherub cheeks.

The park was at the center of town, and the garden club had planted their fall annuals, displaying orange coneflowers in neat, organized rows. It seemed too late to plant them, with frost creeping so close, but the bulk of my garden knowledge was limited to what I grew in my windowsill. I smiled to myself, one eye on the stroller, one reserved for people watching, the town full of shopping bags and good cheer.

The sunshine bared down on us, and the wind kicked up a notch, the breeze kissing my pale shoulders. Both Pam and I tilted our faces to the sky at the same time, letting our cheeks revel in the heat. Mother and daughter, relaxing, letting the Earth supply us, like we were also made of chlorophyll and pollen. A perfect day to round out all the bad ones, that moment a cure for all the late nights.

I smiled, my back turned, keys at the ready. My shift supervisor Lenny was religious about the way we locked up at the J & J gas station. He acted like we weren't a filling station but a bank, having traded our rundown cash register for a vault of ancient valuables that required extra protection.

"Check it twice, Debbie. Always check it twice," he said in his accented English, an accusation found in his narrowed eyes. It was offensive, the idea that I'd cut corners, like my cardigan hid a sleeve of arm tattoos or I moonlighted as a marijuana dealer on the side.

I didn't socialize with Lenny, so he had no way of knowing that I spent my free time at the Salvation Army, opening my wallet before I opened my mouth. Pam liked to brag that I was

God's favorite, but it was anxiety that guided my giving. I needed to cover my bases, so I was rich in good deeds, with feet and finances committed to righteousness. But it was fear that kept me devout and caused me to check the lock twice.

My mom was a strict Baptist, her beliefs written in permanent marker, our family's King James Bible charting out her parenting course, peppered with "thee" and "thou." For her, even smiling could be sinful, and she made me believe our heavenly father had his celestial lightning bolt aimed square at my chest, with no margin for mistakes. She never spared the rod, and I sure wasn't spoiled, so I grew up sleeping with one eye open in case temptation caught me unawares. I never discovered why I deserved those whippings, so I figured sin grabbed ahold of me inadvertently. Mom kept me faithful and fearful in equal measure, and I followed suit ever since.

I completed Lenny's closing procedure, with no bristles on the back of the neck or ominous shiver up my spine. I didn't yelp or turn; my mind was on Grayson's medicine and if the overtime would be enough to cover it. $8.25 was shit wages, but I'd worked enough to fill up my invoice, the days and times dragging onto the very last line. Quantity over quality, and my feet paid the price.

My thoughts were on my fingers, each digit getting stiffer by the second, while I turned the key, making sure to hear the click of the lock sliding into place.

A hand rested on my shoulder, the bulk of it paperweight heavy, already putting force on my collarbone. The heaviness felt misplaced, and my stomach shot me a warning burst of butterflies.

I held the keys in my right hand, my movements stopped. I thought I heard a distant car alarm beep, but no headlights cut through the inky blackness. I begged the hand to belong to a lost passenger off Route 27. We were the last gas station before a long stretch of winding interstate. Just us, the bus stop, and the local hospital marked the bedrocks of Oxford's final offerings before the slew of green mile markers. I'd smile and give directions or apologize for the blinking closed sign, eye to eye with a road-weary traveler who'd made a wrong turn.

But I knew something was wrong. My heartbeat told the truth, the pace quickening, the tell-tale tightness growing in my chest, a rhythm found only in horror movies. I didn't want to turn and face my future. Instead, I held onto the keys and hoped for an escape plan.

His fingers squeezed my skin, and I clocked the thickness of his winter gloves. My mind reassured me, citing the chilly weather, the orange leaves bundled into haphazard piles. My own fingers were slick with sweat, a step away from becoming tiny frozen popsicles.

But my body reacted. My abdomen clenched at the sight of those gloves, my stomach swirling a warning.

"Don't you move," he uttered. His voice was higher than I expected, almost feminine, the squeak of syllables pressed against my ear.

His breath tickled my neck unpleasantly. I wanted to reach and wipe myself down, to keep myself separate from the stranger.

I didn't know if shaking my head counted as movement. Odd that I wanted to follow the rules, to make sure I did the next right thing. But I was detailed even in danger. My anxiety was shown not in my actions but in the puddle of sweat pooling at my hair-line, turning my gray locks soggy.

I felt the weight of him, a cumbersomeness that took up space, his height much taller than my five-foot-six frame. I didn't lean in, but I could feel him hovering behind me, the stench of earth and dirt clinging to his clothes. Something else lingered, a tangy smell both familiar and unknown.

"Inside," he commanded. My body revolted, all locked knees. *If I go back inside the station, I'm never coming back out.* That's what I thought, the outcome like being placed into the trunk of a car, the initial step that led to tombstones and graveyards.

I hesitated. Out of the corner of my eye, I saw a Jeep Cherokee close to the bus stop, its doors wide open. I registered the white leather seats, seemingly vacant, the beeping sound breaking through the silent night. I stalled, praying that the car would move, but the contents remained empty, no passengers found.

"Is that your car?" I tried, hoping that a distraction led to a diversion.

He replied with a sharp prick against my flimsy uniform shirt. The sting of a cut flitted near my left rib cage, the swish of it purposeful, and I gasped. He bore down on the blade, with his arm flattened against my right elbow. I morphed into a statue, chilled and unsure of my next move.

My hands wouldn't cooperate, the swinging keys threatening to drop. I wondered if I could run, throw the keys and go, the preferred protocol when being robbed. Toss a wallet in the oppo-site direction and skedaddle, that was the safest bet in vulnerable situations. But my eyes roamed over my ample stomach, the jean pants pulled too high, my gut jutting out paunchy. I'd never be fast enough. There's no way I could make it three steps, much less to the empty Jeep and open road.

And even more so, I wasn't the running kind. I was the take-it-on-the-chin type, quiet and tender. Fight or flight? No, neither. I was a freezer, through and through.

The keys clinked again, my hands moving to undo the lock. They shook, and it took longer than normal to comply. I registered his annoyance, his impatient breath circling in spurts.

"Come on!" he urged, insistent, unyielding. Another slash to the back, this one making me yelp. Adrenaline caused my face to pour sweat, the fetid smell creating a nauseous swirl in my gut. I wanted to wipe the perspiration away, certain that this type was poisonous. Like a warty toad caught in a jar, the stench of stress bloomed over my body, the foul odor my only weapon.

I gagged, and the lock pulled open. The door swayed a fraction of an inch.

He reacted, pushing me through the opening, his knife again grazing my back as he angled me forward, linebacker rough.

I stumbled, tripping over my beige boots, cursing my clumsy feet. I saw the Cheez-Its I stocked, the blurred red box promising extra-large bags, double toasted, while I struggled to regain my posture. The packaged peanut butter crackers at the front cashier were lined up neat, an easy grab for families on road trips. The lights were off, and the shadows of the reach-in fridges made everything bigger, the effect a haunted house full of jump scares.

A strong shove from behind flung me to the ground, my chin connecting with the floor, rattling all my teeth. The details of the stranger remained ant-sized, limited to my peripheral vision, the curve of his gloved finger over the serrated blade, the green floor tiles cool to the touch.

His breath, ragged; his legs, pinning me down, as difficult to move as tree trunks. The smell of him hit my nostrils, his cologne a forest of moss and rain. Wet streaks of mud stained his gloves, tainting the back of my uniform with dark smudges. Underneath the moss and the grit, I recognized the smell of fresh blood. That was the scent I couldn't name before, but now I knew the truth. He was covered in it.

He wiped his damp gloves across my back, intentional this time, the slime on my skin seeping through my torn shirt. I squirmed at his touch, eager to put distance between us.

And then a laugh, cheerful and girlish. One that spoke of hopscotch and hula hoops. Of merry-go-rounds and swings that went higher and higher, begging to connect with the sky.

He stilled over me, his laughter removed. My panicked stomach rumbled against the floor, the grumblings echoing loud in the dark. I kept silent, barely daring to suck in air.

My scream precluded the plunging knife, my body heralding a premonition before the anguish began. Before I could register my wounds, another assault tore into my backside, getting stuck deep into my tendons and the web of veins and arteries. I saw puddles of my blood forming a line, merging into a ruby-red river that lubricated the floor.

He flipped me over, struggling to hurl the bulk of me face-up. I winced as my back collided with the floor, the torn ligaments alight with agony.

"Look at me," he barked, his tone a full-fledged growl.

But I got to choose, and I wouldn't let him be my last memory.

I refocused, pouring every bit of myself into the moment in the park instead of my leaking wounds. I saw stars, and a whooshing sound thundered in my ears.

I focused on something simple, Pam's hand, our fingers intertwined. In that moment, there were so many things I should've said.

That I adored her completely.

That getting pregnant young wasn't shameful because babies were always a blessing. Especially little Grayson with his grandfather's eyes and his button nose, with bulging thunder thighs under smooth hand-me-downs. I wanted to promise her that he'd grow to appreciate her, that he'd write her sappy cards in rushed cursive, same as the ones Pam gave me.

I'd remind her that life with her had been glorious, full of moments regular people took for granted, those everyday perfections, like shared dinners and family cookbooks. I recalled her dainty face dotted with flour and freckles, her tight scrawl making edits to our pumpkin pie recipe. Or the way we both watched Grayson sleep with his hand arched by his Cupid's bow mouth. All evidence of a love that seemed bigger in retrospect.

My mind realized I was bleeding out on the floor. I could no longer turn my head, and the thump of my heart got harder to hear. But I was listening to the birds tweet back and forth, their chirps autumn's favorite serenade. We sat on the bench, the picture of perfect peace, generations of a family tree silent and pacified.

And I clung to that happiness, while the pain pinnacled into a mountain of hurt. I heard the laugh, but I rejected it. I reached to find Pam's hand, begging for one final squeeze. I found only air.

I clawed for my last piece of free will, choosing Pam and Grayson for my last words, whispered from blue tinted lips. He could take my life but he'd never sever those family ties.

I only wished I had more time.

Chapter 5
Lena Taylor
Date: November 9th, 2007, 7:45 p.m.

I was distracted, my mind far from the curving yellow line. The rain distorted the green sign welcoming me to Oxford, Ohio, another small town in a row of rural highways. The letters looked cloudy, and the thickness of the storm made me nervous, same as it always did. I death-gripped the steering wheel like it had personally wronged me.

The rain summoned me back to age fifteen and the moment when my mother skidded into the car in front of us. It had been pouring, and I forgot my umbrella, making us late for the school drop-off line. The windshield wipers were barely able to keep the downpour at bay, and the deluge drowned out the voices on the radio. I was in the front seat, helpless to intervene, as I watched my future unfold. I pumped a set of invisible brakes on the passenger side to stop the car from fishtailing. I kept pressing my heels firmly into the ground, confused why the car wouldn't obey me. Instead, I heard the screech of wheels and the smell of burned rubber stinging my nose. The crunch of metal on metal came next, the impact shooting me forcefully forward.

We collided with a bumper-sticker–adorned truck, shaken but uninjured, though thirty years later I still hated driving in the rain. For me, every downpour elicited the alarm in my mother's eyes, her knuckles white against the black backdrop of the steering wheel. This kind of storm was especially triggering, the torrent reminiscent of a storm's eye, threatening to overwhelm the road and my visibility.

I'd just passed Mt. Airy, heading south toward Covington, less than an hour away from our planned destination. My best friend Sally was waiting for me, likely watching trash TV with her hair swirled in a towel and a bottle of champagne chilling in the room's ice bucket.

We had poured over the details of this trip for months, and it took a near miracle to align our calendars. We found the time, crammed in between soccer practice, PTA, and part-time work schedules. I made it official when I drew stars around the November dates, anticipation seeping all the way down to my soul, our trip a grown-up version of spring break in Cancún.

I couldn't wait to give my best friend a tight hug and see her new haircut that she swore looked chic instead of middle-aged. A weekend of long conversations, instead of rushed phone calls and quick voicemails, felt luxurious. It provided a much-needed respite before the hectic Thanksgiving rush, plus my family could survive on premade casseroles in my absence. I'd left instructions for every scenario, from food to emergencies, covering all the bases without being asked.

I missed Sally's toothy grin, and the way she could reassure me without words. Raised in the Midwest, she was farm girl sturdy, every inch of her unflappable, the antidote to my volcano emotions. Sally's laughter was my preferred calming potion, an elixir that could cheer me up in half a minute. I functioned as her perennial cheerleader, nagging her to apply for a promotion, reminding her of her worth. Close friends balance each other that way, sanding down rough edges enough to crawl across life's finish line.

We splurged on a 3.5-star hotel because we were no longer the girls who could sleep on spare couches or be content on pull-outs. My back would start a mutiny if I booked a Murphy bed. Middle age had its problems, but it comes with enough cash to provide good linens I didn't have to change. Maybe there was an embroidered robe waiting in the closet, the creamy color pristine, untainted by coffee stains or clothing pills.

But I didn't need the fancy soaps or freebie lotions that were synonymous with luxury. All I required was time with Sally that wasn't interrupted with sticky hands and snack requests. There would be no laugh tracks in the background, no *iCarly* episodes to compete with. Just good wine, gossip, and the opulence of silence.

This was long deserved, even though the trip came with consequences. My husband Brandon shot me a resentful glare, his back stiff, his eyes on the towering stack of dirty porcelain plates. He continued to load the dishwasher, his expression cagey, watching the wheels of my suitcase thud against the floor. He didn't offer to help me load the car. Instead, he watched me struggle, which said it all.

"It's only three days," I reminded him, justification brimming in my voice. After eighteen years of marriage, I could read between his expressions, and he was currently giving me grief.

He nodded a curt response, his eyes upon the pizza sauce runoff in the sink. The frown deepened, and his hands found his hips.

I swallowed my words, pushing down every rebuttal to avoid an argument. I could've thrown the business trips back at him, the weeks where he was gone, leaving me alone with three needy kids. Brandon didn't know how our children were sleeping back then. He had no knowledge of the endless effort it took to feed, clothe, and coordinate schedules. His version of family life was reduced to a summary, concluded in a ten-minute phone call. I updated him the best I could, with quick bursts of stressed sentences, his reactions muffled by the hotel TV in the background. Then he was home and bone tired, his fifty-hour week draining his last energy reserves. Brandon sprinkled us with his leftover attention, but it was never enough, and I resented him for it.

In those days, Brandon was crisp in a pressed Brooks Brothers suit while I was drenched in milk residue, sweat, and stains that burrowed deep into my shirts. I had to toss most of my maternity clothes and start fresh with every pregnancy since the remnants of spit-up and stink changed the very nature of the clothes, soiling them forever. As a businessman, he got to skip over the diapers overflowing with diarrhea, the long blend of nights where I was too tired to care about anything, when even my fingernails hurt and my sanity dangled by the tiniest of threads.

It was easy for Brandon to claim our parenting journeys were equivalent, now that we're on easy street, with potty-trained kids addicted to PlayStations. He'd already whitewashed the worst of parenthood, content to claim equality, though he'd never juggled anyone's needs but his own. It wasn't the fathers who got down in the trenches.

It was Sally who talked me down from the ledge on those late-night phone calls laced with barely-held-together rage. She laughed when I said that's why people murdered their husbands, and she listened to me ramble until I got all the aggression out.

"They don't understand. That's all," she murmured, her voice a balm. "That's why a woman will always need her girlfriends. Because we get it in a way that men never can."

I nodded in response, her words a bridge to serenity. Sally soothed my self-righteousness with understanding, with words passed through generations of females, a collective consciousness that melted my anger away. She held all those hateful words for me, and that allowed me to continue, deflated of my list of grievances.

In those early days of motherhood, Sally was the one who stitched me together, because she'd walked the path ahead of me and stored up a well of advice for when I needed it most. She saved me and my marriage, and yet Brandon was none the wiser.

It would've been easy to take the bait in that tense kitchen moment, to have it out over the suds and dishwater, to singe Brandon with a mother's fury of being overlooked and under promised.

But I thought of Sally and her colorful fingernails, and I scaled back my bitterness. The winding nature of our shared history was worth every bitten tongue. As friends, we'd scaled larger dragons, in our dorm room at the University of Ohio, decked out and half-drunk on our own self-importance. Sally was a dream roommate, effervescent with her easy laugh, quick to shrug off little annoyances. Even though she was a neatnik, she never bitched about my dirty clothes heap or the pizza boxes piled beneath our full-length mirror.

Instead, Sally read poetry, content to soak in Byron and Rumi, humming pop radio jingles while she studied. She popped a bag of salty popcorn and split it with me each night, handing me a bowl and a highlighter, anticipating what I'd need before I even asked.

That kind of friendship was worth eating every indignant word, and I held in my critiques like I was fortifying a steel wall. This weekend was a reminder of who I was before I had a mortgage and life insurance, before scribbled grocery lists and end-of-year teacher gifts.

With Sally, I got to be that girl I used to be, when I was Lena, not Mom. To her, I was the girl who loved Bob Marley and tacked up posters with putty, never caring if we got our deposit back on our first apartment. She catalogued all my immature moments, including my twentieth birthday when I sang a horrendous rendition of Garth Brooks karaoke until I passed out. Sally was there through my first breakup and graduation, long before worries about stocks, Costco memberships, and Kindergarten Roundups.

There were days I didn't remember that person at all, but Sally did. She stored the me I used to be away, and in her memories, I found myself there, young and sparkling, not a forehead wrinkle in sight. Friendship like that was a time machine, bubble wrapping all our favorite moments, a happy timeline of two.

Instead of quarreling, I wrapped my arms around Brandon,

breathing him in. After all this time, I still liked the way he smelled, like fresh grass and Tide detergent. I put down the urge to wound and instead embraced him from behind while he rinsed a final broccoli-laced bowl. We had a dishwasher, but he believed in the pre-rinse, precision found in chores, work, and his golf game. That's the kind of man he became, the one who checked everything twice, and most of the time I was thankful for his aversion to shortcuts.

"Thanks for taking care of the kids, baby," I acquiesced, my voice soft against his neck. I hugged him tight, pressing my chest to his back.

I felt him stiffen, then relax, and his faint heartbeat pumped a greeting. I knew then that I was good to go.

"It's okay," he conceded. "You deserve a nice trip with Sally. It's been too long. I know that. But it's harder when you're away."

I hugged him tight, one more time, a show of gratitude and not ill will. He gave me a quick smile before drying his hands on the dish rag. He eyed my suitcase, and went to fetch it, feeling chagrined about his prior sour grapes.

The harder part was saying goodbye to the children. The clingiest one was Tommy, six years old and a momma's boy to his very core. His lip trembled, causing my heart to flip flop in my chest. Tommy was made of one hundred percent sugar and seemed so fragile, the kind of kid that protected every bug outside and procured wildflowers for me on the walk home from the bus stop.

While most boys were rambunctious, my second son was a different breed, quick to find my lap and touch my hair, wrapping it around his fingers like wedding rings. I couldn't imagine him ever tiring of my attention, and the feeling was mutual. Even on my most frustrating days, when there wasn't a moment to gather my thoughts, there was something in Tommy that comforted me. His need for me was a force of nature, his smile my lighthouse beacon.

Tears already brimmed in his eyes as he moved forward to hug my leg, trapping me in his spindly arms. I let him rest on my legs, my hand patting his head, stroking the curls I found there.

Cora was a confident and savvy redhead, who even at ten made sure she was the loudest person in the room. I loved her for it, that ability to take down her brothers and anyone else at a moment's notice. She was born with her preferences tattooed on her skin and an air of haughtiness that she wore like a crown. Cora was a picky eater, and a planner, with goals carved into stone, as official as the Ten Commandments. My love for her exceeded her list of daily frustrations, though sometimes it felt like a draw, since her predilections came with no wiggle room and very little patience.

Cora only liked red mechanical pencils, and all her clothing had to be starched, not a wrinkle out of place. I had to wake up ten minutes early to iron her unofficial, but non-negotiable, daily uniform. A knee-length navy dress, paired with a white button-down, her look both polished and retro. I joked she'd be a Supreme Court justice in no time, and Cora didn't even flinch, the humor landing like a premonition. She already made her Christmas wish lists months in advance, so Harvard Law didn't seem that farfetched.

But she was still soft in all the little-girl ways, still secretly talking to her stuffed animals at night and wanting one last kiss to keep any lingering closet monsters away. Having a girl like that was a privilege, even though parenting Cora was more wrangling than raising.

The oldest, Tim, was my thoughtful type, fourteen, and full of shrugs and sullenness. Teenage angst had descended upon him rapidly, with hair covering his brown eyes and a crossed-arms attitude appearing out of nowhere. He had always been quiet, but now he scowled all his replies. A touch from me could cause a skittishness that never existed before, and Tim's current speech was limited to eye rolls and sighs. I'd promised to roll with it, to summon up my waning patience, though this version of Tim was the most difficult.

I longed for a way to remind my firstborn of our connection, his entry into the world so brazen it took my breath away. I'd barely pushed through four contractions when he appeared, perfectly pudgy, with a full head of dark hair and a cry heard down the street.

He needed me, too; I was sure of it. I only had to re-learn the guidelines again, to acquire a degree in teenage turbulence, to know when to push or let loose. Such was the nature of motherhood; once I understood it, all the rules changed. The only way to win was through perseverance, with a side of checking their search history, and a whole lot of prayer.

"All right, kids. Dad's in charge. I'll be back before you know it."

A whine escaped from Tommy as he continued to grab my legs, holding on tight.

"Don't go! Why do you have to go?" he urged, even though we'd had this conversation five times.

"You know why, baby. Aunt Sally and I need time to hang out and see a new place."

"But why can't you take us with you?" he questioned, certain that his presence was always welcomed. Tommy said it so fixedly, like it was ridiculous to want time away from him, while a tantrum brewed on the horizon.

Cora patted his head, smiling. "It's all right, buddy. We'll be okay."

I shot her a thankful grin while she distracted him, grabbing his sticky hand with care. They weren't used to me leaving, which was also why I ached for time away. The guilt of motherhood threatened to topple me, the push-pull of love competing with happy hour and no alarm clocks.

It was time to leave; more farewells would only encourage meltdown mode.

"You all be good. Cora, Tim, be sweet to Tommy while I'm gone."

Cora gave me a reluctant nod as Tim turned to jut up the steps, back to whatever PlayStation game currently held his attention.

"And bye to you, too, honey!" I called after Tim and received a grunt in reply. I shrugged and winked at the other kids; both were used to the game of pacifying the hormonal teenager. I knew I had five minutes or less to get gone before Tommy prolonged my getaway. Cora held him tight, allowing me safe passage.

One last peck from Brandon and I was in the Jeep. I'd had my Grand Cherokee detailed, and it smelled brand new, no whiff of stale French fries to be found, no splashes of Coke on the center console. The quiet felt so welcome that I sighed in relief.

Other women might judge me for wanting to leave my family, for having that little voice inside that yearned for irresponsibility. But I had curated a playlist on my new iPod Touch, full of sweet reminisces like Mariah Carey's *Fantasy* CD, with bubblegum-pop anthems created to make me shimmy and shake. I was road trip ready, and I pushed off any feelings of remorse. The open road and my best friend awaited, and not a moment too soon.

The drive seemed so much longer than I'd expected. I was lost in thought, cruising five miles over the speed limit, through a cluster of outlier towns. No amount of caffeine would keep me alert, and I wished, not for the first time, for an IV of the stuff, shoved straight into my veins. The scenery was monotonous, full of downtowns with hidden homegrown cops, waiting to catch me gunning it.

I turned on the radio to break up the boredom while cursing the limited iPod battery, but it was no help. My options were limited to static and talk radio, with political heads droning on about Senator Mike Huckabee and the chances of an Obama presidency. I had no opinion of politics since most of my day was juggling crockpot meals and Tim's sinking Algebra 2 grade. I turned off the radio and listened to the rain, my windshield wipers working overtime.

A deluge began to beat down in earnest. I passed a tiny hospital, empty of its ambulances, looking low funded and ill prepared. The red cross was blurry in the evening light, and my eyes felt dry as I skidded through another blink-and-you'll-miss-it town.

I yawned, glancing down at my cup holder to see if there was anything drinkable left. Just empty coffee cups, the dredges a chestnut brown, drained of everything useful. I contemplated stopping again, but I was too close to pull off now. I needed to push myself further, a long-distance runner in the last heat.

Out of the corner of my eye, I saw a glimpse of someone standing on the shoulder of the road. An awning tried to keep the stranger covered, but the rain swirled, the overflow transforming the bus stop into a lean-to. The florescent lights of the gas station flickered, a strobe light cutting through the incipient darkness. The flicker of the J & J sign created a halo over the young man, bringing him into the spotlight.

I slowed and studied the drenched student, his posture stiff and shivering. His thumb was out gingerly, a deferential gesture, unsure and ready to change his mind at a moment's notice. Maybe the bus was canceled, leaving in its wake a soaked passenger having a dreadful day.

Hitchhiking was no longer in vogue, but there was a time when my generation leaned into the generosity of strangers to get us from here to there. The end of the 1970s was a simpler time, and Sally and I used to hitch together when our platforms were too high or the walk felt too far. I hadn't picked up anyone in forever, but he seemed pitiful, hunched and hollowed out, waiting for his luck to change.

I rolled down the window, but he couldn't hear me over the rain. The water weighed down his clothes like dumbbells as he sloshed forward. He moved with effort, clinging to his dripping black parka which was almost comically saturated. He was still in his twenties, an awkward college kid caught in a thunderstorm. He wore a backpack, juggling it poorly on his shoulders, his face asking to be rescued.

I was an unlikely forty-six-year-old savior in my skinny jeans and worn sweatshirt, but I pumped the brakes anyway, content to take on a weary passenger. Some good conversation could keep me awake and give me the jolt I needed to keep driving.

I pulled to the side of the bus stop, gesturing through the cracked passenger window while the rain splashed onto my white leather seats. I reached over to scoot the droplets off, even though he was already soaked. My grandma called that kind of wetness being a drowned rat, and I smiled when he squished into my passenger seat. His hair dripped, long and black, shielding his face. I kept the engine running but placed the car in park, flicking on my hazard lights.

I wasn't sure about the current hitchhiker etiquette. I expected him to be thankful, seeing that my car was an obvious improvement to his previous sea of puddles. When he didn't speak, my gut furrowed, but I gave him a moment to find his bearings. His knees bounced, in danger of hitting the passenger seat dashboard, his legs too cramped for comfort.

"Oh, I'm sorry. You are much taller than my fourteen-year-old. He's the one who usually rides shotgun. The thingy to move the seat back is on the side, near the door." I suppressed the urge to point it out, to show what I meant. My kids listened better if I did demonstrations, but the hitchhiker was grown, and I smothered the urge to be helpful.

He didn't make any moves to fix the seat, and his body remained slanted away from me. His pallor was pale, but I couldn't tell if the rain exacerbated that, making him look a bit ghostly. His arms were more muscular than I'd first assumed, his jacket clinging against large biceps.

"Thanks," he shrilled, his voice piercingly loud. "I was stranded at the bus stop over there. But the rain, well, it got delayed." He avoided eye contact, his jaw tight and tilted. I drummed my fingers on the steering wheel, trying to decide if I'd made the right decision. He continued to fidget, his fingers tucking his tangled locks behind his elfish ears. His movements made me restless, but I couldn't kick him out into the monsoon now.

I decided that expectation setting would smooth out the initial awkwardness.

"It's no problem. Rain like this can soak you in a second. So, I'm headed toward Covington, about an hour away. Or at least, I think so, if this thing can be trusted." I motioned to my Tom-Tom, the route inked out in blue and black dots.

He continued to fidget, fiddling with the zipper on his bag. Silence infused the vehicle. It had been so long since I'd had a passenger that wasn't my family, but the sluggishness of the drive was tangible. He appeared a bit odd, but I needed a distraction, and the storm had already linked us together.

"Where are you headed? I'm not from around here, so I'm not sure I'd know where you are going," I rambled, nerves making my voice increase an octave. "My best friend and I are going for a long weekend, but this rain has made the trip so difficult." I didn't know why it felt important to tell him that someone was waiting for me. It was strange the way he kept tinkering with his backpack, while simultaneously keepings its contents hidden.

I chattered on, covering up my unease with words.

"Well, I can take you as far as Covington. But after that, I'm afraid you're on your own." I added a smile at the end, a show of politeness that I hoped he'd reciprocate.

But he continued to gaze at the floor, his eyes never finding my face. A rush of anxiety permeated the car cabin, swirling around me in tight circles.

"It's not, there's no… issue," he replied, his long legs bending in my direction. The straps of his backpack were chafed, and a smattering of acne maligned his cheek. His dark-rinse jeans were bathed in rainwater, but his gloves looked custom fitted. They were buttery black leather and expensive, the fit precise, as if curated from a wax model. They weren't meant for cold weather or ski slopes.

My heartbeat sped up, transmitting a warning. His gloves made me uneasy, though perhaps he was preferential like Cora. I smiled, shyly, imagining chauffeurs and Europeans buying driving gloves in stores with hard-to-pronounce French names. Those millennials have their own style, and it had been years since I'd perused any store except Target.

I balanced one hand on the steering wheel, and gripped the gearshift with the other, ready to make the best of things. A shy companion was better than nothing. Until I saw a shade of silver reflected in the side mirror. He'd removed a lengthy carving knife from his backpack and displayed in on his outstretched leg. It was flashlight bright, longer than an envelope, with multiple serrated edges. It was slightly curved, the handle maroon and intimidating. He paired it with a knowing smile, his green eyes too close for comfort, daring me to move.

Chefs and boy scouts had no need for a knife like that. His was purchased at a pawn shop, all cash, with a withered look from a clerk with no teeth. It was the kind of knife used for dreadful deeds, too sharp for the pantry, too long to cut fishing lures. It was the kind that killed.

When all else fails, run. My father's words ricocheted in my brain, his wisdom curated on evenings spent target shooting, when the sky was clear enough to see the moon in the daytime. He schooled me in little snippets of self-defense, between bursts of his favorite twelve-gauge. In adulthood, I hadn't needed a gun since safety in suburbia meant neighborhood HOAs and alarm systems. Now I wished I'd made a different choice.

"Run, Lena," Daddy would say, reloading his gun. "There ain't no shame in it. If you find yourself in a situation you don't know how to handle, it's fully acceptable to get the heck out of Dodge."

His voice gave me all the direction I need. Keys in hand, with a quick burst of movement, I rushed out my driver's side door. I left everything else behind, my Nokia secured in the center console, my purse slung across the backseat of my Jeep. Hell, maybe that's all he wanted. He was welcome to it, and I'd circle back later to count my losses.

I crossed the highway in a flash, the long stretch of woods directly ahead of me. I gripped my keys vice-like and sprinted, going full speed, despite my shoes threatening to slip on the wet concrete. I ran away from the J & J station, straight into the tree line up ahead.

I didn't look behind me, certain that any pause would slow me down. I kept my eyes on the first tree that I passed, then the next, trying to find a rhythm in my steps. I gasped, out of breath and out of shape, running blindly into the damp undergrowth. My knees ached already, but I pressed on, determined to put space between us.

I couldn't hear anything behind me except the rain, and I lied to myself. I hypothesized he had second thoughts. He hadn't followed me; he'd stayed in the car with the knife, content with the spoils found in the SUV. I kept a running log of reason while I ran, warding off panic with every step.

I zeroed in on my feet hitting the ground, the wind whipping around me, the forest sounds muted by my overtaxed lungs. A log jumped out of nowhere, and I stumbled, dropping my keys into a mound of damp leaves.

I'll find them later, I promised myself, using the moment to gulp air and regain my balance. I ran on, my shoes sticking into mud that was more quicksand than dirt.

From behind me, I felt a breeze, the feel of almost fingers finding purchase. I sprinted but heard the unmistakable sound of an exhaled breath nearby. Ogre footsteps pounded into the under-growth, a second away from catching me. I kept my head up and darted forward.

If I saw him, it was over. He'd overtake me, the end. If I kept moving, I could pretend that I was running a race, and all I had to do was be faster for longer. It was just a game of tag, not a dash for my life.

A fingernail caught my ponytail, snagging it briefly. I leaned to the left, but gloves grabbed my hair, pulling out sensitive strands. I tried to keep moving, wishing that he'd claim my hair as a souvenir. Then I could continue, bald but safe, my losses venial and temporary.

That's not what happened. Instead, he tackled me, and I collapsed face first. I fell, my lips licking slimy leaves, the curve of my ankle connecting with a rock. Pain shot through my leg, a jagged flurry of surprise. My nose slammed into the soil, the impact warping it into a curved fishhook. I bit my tongue in surprise, my saliva replaced with the taste of rust.

I tried to slither away, my movements bulky in the wet dirt. He found me, using his sharp kneecaps to grind into my backbone.

I cried, the rain drowning out my words.

"Please! I have a family. I have child—"

The knife tore through my back, the gash threatening to remove my whole spine. The force of the cut felt like he'd removed my bones, turning my vertebrae into playroom building blocks. He wielded the knife again, heaving into me, the torment overwhelming my senses. The knife tore a jagged trajectory down my backside until no skin was left.

He flipped me over, grunting, his gloves mashing against my open wounds, my screams combined with the rain's pitter patter. Water dripped from his nose, the teardrop landing upon my right cheek. He leaned on his elbows, showcasing his widening pupils, pleasure spreading over his features.

A smudge of mud rested on his forehead. I stared at him, uncomprehending, the burning in my back advancing into uncontrollable muscle spasms.

"Look at me," his voice commanded, his rancid breath hot against my mouth.

Instead, I closed my eyes, scrunching them hard, like a child refusing to eat Brussels sprouts.

He pulled on my eyelids, screeching, more wolf than man. Someone would hear, and I willed him to yell or howl, anything if it led to my rescue. I was still conscious, but the shivers had started, along with my teeth chattering involuntarily.

"LOOK AT ME!" he shouted, each word non-negotiable, his bellow a gauntlet I chose to ignore. I kept my eyes closed and listened to him wail, resisting his last request with a telepathic curse word.

"Mmbep tildo." I gurgled a gauntlet, but it came out as nonsense soup.

The knife plunged into my left arm, the effect akin to a nail gun shooting through my skin. My hearing dimmed, and my vision blurred. I fought off the desire to rest, to allow myself to be weary. I wouldn't get pulled underneath these wounds.

I squished my eyes together, and I summoned Tommy, coloring a card for me for Mother's Day, his writing all pinched together and illegible. *Keep it, Mommy*, he told me, *keep it forever*, and now where was it? In a back drawer, amongst old receipts and bills.

I thought of Cora, her hair braided, standing in our yard with her lemonade stand, a look of determination blazing on her face, a sunburn threatening her freckled shoulders.

I called for Tim, and the happy tilt of his laugh when Cora bested him in arm wrestling. The hoot of pleasure, so unassuming, the moment frozen and precious.

And Brandon, who cried so hard when I walked down the aisle that the preacher had to stop his homily. My husband didn't even blush, even when our first wedded kiss tasted like saltwater. My Brandon, who yelled, "Lena! Remember! Pushing feels like trying to shit yourself!" when I needed to force Tim out during childbirth. The nurse giggled, but it worked. His methods were crass, but the result lay cradled in our arms moments later, tucked in tight.

My sons, my daughter, evidence of them found in the stretch marks crisscrossing my skin, their names a shortcut to every happiness. My devoted husband who was never too tired to wrap his arm around me and snuggle in tight. My bottom curved into the dip of his legs like LEGO pieces meant to fit together.

My breath shuddered, no longer connected to anything permanent, my lungs ragged and wheezing. Another wound ricocheted into my right shoulder, sending my arm flailing, my body no longer within my control.

I felt a gash chisel into my chest, but I kept my focus on my dearest ones, with ping-pong thoughts traversing space and time. I prayed that God and Sally would look after my children, that my best friend would feed my kids their favorite fettuccine casserole, peppered with dinnertime stories about me. I prayed that my family's future happiness would not be rooted in this present grief. And above all else, I used every bit of my energy to project a message of love. If miracles existed, they'd feel it.

My babies, I thought, against my compressed chest, the air hissing out of my lungs like a flat tire.

Sally and Brandon, I commanded from my mind, *ensure that my children remember less of my lectures and faults, and more of the things that made us a family, our history written in my womb and bones.*

The last of me manifested all my devotion, despite the cuts that showered my arms, legs, and face. The last of my consciousness yearned for my family, reaching across the forest, the high-way, and the town, to land soft against their cheeks. They'd pause, feeling the imprint of a soft kiss, one shared last graze, the sum of a mother's dying wish.

Chapter 6
Saanvi Kapoor
Date: November 9th, 2007, 4:45 p.m.

The collective weight of my classmates' eyes was unbearable, causing hives to erupt in itchy molehills across my neck and chest. The desks hemmed me in, blocking every exit, trapping me in a sea of righteous judgment.

It's not paranoia if it's true, I reminded myself. You'd think I'd be used to the stares, being that I was a woman, and a minority, in the chemical engineering field. My whole master's degree had been a combination of murmurs and side-eyes, a swirl of unspoken questions and insults that I was lost or filling a quota. I'd earned my place, but never adjusted to the glances that settled upon my shoulders, taking up residence and planting a homestead. They said looks can't kill but I begged to differ.

Currently, a barrage of well-timed coughs and pointed fingers continued to interrupt class and left no doubt about my peers' insinuation. I was the topic of the day, not biophysical chemistry, their snippets turning me into an Indian Hester Prynne.

I shifted in my seat, aware of the looks that lingered, the thick dose of gossip with frowns aimed like bullets in my direction.

Before, I was an anomaly; now, I'd been reduced to the pariah level, which was an obvious social demotion, even for an outcast like me.

I knew I should've skipped today, but what excuse could I offer? *Excuse me, Professor, my kind-of friend made national news for being an alleged serial killer, so can I please take a mental health day?* That explanation would cause an uproar and confirm what everyone was already thinking. I learned, because of Jason, that guilt by association was a tough label to lose. So much for innocent until proven guilty. *What a sham*, I mused, my bad mood threatening to come out swinging, no prisoners taken.

The campus of Miami University was nicknamed high school with beer, its midsize stature pitted against the sprawling campus of Ohio State. The smaller size guaranteed that my peers had seen me with Jason LeDown last summer since most students were local and commuted to campus. They experienced college life with a side of their mother's home cooking, tucked safe in their childhood beds. It also meant they all knew each other, their faces yearbook familiar, the next four years another accolade in the same small-town story.

I came here on scholarship, so I lacked ready-made friends, and my transition to Miami University was full of stops, starts, and wrong turns, a bumpy road in my search for desirable higher education. Plus, my dark skin color created an obvious multifariousness, a flashing beacon of diversity. We made quite a pair, the yin of my double nose rings, matched with the yang of Jason's red polo, a preppy dissenter in a sea of camo. Our skins, one stretched, one brown, left a wave of silenced conversations in our wake, full of crossed arms and squinty eyes that we pretended to ignore.

That was a year ago, before Manib and his coffin, before the life I had ended and another lesser life began.

I doodled on my notebook, willing myself not to cry, as I thought of those *before* times, notable only because I was naïve to the tragedy waiting to drown me. For those who'd lost someone, that demarcation wasn't a line in the sand. It's made of concrete, the markings written in lost sleep, and time that changes but remains stagnant. Grief compounded takes no prisoners, with calendars marred by trauma.

Previously, I was focused on highlighting the discrepancy between Miami University and UNC Chapel Hill. One was an almost Ivy League institution, full of oral history and baby-blue jerseys, its alumni including Andy Griffith. The other was a pinprick on a map, in a town that was resembled a *Sim City* video game. Oxford, Ohio, was never meant to house a top-tier university. Its offerings remained stunted, with a downtown that might not survive the next recession, the multitude of boarded-up windows on High Street just waiting for an excuse.

I knew Jason wouldn't be impressed, seeing as we spent most of that summer in the state-of-the-art lab together, with brand new equipment and an organizational structure that rivaled the Dewey Decimal System. But I wanted him to witness my ascension, from the scruffy basement dredges stocked with broken beakers to the pristine lab of the summer. I was the dog in *Lady and the Tramp*, but I'd shucked off my mangy status and traded it for the high life. And he'd been complimentary, his eyes wondering over the cracked equipment, threatening a papercut or worse.

"Oh, Sammy. You described it well, but it's worse than I imagined." Jason shuddered. "You have to overcome so much!"

I smiled, feeling accomplished, choosing to ignore my American nickname, with its offensive subtraction of vowels, curbing my culture into something house-cat appropriate. I allowed it because it meant securing Jason's approval, which was not easily obtained. Jason lobbed his best eye rolls for other students in the class, eviscerating the ones he deemed lazy, his criticisms quick and cruel. At the time, I felt lucky to be in his good graces; now I wondered about the implications of him writing people off with ease.

We'd spent the rest of his day trip drinking PBR in the downtown dive bar, known for its sticky floors and cheap draft prices before he caught the bus back to Chapel Hill. His goodbye wave from the bus window was the last time I'd seen him in person, though we still chatted on AOL Messenger occasionally. Our last communication surrounded Manib, and Jason was eloquent but brief in his platitudes.

> Chem4life: So sorry for you and your parents, Sammy. I know what your brother meant to you.

> SKRulez: Thanks.

> Chem4life: Thinking of you, there's no logic in this.

> SKRulez: Agreed.

Words did nothing to ease bereavement, though I appreciated Jason's succinct attempt.

A novel rush of fear swept through me. I wondered if I should clear my hard drive of any communication between us. I imagined FBI agents in black bomber jackets scowling at me, their gloved hands cradling my computer like a fragile bomb, the swish of their windbreakers paired with serious accusations. I knew next to nothing about scrubbing computers and allowed my head to rest in my hands, covering up the world for a moment. The seriousness of Jason's crimes would cause everyone to review our interactions through a critical lens. And that meant I was way out of my depth, now that my lab partner was infamous, armed, and dangerous. I had the weekend to ruminate and develop a strategy if I could just survive this last Friday class.

A swift kick to the back of my chair reminded me I was still holding court in class. I tried to lock into the lecture, but my thoughts were far from quadratic equations. My attention was centered upon last night's 11-Alive news bulletin, the moment seared into my brain for eternity.

The television broadcast roared to life right before midnight. With solemn grimaces, the reporters stated that a senior college student was the victim of an attempted break in at Jason's university, UNC Chapel Hill. They paused, then delivered the punchline, after making the viewers wait for it. The Co-Ed Killer had been identified, caught because of a discarded ski mask, the saliva and fingerprints matched to a current graduate student. The subpoena alleged that the killer matched fingerprints on file, the result of a teacher's assistant background check.

When the newscaster flashed the photo of Jason LeDown,

labeling him as the suspect in the Co-Ed Killer cases, my cereal bowl missed my hands, spilling onto my apartment floor. The milk seeped into the carpet, but the plastic bowl remained upright, no porcelain to be had on my meager stipend. I raced to the TV, turning it up full blast, my fingers shaking while the reporters confirmed that Jason was on the run, current location unknown.

"Oh shit!" I yelled, my thoughts scattering into icicle shards. The shock threatened to dismantle my mind. I steadied myself the only way I knew how, by memorizing the facts like I'd be quizzed on them later. Type A to the core, even in peril, forever a student first. The reporters condensed the facts, and I wrote them down for review.

Charlotte, a senior at UNC Chapel Hill (her last name redacted to protect her identity), had reported that Jason broke into her apartment with zip ties in his hands, a morbid welcoming party greeting her at dusk. She'd been armed, and that discouraged Jason from a further assault, then he fled the scene. Based on her description and the uncovered ski mask, Jason LeDown became suspect number one, paired with an unflattering headshot that flashed across multiple news channels. In it, he looked pale, his porcelain face unperturbed under a halo of black hair. He looked wane and supercilious, though no one looked like themselves in a yearbook picture, his expression far from the polished teacher's assistant I recognized. I zoomed in on his features, uncertain of what I missed.

Last night, I'd slept poorly, my internal monologue a manic jumble of concern and doubt. I wondered how Jason went from genius biomedical phenom to murderer overnight. Whatever was wrong remained latent, because I only recalled his cat-scratch notes, his routine of cleaning every beaker before starting the day. To me, he was every inch a budding scientist, a man obsessed with facts, figures, and equations. A knife-wielding maniac was a stretch. Instead, he kept meticulous data in tight columns, washed his hands at hourly intervals, with a smile tight and predictable, aimed in my direction.

It was difficult to believe the accusations were true. I tried to match the buttoned-up lab rat with a blood-soaked killer, his face lined with droplets of ruby red. If it wasn't so serious, I would've laughed, imagining Jason running around campus in his lab coat, a literal rendition of Dr. Jekyll and Mr. Hyde.

But he was dismissive, quick with his vicious impersonations of Dr. Parker behind his back, and the quips that made me laugh but caused my scruples to send up a warning flare. Jason was a prodigy, but he wasn't kind, and with him, I became bitter, too, a sarcastic student I didn't quite recognize. We bonded over what we disliked, but I remained safe for his brutal asides. I was the dutiful sidekick, ready with a comeback and a bark of laughter. But I'd witnessed Jason's anger, set to a quick boil, ready to catch idiots in the crosshairs and take them down.

For Jason, non-intellectuals deserved their demise, whether that's low-paying jobs or a blue-collar life with its calluses and food stamps. No empathy was found for those with lesser scores, who worked long hours for less pay. Instead, Jason sneered at their toils, his haughty head imbued with tenure dreams and a six-figure salary, his future an ivory tower of academia.

I listened to those lectures and never mounted a rebuttal, though I was a scholarship student from working class roots. His haughtiness was incredibly offensive, but I kept my mouth, and my family's SES status, to myself. In the darkness of my bedroom, my thoughts vacillated between guilty and innocent, no consensus found. I gave up the ghost of sleep and pounded some coffee instead, but it did little to clear my head.

There were good odds that Jason would come here. He had limited friends and fewer acquaintances. I was his confidante, though I knew only the basics surrounding his personal life. I admired his intellect, but we spoke the language of numbers and late nights, of math pages that became notebooks, which became volumes. We bonded over things we couldn't yet articulate, theories that existed in the realm between what was real and what was possible. I understood him, sure, but I didn't know his predilections, his secrets, the things that made him tick. He made me feel less lonely, but only because he understood the sacrifice of higher education.

We spent our Saturday nights rechecking the lab data, and I hadn't been on a date since before G.W. took office. Jason walked the same stringent path, trading lovers and keggers for measurements, scales, and *summa cum laude*.

I wondered where he'd go and who he'd ask for help. If the situation were reversed, I'd show up here. I paced, wondering how to approach a person of interest and the legality of harboring a fugitive.

I had no one to talk through the facts, to decompress the data I'd acquired on Jason and his alleged offenses. I was worlds away from my Facebook-obsessed peers, who scrolled while I studied, trading bar crawls for distinction and the Dean's list.

That's why Jason and I were combustible because our brains

were linked, not our bodies, our conversation the result of firing synapses, the downregulation of dendrites, resulting in theories taking flight. I liked to picture our initial camaraderie like an action potential rendering, a neuron becoming an electrochemical cascade, positively charged and in motion. Our friendship felt electric, because of our devotion to the purest of all subjects, chemistry. Lavoisier's oxygen theory of acids started our spiral, and we took up the mantle, eager to modernize the ideas found in those tired textbooks.

For one summer, we were inseparable. Working side by side, swollen with junk food and caffeine, our partnership seemed both official and natural. He picked up where I left off during our practice equations, with Jason's poor handwriting rivaling mine. We both had to squint to make out the numbers. But he'd also commanded the lead, his confidence unquestioned, and on every paper he signed his name first, his brilliance reserved for the top spot. I let it go, though it bugged me, a chip in the friendship armor written in bold cursive.

The class bell cut through my anxious thoughts. I sprinted out of class, flushed, the clock finally granting my release. I continued to feel the sting of my classmates' convictions, but I jogged on, brushing past the double doors of Pearson Hall. I tightened my pace, impatient to outrun the whispers, my tiny apartment close by and private.

I called it an apartment, but with its dismal square footage, it barely qualified. My time at Miami University had always felt temporary, with my silverware remaining in cardboard boxes, the living space sparse and white-walled. I'd applied to other internships across state lines and would soon learn about my next assignment. No use in unpacking my paltry possessions. I'd reduced my outfit to a predictable pair of jeans and a white button-down shirt. My life read like a bumper sticker: no muss, no fuss, just math.

There's comfort in regimented days, the consistency safe and banal, with no deviations from the mean. My security was found in structure, whether that's a predictable pattern or an Excel spreadsheet. This year had packed enough drama to power a nuclear warhead, so I whittled my life down to the smallest of highly foreseeable parts.

I learned the hard way that straightforward was safer because it kept sorrow at bay. Grief remained unpredictable, with little reminders of Manib buried like minefields throughout my day to day. That's why death was a son of a bitch. Soon as I understood it, it gave me the slip, sneaking up on me with another wave of mourning, without recourse. There were days devoted to missing my brother, when the depression would slink into my room, threatening to wreck everything I'd built. It took all my energy not to succumb, and that was not a victory. At best, heartache offered a stalemate, never a reprieve.

I barreled inside my apartment, my stomach grumbling from a coffee breakfast and a nonexistent lunch. I heated up a Lean Cuisine, ready to play another game of morality Russian Roulette, insulated from the world in my kitchen, surrounded by white blinds and a vintage microwave. As the powdery pizza cooked, I cross-examined myself, pondering if friendship constituted a legal privilege.

If Jason was a killer, then I should turn him in; that's not even up for debate. But there was plenty of evidence to suggest he was

wrongfully accused, including Occam's Razor. If the easiest explanation was the right answer, then Jason was exactly who I knew
him to be, someone who'd rather discuss cryogenics over murder
weapons. He'd aced thermodynamics but complained it stole
every second of his spare time. His studies dominated his schedule, and his academics were too rigorous for a slasher side hobby.

That's some dark humor, the idea that only C-plus students
could balance killing and coursework. But it felt true. Advanced
coursework like ours left no wiggle room for stalking and break-
ins. We could barely find time to eat dinner, much less run
surveillance.

And I'd been in Jason's presence many times, the two of us
alone at dawn, furiously calculating mass transfers until we
induced serious headaches. With all that alone time, he would've
had numerous opportunities to overpower me, if that had been
his intention.

Jason wasn't inherently chauvinistic. He'd reserved his worst
diatribes for Josh, an older student with bifocals, who needed
extra time and individualized instruction. Jason would cackle at
Josh's ineptitude and would actively try to undermine him in
front of the professor, highlighting every mistake his adversary
made. It upset me, the way Jason persecuted Josh, crowning him
with a figurative dunce cap while the class laughed. But I was
happy to avoid Jason's denunciations, my status as his lab partner
ensuring safe passage, though my reasons for pairing up with him
were personal, not strategic.

Jason's mannerisms reminded me of my brother Manib. That
had been the initiating fuse of our friendship. The sound of his
name made my heart clench, the equivalent of pressing hard on a

bruise. The road of Manib only led to heartbreak, and crying spells, and days when I had to drag myself out bed, bereavement consistent in its haunting. Losing someone to suicide could do that, whittle you down, until all that was left were unanswered questions stored in my skeleton body. Sadness upon sadness, and then deeper still.

Physically, they looked nothing alike. Manib had the mussed hair of Harry Potter, black and sticking straight up, his brown skin covered with sardonic band T-shirts and ketchup stains. Jason was pale and sturdy, a trellis in J.Crew trousers. But the way their minds whizzed, breaking every bell curve, was beautiful. They could learn by listening and crushed every test, confident going one-on-one with a blackboard. I wanted to break apart their brains, to dissect the gray and white matter, preserved in formaldehyde, two perfect case studies in next-level intelligence.

I believed that if I could crack the code of their brilliance, I could've won multiple Nobels, toppling the science community in one fell swoop. Two men, both outliers, and I was the bell curve that held them together, the wiring that kept them stable.

Those similarities created a sisterly tsunami of affection. I pushed the memories away. Jason was not my brother. My brother was dead, and was always more fragile, his bleeding heart two sizes too big, wanting to cover the world with love and call it cured, until depression took him to a place where no remedies existed.

I bit into the pizza to distract myself, the cheese burning the tip-top of my mouth, searing it with sauce and pain. But the burn did its job, distracting me from my reflections, rooting me in the present.

I chewed, swishing the lava-hot pizza across the sides of my mouth. I took another bite, the heat making my eyes water, when a light knock rapped on my door, so soft I might've misheard it. I waited, eyes on my plate, eager to be mistaken. I heard another tap, then two. Someone was at the door, and I knew who it was. I had been waiting for him, with scatter-brained contemplations, certain in my soul that he'd show.

I should've followed a script when Jason appeared on my front stoop, drenched and chagrined, his hair flat against his forehead. I should've pretended to be gone and left him dripping on my welcome mat. But the selfishness of his presence hit me in the chest, and I wanted to vent my anger. Even if he were innocent, by showing up here, he'd made me an accomplice, my name attached to his story, as immovable as concrete.

I longed to string curse words together, to lecture him about the inappropriateness of this visit. Instead, I warily cracked the door, pinky finger wide. Knowing him now came with a risk, as well as a possible aiding and abetting a fugitive charge. Not to mention the betrayal of my gender and every democratically held belief if I assisted a serial killer who targeted women my age.

"Sammy. Please," Jason began, his voice hushed. "You know I've got nowhere else to go." His squeaky voice was hot and familiar, but his bowed head was not, his posture a prayer for my mercy.

I'd expected a litany of excuses expounding from his mouth, not outright begging. It startled me, to see him so insecure and hollowed, a valedictorian drained of all accolades. Or was it intentional, the way his body shielded inward, safe from the streetlights in the distance, designed to illicit my sympathy? I hesitated, insecurity trembling the pendulum between right and wrong.

"Please, you know this isn't me. You know this *couldn't* be me," Jason tried again, his voice thick with sorrow. I paused, the door continuing to open another inch. I needed him to rid me of the sudden queasiness that swashed beneath the surface. He'd have to convince my gut, not my mind, of his innocence. Bile rose in the back of my throat, my belly aching for the toilet, a moment away from locking the door and deadbolt.

"I'm going to be sick, Jason. You better go."

"I don't deserve your help, Sammy. I know that. And I wouldn't be here if I had any other place to go." He sniffed, his voice high-pitched and agitated. "But you know I didn't do any of these things, that I'm innocent of these charges. And, well, you're my only friend. That's why I'm here. I know I can trust you. Please trust me, too."

He stared at me, his features broad and blameless. Jason held my gaze, and I imagined him trying to channel doe eyes, Disney movies, anything but murder, blood, and mayhem. I allowed him to plead, but I didn't swing the door open, not yet. His expression seemed inauthentic, his eyes too wide, a wolf in grandma's clothing with the sharpest of teeth.

"You shouldn't be here, Jason. The police are looking for you. I really don't want to get involved in this." I channeled a firm voice, meant for a courtroom or a district judge. With a steadfastness I didn't feel, I continued. "This isn't good for me."

I needed something heavy to hang on to, to combat the churn of uncertainty, my next move still undecided.

"Sammy, please. Let me in. I got here by bus, and I need to rest. I've got a plan to clear my name. I need a break, then I'll be on my way. Please, Sammy, for me."

His voice eked out into a whine, so different from the certainty of the being the best and brightest. For someone with a genius IQ, he appeared humbled, with a dirt smudge on his cheek and hands clasped casually. No way this was the same man who used zip ties and bindings, who broke down doors with blades and malevolence. The likelihood of that was statistically impossible, it had to be, and I made my choice.

I creaked the door open, the awkwardness between us palatable. He pressed gently against the doorframe, his foot crossing over my apartment threshold. I didn't stop him, and I wondered briefly if I could have. Would he have turned on me, with narrow red eyes, monster-like in his resolve? I didn't test him. There were no tricks up my sleeve. Instead, I stood still and watched his movements. He seemed comfortable once he was indoors, regaining a bit of his confidence. His clothes had lost the battle to the earlier rainstorm, and he sidestepped onto the rug, politely trying to drip less onto the bare floor.

"Thanks so much, Sammy. You have no idea," he uttered, giving me space to back up. I didn't move to close the distance between us. This situation was all business, no hugs or comfort offered, and I let my body language set the tone. My arms remained firmly crossed, protecting my chest, the stance of unamused women everywhere. I kept facing him, walking backward into my kitchen, clear I was taking no chances.

He resembled the friend I knew. This grimier version donned sagging jeans and had dirt under his fingernails. His black parka covered his torso, keeping him warm in the November cold. His eyes adjusted, scanning my colorful rug, the tug of a smile on his face. Jason had never viewed my living room, with the ant-size

TV, the trash can overflowing with graph paper, and the crumpled Belvita wrappers on the kitchen counter. Every atom of me should've been on high alert, blaring SOS signals.

Instead, the nausea eased, and it felt natural to welcome my fellow numbers nerd into my cramped space. The current Jason, in his rain-soaked Nikes, was the same student who loved Nacho Cheese Doritos, who licked the pepper flakes and salt off each finger. He kept time by pencil taps, in creaky vintage chairs, and shared his Dr. Pepper with me, pouring half in a cup so I could save my quarters for the laundromat.

His tall frame dwarfed my diminutive kitchen. All his worldly possession were stuffed in a ratty backpack. A nondescript baseball cap covered his locks, the brim low on his forehead, his features lost to shadows.

"It's been madness, Sammy. I headed straight for the bus stop, knowing that Chapel Hill was no longer safe for me. Luckily, I purchased a ticket to Fairfield, and no one checked ID," he continued, his voice rushed and raspy. "I kept away from people and walked the rest of the way here. I knew if I could make it here, you'd help me. You'd know I was innocent." He stepped closer, waiting for me to agree.

I didn't offer any opinions or assurances to keep the dialogue flowing. To promise anything felt like a trap. I knew we had to be fingerprinted because of our privileged lab access. Our professor opined that he was taking no chances about handing over the keys to his multi-million-dollar kingdom. We all submitted because by then our internship had begun, and we promised to be mindful of broken or missing items. How Jason's prints landed on that ski mask was the most difficult piece of his narrative to explain.

It was suspicious, but too soon to offer any official stance. I kept our interactions purposeful, like the scientist I claimed to be.

"The most pressing matter remains your plan of action." I clarified, orienting us onto a concrete topic. I put space between Jason and myself, idly heading behind the kitchen island. I moved incrementally, but with the intention of enforcing a barrier between us. The interaction felt off-kilter, with me functioning as a travel agent to a tourist. His presence filled my breakfast nook, with drops of water glinting off his hat and plain clothes.

"Well, first, I need food, any kind, whatever you've got. I'm starving. And water, too. Maybe some decent conversation with someone I can trust." Jason's tone was bleak, switching back to hangdog deferential.

I replied by rummaging through the dusty cabinets, but my offerings were scant. As a graduate student, I barely cleared sixteen grand per year in stipends, so everything I owned was of the cheap and bad-for-you variety. Normally that would embarrass me, but I knew Jason was the same, our poverty a shared joke during happier times.

"I've got the usual: granola bars, peanut butter crackers, Goldfish, and I think the juice in the fridge is still good but let me check." I busied myself while he sat down at my secondhand breakfast nook, resembling a giant placed at the kiddie table. Before, I would've laughed, watching him squeeze his tall frame into the barely held together chair. Today, I kept my remarks quiet, no longer certain I'd say the right thing.

I gathered up what I could, pouring him a glass of OJ and water into stolen restaurant cups. I liked the red plastic tumblers at Pizza Hut the best, since they could easily hold thirty-two ounces of Diet Coke and were dishwasher safe. Stolen glasses made up half of my cupboard, with Goodwill curations completing the mishmash ensemble.

I didn't slide the plate over to him like a criminal guard, but I didn't sit next to him, either. I remained out of reach, depositing the donations in front of him. Manib always joked I had Inspector Gadget arms, and now their length came in handy. The skittishness of our encounter continued to feel unpleasant, an ominous trick that turned familiarity sour.

If he noticed the thrifted cups, he didn't mention it. Instead, he tucked into the food, barely pausing to chew, a feral animal preparing for hibernation.

"Thanks, Sammy," he said in between gulps, his Adam's apple vibrating between chugged drinks and cracker containers. He inhaled the snacks with the ease of a hot-dog-eating contestant gunning for first place.

My mouth opened, forgetting my own manners. I'd never seen Jason so discombobulated, the opposite of his previous put-together nature. His dull clothes were at odds with his prior slick-backed hair and ironed shirts, his glasses polished, his books aligned. It knocked me off balance, the dichotomy between past and present. I watched him devour the snacks, his arms taut, the bulk of him able to overpower anyone, if he used his height to his advantage. He consumed the granola bar in one bite, his crunches untamed, an uncontrollable urge to feast. The overhead bulb was threatening to burn out, the flicker of it suitably eerie.

I shivered, though it wasn't cold. What would my brother say now, if he could see me, all passive and uncertain? I could hear

Manib's voice in my head, between my ponderings and Jason's chewing.

"You, Saanvi," he clicked at me, "want to know everything about one thing. That is exactly how you ended up right here." He would smirk then, a dimple on his cheek. "I told you that makes you only smart at one thing. Me, I want to know everything about everything."

"That's impossible."

"We will see, Behen. We will see, eh?" He would spin in his chair, a confident swirl, relying on the carefully practiced wit of close-in-age siblings.

I almost smiled at the memory until I realized Jason was speaking.

"Can you tell me what they know?" he asked, his mouth still full on one side with a pocket of food. He resembled a chipmunk, preserving food reserves in his cheek for a long winter.

"I don't..." I hedged, trying to find a polite way to be assertive. "I don't think I want to talk about that."

His eyes narrowed, a grimace spreading across his face. I felt guilty that I couldn't be open with him, but my mind was whizzing through legal notices and prior knowledge, bursting with questions about what constituted breaking the law. The news anchors had urged anyone with information surrounding Jason's whereabouts to call the tip line, but I didn't know if that was a precedent or a request. My head spun, and my fingers gripped the table tight, working to keep me vertical.

"What do you mean?" he queried, his voice sharp, his gaze a laser, intent on elaboration.

"I mean, Jason, I can't get involved with this. A crime, a

manhunt…" I searched for the right words to convey the trouble he was in. "I am not sure if you're aware, but you made the national news. Everyone is looking for you. They probably will come here, maybe even soon, and explore all your known contacts."

"Shit!" he screamed, banging his fists on the table, the sound a jump scare, causing me to yelp. "Sammy, why the hell didn't you lead with that? Damn it!"

I'd never seen him furious, with his jaw tight and lips pursed into an intense straight line. He looked irate, but worse, more significant. *He looks guilty*, I thought, ever the unstable lunatic, ready to pounce.

"Hey, take it easy." I forced myself to sound casual, but the words bounced off him. His head whipped over his shoulder, hypervigilant to the possibility of the Feds and a battering ram.

"I thought I could stay here, Sammy. That's why I came here. I assumed you'd let me stay, but the cops are too far ahead of me." He swallowed his snack crumbs, scattering the rest across my scratched table.

I shook my head. On this, I was firm.

"No way. And not only because I want to limit my involvement, but because they will come here, Jason. We both knew you'd visit, and they realize that, too. It's only a matter of time until they arrive, and I really don't know what to say when they do." I bowed my head, the truth hovering in the air, drastic and undetermined.

He sighed, dejected and wet, the curve of his back producing a slanted C. He cradled his knees, drained of all the right answers, and I felt sorry for him, the way he became deflated, removed of all energy and strength. I pitied him, and yet, I needed him to leave fast. My favor had reached its time limit.

"I'm sorry, Jason. Probably best if you head back to the bus stop."

"Yeah, there's no other option," he replied dejectedly, stuffing the remaining contents into his pants pockets. Crumbs continued to rest on his upper lip as he stood, his pants leaving a ring of water on the chair.

"Hold on, just—hold on," I replied, dashing up the stairs. I got a towel for his hair, the worn cotton feeling soft in my hands, a meager peace offering. I ran back to the kitchen, the towel dangling in my arms.

"Here. Take this," I urged. He shot me a grateful smile.

"Thanks, Sammy. Thank you so much. I really appreciate this, even though my plans changed. I need a ride to the bus stop, then I'll be out of here, I promise. My ticket's still valid, and it's faster if you drive." He'd pivoted, trading a hideout for a runaway dash to places unknown.

"And I won't tell anyone that you helped me," he added as he dried off his hair and patted his clothes. Relief flooded through me, and I released air I didn't know I was holding. I wanted him to promise to keep me a secret, but I didn't want to spark another tirade.

A lightning strike sounded, the crack of it close by. We eyed each other, both acknowledging his attempt at drying off was futile. He shrugged his shoulders, folding the towel carefully, placing it across the couch armrest. The way he cradled it was gentle, the antithesis of violence. Jason heaved his black backpack onto his shoulders, more hiker than mugshot, braced for the rain and whatever came next.

I grabbed my keys from the living room table and led the way to the parking lot. He waited while I locked the door, purposefully keeping six feet between us. I felt chagrined, crimes weren't contagious, and yet I appreciated his efforts. And the worst part was he knew it. Jason moved deliberately, never darting impulsively, no actions left unchecked. Whatever happened had already changed him, and his mannerisms slowed to a steady, predictable pace.

I wasn't sure if he was projecting a safe image or becoming a better predator. The only certainty was that the Jason I knew was long gone, and in his place, a man who kept me guessing.

He spotted my red Nissan and grasped the passenger side door. The parking lot was empty, but the sky turned a deep gray as another rumble of thunder made itself known. We didn't have much time before the sky would open and pour, and I hadn't grabbed an umbrella on the way out.

"The bus station is near the hospital," he instructed, fastening his seat belt. He'd done his research, but I didn't need directions. The bus stop in Oxford was saddled between the hospital and the J & J gas station, and I'd waited through storms and sunshine to catch the number 5 bus. I could take us there blindfolded.

He checked to make sure his seat belt was tightened. It seemed unlikely that the next Jeffrey Dahmer would care enough to abide by the seat belt law. It was so innocuous that I almost joked about it but instead put the car in gear.

It took ten minutes to drive past the county hospital, the red ambulance signs shining in the darkness like a talisman, the storm taking ownership of the sky. I parked, resting my hand on the gear shift, unsure about his send off. It didn't seem appropriate to wish Jason luck, but I also didn't want to leave him without a goodbye.

I thought of the last time I saw Manib. He'd slept in, his hair damp with sweat. I was already late for class, my mind on my pop quiz and back-to-back schedule. I rushed by with a strawberry Pop Tart dangling out of my mouth, my hip balancing against the doorframe.

"I love you, sis!" he said, his voice slightly winded. I wanted to respond, I heard him but couldn't sacrifice my only sustenance shoved in my mouth. I nodded my goodbye, taking the front steps double time. It was only later that I realized I hadn't responded, after Manib's body was found in the garage, his neck red and wounded, his eyes bulging and swollen, a body swinging where my brother used to be. His Rakhi remained tied against his wrist, a symbol of protection and sisterly affection he no longer needed.

I learned to treasure my farewells after that.

"Jason." I angled my body, tilting my shoulders close to his. "Take care of yourself, all right?" It wasn't a reprieve, but a hope, an assurance that he'd be okay.

He looked at me and nodded once before his fingers found the door handle.

"Thanks again, Sammy, for everything." He closed the door softly and walked at a brisk pace, the rain beginning to sprinkle my windshield and his jacket.

He turned, then faltered, facing the passenger side door with a quick knock on the window and a motion to roll it down. I followed his cue, winding down the window, the gust of rain swirling around us.

"I'm glad I got to see you, Sammy. You're one of the good ones, the kind of woman who knows her place, who lets me take the lead, and I've always appreciated that. You're so different from the fun-time girls, with their tanning lotions and their ponytails, the opposite of clever and much too trusting. They have the intelligence of a snail, and eyes full of fluff, a brain of no use, with nothing left to give, and no modicum of respect."

He grinned, and the wolf was back, hiding in plain sight all along, his words a motive, his intention clear. Too shocked to reply, I watched him settle under the bus awning, his backpack high on his shoulders, content with a long wait.

I grabbed the steering wheel, wondering if my Jiminy Cricket conscience would intervene. My stomach growled, and I waited, until the silence got to be too much, the car cabin a vile reminder of Jason's parting words.

The sounds of Outkast blared from the speakers, instructing me to shake it like a Polaroid picture, the bass slicing my eardrums. I turned off the radio, registering my mistake. My fingers wound around the car door handle, along with a rush of bile that blanketed the asphalt. Chunks of undigested pizza littered the ground, the sting of throw-up burning my nose. I emptied my dinner in the parking lot, with remnants of tomato sauce splattering my shirt, the degree of my sickness catching me by surprise.

It was a sign. Deep down, where biology was housed, my body reeked of wrongdoing and created a putrid wedge in my insides. I vomited up my morality, my fingers rushing to keep the hair out of my face. My body knew the score and judged me harshly.

Jason was not my brother, no matter how many characteristics they shared, no matter what test scores and aptitude showed.

I'd made a terrible mistake. My body concurred, and another round of sickness poured from my throat, while the rain attempted to wash away the evidence of my sin.

Too late, my throat burned a reply. Too late.

I didn't call 911. I didn't place an anonymous call to the police. I did none of the right things. It was self-preservation, and I made the horrible choice eagerly.

When the sickness eased, I put the car in drive and sped away. My only goal was to rid myself of further wrongdoing, and any lingering connection to Jason LeDown.

Chapter 7
Charlotte Winder
Date: November 7th, 2007, 2:30 p.m.

My backpack and mood felt lighter, the absence of my heavy books and test anxiety allowing my hunchbacked shoulders a reprieve. My acute worries should evaporate, now that finals week was winding down, with graded tests and calculated averages soon slated for student viewing. But my insides remained tightly coiled, my university a location where serenity had long since abdicated, leaving behind a legion of concern that couldn't be solved with Tums or alcohol. As a student body we'd experimented with that playbook of coping skills, though it did little to ward off a serial killer.

The collective campus attitude paid little attention to words of caution, echoed by police officers and buttoned-up administrators. My peers were hellbent on rejoicing, the pit, or central location of campus, toilet papered and properly celebrated in spite of the recommended curfew. The students were at a fever pitch, eager to throw off textbooks and responsibility, but I remained on the outskirts, eyeing the parties from afar, unwilling to shake off the wariness I felt.

You'd think others would practice restraint, given that a literal murderer was on the loose, but danger wasn't going to thwart the beer pong championships off fraternity row. If anything, it added to the sense of adventure, with students skirting off paths, screams turning into jokes about how Chapel Hill had embraced Halloween overnight. Seniors dressed as final girls, and slasher costumes were ubiquitous, in poor taste but still so popular, certain of their safety in numbers.

My friend Hilary, a self-proclaimed true-crime aficionado, stated it was the same reaction that some had to Bundy in the late '60s. When he escaped from his hearing, spelunking off the side of a two-story building, there was mass panic, but also a subset that devoted their attention to selling merchandise and inventing silly cocktails for the killer at large. Human beings survived on trading shitty defense mechanisms to combat a loss of control, even in the new millennium.

There was no permanent way to divert our fear. Under every episode of binge drinking and nights spent heaving over the toilet was a livewire of terror, paired with three names. We all knew their stories: Chrissy, Sheena, Sherry, the death trifecta, chanted in order like a rosary, a trio of sacrifices made to the Co-Ed Killer. There's no amount of Jell-O shots that could remove their memory.

I'd felt haunted or hunted all week, my sixth sense working overtime, compounded by my mother's warnings ricocheting in my head. The breaking news voiced the macabre script on television, declaring that UNC Chapel Hill was plagued with a serial killer. Ever since the third female victim was found, desecrated and hog tied, the media and my mother had blared advice with increased fervor, until it was impossible to ignore.

"Don't walk at night. Don't risk it, not now, not when you are so close to graduation." My mom's familiar refrains amplified into a chorus of warnings about wickedness, shadows, and dangerous men. She lowered her voice to let me know she was decidedly not joking, her tone hushed and grave.

I listened to the talking heads reinforce her every concern, labeling UNC Chapel Hill the equivalent of a murderer's playground. Nicknamed the Co-Ed Killer, or on some stations the University Binder, an unknown man was making the rounds, stabbing his way onto the most-wanted list. The campus police force doubled, with walkie talkies hissing commands, hoping more uniforms increased student protection.

Before it was easier to dismiss Mom's fears as trivial, but Chapel Hill was a city at odds, part code red, part rabblerouser, and I was stuck squarely in the middle. While my peers were content to role-play the movie *Scream*, with ghost costumes and camera flashes, I picked up the pace on my way home and avoided all shortcuts. With a madman on the loose, it felt safer to treat every alleyway like an opportunity to be jumped. Still, even on the main streets, every breaking twig and fallen footstep seemed sinister.

My personal skittishness was dramatic. I scolded myself that the only stalker I'd attract was Kevin, my ex-boyfriend, who yearned to give our relationship another try. He and his beer belly were the only uninvited guests I'd encounter, along with another round of breakup bingo through gritted teeth. Annoying, but harmless, and the conversation would end again with Kevin's tears snaking down his bulky cheeks as I handed him a tissue instead of my heart. Each time he left, I only felt relief, reinforcing that I'd made the right choice to call it quits.

But I couldn't shake the unpropitious belief, my ears registering every sound, searching for the unseemly. I glanced behind me. There was no one following me, but the fog of unease remained.

I wasn't unprepared for worst-case scenarios. My dad said that our bloodline was blessed with copious ammo and 20/20 vision. Most members of our family tree did a stint in the service, earning national defense medals instead of Olympic ones. Dad told me that whatever was Latin for hypervigilance should've been our family creed, joking that the Winders would always be locked, loaded, and ready for action. He'd been in the Marines, and never lacked patriotism or belief in the right to open carry.

When I went off to college, my parents gave me their patented platitudes about not walking to the bio lab at night, same as any undergraduate family. But they also gave me a 9mm handgun, the parental version of a contingency plan. That was in addition to the .38 special revolver they'd purchased as my initial concealed carry.

My dad handed me the pistol like it was an engagement ring, his smile broad, his lips urging me to shoot first and ask questions later.

"That's basically our motto," he joked before turning on his serious eyes. "But also, it might keep you alive. A young woman, living alone, who knows how that story ends? But my daughter won't be caught unaware."

For my father, guns were shorthand for guaranteed safety. I grew up hearing that the military saved my father's life by teaching him to always be prepared. But my mother said being a military wife taught her life lessons as well. She peppered our conversations with reminisces about the early days when Dad was deployed, and she had only a toddler to keep her company. Being alone made her recommend gun ownership, because Mom's snub nose became a dependable guardian angel in her faded yellow purse.

"Sometimes, I'd tap it, making sure it was still there," she added, scurrying around the kitchen in her favorite apron, the one embroidered with ducks and rabbits. "And it made me feel reassured, knowing a weapon was close by."

The juxtaposition always made me laugh, my mother, the housewife, cooking a chicken pot pie with a loaded gun resting by her coffee mug. She was schooled in Southern hospitality, baking pies from scratch for funerals and functions, while also holding her own at the range, a finger on the trigger, both eyes on the target. The lesson there was don't take my mom at face value. She looked prim, her lipstick matching her nail polish, but underneath her manners was a skilled sharpshooter, packing serious heat.

I'd stowed the guns in a safe within my closet, the opposite of armed to the teeth, until recently. The events on campus encouraged me to dust them off, ready for a dose of easy courage. I'd deposited the guns in my nightstand, the bullets secured, their presence an uneasy acknowledgment that something serious had sprouted in my world.

It was incongruent that a posh university like UNC Chapel Hill was now the subject of chronic violence. Previously the biggest local crime consisted of stealing a term paper or buying quick-release Adderall for finals week. The school body was comprised of scholarship nerds, decked out in Tarheel Blue, immune to anything outside of the university zip code and their own privilege. The professors lived near the campus, continuing to promote the scholarly research triangle, with Duke and Wake Forest Universities offering fantastic co-partnerships for the studious set. UNC Chapel Hill was built for academia and excellence, not for malice and madness.

My hands were a fumbling mess, suddenly clumsy when presented with my apartment door. The foyer was motionless, but I entered the hallway like it was a crime scene, scanning left to right. The kitchen was clear. I tiptoed down the hallway to open the bedroom door with the tip of my foot. No monster awaited my return, but the pinprick of fear persisted.

There were no creaks, no rustling curtains, but a whisper of uncertainty swirled. Nothing ducked, or moved, no item out of place. I turned on the fan, and I watched it spin. I counted to ten. The house creaked, and I waited, a statue.

Everything was in order. No jewelry was missing, no credit cards misplaced in my wallet. My dirty towel lay bundled on the bathroom floor, my sports bra lying beneath it. The bedsheets were in disarray, the dirty dishes lined the sink, and all was as it should be.

I shook my head. My fears were skyscraper high, not only

because of the recent string of violent crimes, but also because of graduation. In May, I'd leave the university, and its stone walls, for the uncertainty of the real world. I'd been cocooned here for four years, resting in the laurels of early classes and campus wishing wells.

I smirked, remembering how as a freshman, I'd trekked down to the Old Well, full of bravado and algae water. Tradition promised that one sip of the alkaline water would ensure top honors, but the upperclassman snorted behind cupped hands while undergraduates tried not to heave, all in the name of university custom. With seniority, I'd given up on the Santa Claus dreams of good grade point averages being attributable to anything other than hard work.

But with graduation approaching, I'd caught a bad case of transition anxiety, my head overloaded with hesitancy. It was a big ask, to leave the sanctity of professors and midterms into the great unknown. I wished for a little bit of magic, the lure of a wishing well, something that would guarantee my future would be as happy as college had been.

My plans were basic. I'd renewed my lease for the upcoming year, allowing me to tread water until something better arrived. I could work part time and stay connected with friends before becoming an official grownup.

I should take a shower, the smell and grime of the day seared into my skin and stinking up my armpits. The wetness under my shirt felt sticky like duct tape. My stomach had other goals, recapping my smoothie and non-existent lunch. I headed to the fridge to survey dinner and was disappointed to find nothing appetizing.

I perused the shelves, but only a bruised banana and a suspicious-looking clementine remained.

I sighed, wishing I'd prioritized my pantry with my basic staples, like Ritz crackers and fancy Brie cheese, paired with a bottle of good Pinot. I shut the fridge door, harder than I intended, my frustration and hunger launching an inadvertent ambush on the appliance hinges.

Another evening of college food offerings would have to do. I should get my fill of undergrad grease, let the oil leave traces on my scale and my fingertips, since my student discount was a ticking time bomb. Plus, Time-Out chicken had served me well, the fried food soothing both rumbling stomachs and jangled nerves. The restaurant was close, the path well-lit, and my appetite urged me to hurry up and head out.

Scores of Northface jackets tumbled into the restaurant, the dinner crowd antsy and ready to throw down. I spied an open table by the bar, a rarity during peak happy hour times. Ava from my Anthro class appeared at my shoulder, her tray wobbly with a tower of potatoes.

"Caroline! Eat with me and share these fries. The bartender is cute, but he gave me too many." She gestured to the table, her frizzy hair damp and fashioned into a very messy bun. I surveyed her mountain of fries, then signaled I'd be back.

She was right; the bartender was handsome and bursting with easy grins. He loaded me up with chicken tenders and a pitcher of wheat ale on draft. He winked, and I scurried back to Ava, barely balancing my twin turret of fried food offerings.

I was happy to have company, especially Ava, though her Pollyanna enthusiasm could shine too bright during our eight-a.m. class. She scooted closer, making enough room for both of our trays. Ava smiled, and a rush of affection for her took hold. I'd take that grin and save it, its memory an amulet to defend against the horror wading through campus.

"He's so cute, but he flirts by giving out food, which is kind of strange. Please help me eat these." I gestured to the overloaded plate. "It's enough for four people!"

Ava cackled and dabbed ketchup on her fries.

"I'll take it," she countered. "I like a man who appreciates that I like to eat." She munched openly and glanced back at the bar. I followed her lead, letting the chorus of college students provide background music, as we drank our beer and satiated our hunger.

"Thanks, Ava, for the fries. That hit the spot." I patted my stomach, a soft sign of leaving. "I gotta go, though. You can finish the pitcher. I still have one last paper to write for Professor Brandt's class."

She pouted. "Are you sure? Carolineeeee, we don't have much time left. Wasted Wednesday is already beginning!" She tipped back her chair and surveyed the crowd. The dinner crowd was ready to get rowdy, evidenced by the increased volume of music and lack of personal space. She glared at me, like I'd breached a contract by eating her fries and ducking out early.

It was tempting, the dollar shots, and the feeling of false camaraderie that came with expensive bar tabs. There's strength in numbers, and I wanted to be surrounded by other seniors, to watch their foreheads glisten in sweat and good favor. I yearned to sink into the noise, to get a break from whatever was tap dancing around in my subconscious.

But I heard my dad's words in my mind, megaphone loud,

warning me about the dangers of too much of a good time. His advice echoed inside my head, a stern proclamation.

"You can drink on the weekends, Caroline. As a father, I can't keep you from it, and I doubt you'd listen anyway. But I'll tell you, the people I know that got into trouble in college were the ones that drank during the week. First, it's a drunken Thursday here or there and missing a morning Friday class. But then it starts becoming more frequent, and they only realize they're failing when it's too late to clean up their act." My dad had shot me a warning look, classic squinty eyes and judgment. I'd listened, reserving fun for the weekend like the adult I'm becoming.

"I want to, but I still have a couple more classes until I'm done. I can't let up yet."

She frowned her rebuttal, not quite ready to acquiesce.

"Grades are almost done. Come next door with me for one drink. One and done! Then you can go home, I promise." She grinned, a hint of ketchup on her lip.

I imagined the condensation on the frosty mug, the sticky bar, strewn with paper coasters. I grabbed my keys, ready to give in, but my fingers lingered on the keychain from my mom. It was a heart with our initials in the middle, and the fun-time feelings vanished, flatlined by responsibility.

"I can't, I really can't. But I promise I'll go out with you this weekend!" I flashed Ava my best Girl-Scouts-honor smile. "Seriously, I will. I have to make it to class tomorrow, then I'm yours."

Ava let me off the hook, her eyes drifting toward the bartender and his curly brown hair. I signaled for the check, paid, and aimed a quick hug her way. She squeezed my arms before letting go, her attention already diverted to the winking barkeep.

"Hey, and Ava. Be careful." We'd gone the whole meal without mentioning the murders, which was a personal record for me.

"Caroline, if all goes well, no way I'm sleeping alone tonight." She winked and sauntered to the bar, her confidence conveyed with a swish of her hips. She turned, heels clacking, to yell, "And if it goes very well, we'll have free fries and beer here for life." She blew me a theatrical kiss, and the crowd swallowed her up.

I trudged outside, already missing the buoyancy of the bar and the sound of people laughing, like only good times and last calls mattered.

The walk home made me feel even worse. Living alone was my choice, and one I usually championed. I liked the silence and the ability to come and go without anyone keeping tabs on me. But lately, it felt lonely. What was once independence now felt like desertion, and the quiet led to paranoia. Maybe I needed a pet, a loveable companion to greet, instead of a threadbare couch or a thirsty plant.

As I stepped onto my front stoop, I heard a noise in the bushes. It was a quick clatter, then nothing. I summoned my courage and peeked over the hedge. It was dark, and hard to make out anything except the red brick wall. I waited to see if anything would move, but nothing happened.

Likely a chipmunk in search of something tasty, I reassured myself, twisting my key in the lock. It clicked open, signaling the end of a long day.

I dropped my purse onto the chair, promising myself a quick cleanup before I started on my paper. The hum of the shower eased my tension, and I picked out my favorite pajamas, a worn-in track T-shirt and athletic shorts. The comfy clothes urged me closer to sleep mode, my gaze on my flannel sheets atop my queen-size bed.

Reluctantly, I hopped back to my kitchen table, powering up my Acer laptop and correcting a couple of last-minute edits. Professor Brandt was a stickler for grammar, his classroom a kingdom where he ruled in Times New Roman. I checked the word count and re-read it one last time, then powered down my computer after hitting submit.

Everything felt dangerous in the dark, the kitchen a minefield, my feet full of stumbles. I navigated back to my bedroom, but my eyes focused on the popcorn ceiling, rejecting the rest I needed. I flirted with sleep, my gaze tracing patterns on the wall. I told myself not to look at the clock, gave up as the numbers clicked from two, to two thirty, to three a.m. I turned on my side at five a.m., the intractable insomnia weighing heavy on my chest. I decided to call it and swung my legs over the side of the bed, awake but not relaxed.

I brewed the max amount of coffee my Mr. Coffee pot could hold and drank it down fast, though the jolt of caffeine did little to improve my mood. I knocked my knee against the familiar outline of the barstool, the pain of it alighting down my leg.

"Damn it," I cussed at no one, my leg throbbing at my clumsiness.

Another quick shower helped me jumpstart my day, providing a dose of wet hair and resolve. My Thursday classes were full of last-minute to-do lists with checked-out teachers, their voices a collective monotone. The halls were emptier than usual, and it all started to feel a bit morose, more wake than celebration. The race to the finish line of college had slowed from sprint to slosh, the graduates plodding over the finish line with shrugs and bad breath.

My classes were spread out, causing my legs to burn their complaints. The other students made an identical pilgrimage, heads down and hoodies up, clumped in groups of twos and threes. They moved ploddingly, zombie-like, their fragrance a combination of stale tequila and sweat. I was tired enough without a hangover and rewarded last night's sobriety with another cappuccino. I needed one last stimulant push to manage my maxed-out schedule.

I made it back to my apartment a little before five, thankful for the canceled meeting that provided unexpected downtime. My advisor had wanted to talk about the next steps but then canceled last minute, her voice made of sniffly cracks and sneezes. I doled out some concern but was glad for the break, and the promise of a warm blanket and herbal tea. The granola bar I'd scarfed down for lunch was long forgotten, and the threat of rain glinted in the sky.

I unlocked the door and was again reminded of the absence of appropriate food in the fridge. In my busyness, I'd forgotten to stop by the store, the basics of self-care disregarded in favor of a plethora of to-dos. I'd duck into my room to change, then I'd wrestle up the energy to go grocery shopping. Hell, I'd even spring for a ten-dollar bottle of wine for the upcoming weekend, no Boone's Farm for this girl. I deserved the good stuff.

I swept past the kitchen, pushing myself because I knew if I stopped, I'd skip dinner in favor of television and sweatpants. The day was tedious, and I craved some rest, curled up with the anonymous chatter of sitcoms to keep me company. It already sounded good, taking off my bra and changing into my old track sweatshirt, letting my neck rest on the back of my couch until sleep wormed its way into my brain.

I glanced at my closet, knowing my familiar hoodie was hanging there, the logo long since made illegible from frequent washings, the writing reduced to flecks of white.

I smiled, opening the door to my room, breathing in the scent of lavender from the Glade air freshener. I stood in front of the closet, debating. My fingers wrapped around my collared shirt, my nails brushing against my belly. I knew then that I'd surrender to the lure of the TV, my hand drifting to remove my bra.

I'd pulled my shirt halfway off, the cotton swirling around my head, when I heard it. A sound, no louder than a cough, coming from my living room.

My body went on high alert, but I remained frozen, my ears trained on what I thought I'd heard. It sounded like a sigh from a winded runner, a touch above a whisper. I waited, barely daring to breathe. The apartment was quiet, no more grunts or loud foot-steps. My eyes zeroed in on my bedroom doorframe, and I slowly released my shirt. Nothing moved.

I remained by my closet but scooted toward the nightstand, my eyes never leaving the door. My 9mm gun was closest, tucked in tight, already loaded. I grimaced and jiggled the nightstand drawer, wincing at the noise it made, a high, brassy clatter. My bottom rested against the nightstand handle, and I slowly shook it open with careful fingers. I prayed it wouldn't squeak. I moved with patience, like I was playing the game Operation, continuing to remain front and center, my movements obscured behind my back.

I used my fingers to claw into the drawer, and they gripped

the butt of the gun, the reassuring smoothness connecting with my hand. I'd just grasped it when a noise from the doorway caught my attention.

An unusually tall man, dressed in black, loomed in my doorway. He wore thick gloves and a black ski mask, the top of it forming a triangle, pointed like David the Gnome's hat.

In his right-hand dangled plastic zip ties, his fingers rocking them back and forth. His movements mimicked a Newton's cradle, the series of swinging balls. He leaned against the door frame without fanfare, his lack of invitation causing no noticeable anxiety. He paused, his eyes finding my face, his girth blocking my only exit.

The intruder puffed his chest and spread out his arms, wide open, a sinister Jesus on the cross. I couldn't see his mouth, but I knew he was grinning, his pose cocky, meant to take up space.

He raised his arm, and I watched it drift to his face, pulling his mask over his chin. He removed it, strip-show slow, letting the mask reveal the puzzle of his face in increments. His hair got caught in the process, and he yanked the mask off completely, irritation bathing his features. Each new detail, like his green eyes, and the black strands of hair that creased his forehead, robbed me of air.

It chilled me, the way he wanted to be seen. His movements meant I wasn't supposed to make it out alive, because if I could identify him, then I could stop him. But he didn't know what I held behind my back, my finger against the trigger, sweat already making my hold tacky. I watched him, while my brain registered the heaviness of my weapon, the weight of it dangling in my right hand, cool to the touch, the metal a black ice cube.

My thoughts flashed to my dad. He'd raised me on all the Western classics, like Judge Roy Bean, *Unforgiven*, and any movie that paired John Wayne against a weak yet noble Jimmy Stewart. In addition to loaning me his heroes, he also took me to the shooting range every weekend. He told me there's no need to give a villain the benefit of the doubt. I watched those movies, and then I learned to shoot straight, cowboys and my father teaching me all I needed to know about taking a life.

All right, then. I had it all loaded, ready to deliver a full metal jacket justice.

He stepped into my bedroom, his eyes never leaving mine. His hair was gathered in a haphazard ponytail that grazed his shoulder blades; one thick strand wiggled beneath his hair tie, a wiry snake, out of place.

I stopped his progression by aiming my gun at his chest. He gazed at my drawn weapon, the muzzle pointed at his heart.

"That's right, mother fucker. I'm armed and permitted, with the right to carry." I forced my voice to enunciate, channeling every bit of bravery I could muster, praying I sounded fiercer than I felt. The swearing helped sell it, pairing profanity with righteous indignation.

He judged the distance between us, and I was certain he was looking for a way to continue. That was another thing my father taught me, that a man would disarm a woman two to one, just because he could. I waited for him to make his move, every synapse anticipating his next strike.

The stranger looked at me with hunger, like he'd already decided I was going to be next on his list of trophy kills. He licked his lips and showed no emotion. He didn't retreat.

"Not today, you son of a bitch." I clicked the safety off, continuing to hold my arms aloft. I was learning how heavy it was to continue to aim, and my arms shook from the effort. I should've done some upper arm work to keep the gun tight. My arms wiggled, but I kept them taut. A flash of panic made me wonder how much longer I could hold it out straight.

"Turn around or I will send you straight to hell." I frowned, waiting for him to intervene, confused that he remained unruffled by the door. If he was coming to disarm me, and certainly he was, he moved only incrementally, his eyes scanning my body, up and down. The motion was distracting, his gaze intent on my chest, my legs, reducing me to property he'd own and operate.

He smiled then, a soft and intimate grin suitable for a first date. It made me shiver, the way he recognized me, his eyes alight with an almost gratitude.

All my thoughts clicked into place. This wasn't the first time he'd seen me. He was the one who had been here, watching me, studying my schedule. He'd counted on my meeting with my advisor, reflected in black ink on my kitchen calendar. But he hadn't known she was sick, the late cancellation messing up all his voyeur plans. I'd caught him here, during his joyride, perusing through my private things.

He raised his arms up, palms out, a false show of surrender, his gloves mimicking jazz hands. He backed out of the doorframe, taking his time, each step minuscule. I braced, waiting for him to change his mind, to duck and catch me off guard.

He continued to face me, walking backward at a turtle's pace. I debated shooting him, letting my gun do the talking for me. He was the one they were looking for; I could feel it in my gut, where all good wisdom was housed. He was the murderer, the reason for the break-ins, his face the last thing those young women saw. Here he was, less than dapper, in his shabby burglar costume, looking homemade and half-off. The world wouldn't miss him.

But he didn't charge or try to tackle me, preferring careful footsteps to impulsivity. Shooting him without delay, no assault, no attack, was vindictive, and legally iffy, since I couldn't prove anything other than a break-in.

I kept myself braced for an onslaught but knew I wouldn't shoot without cause. Letting him escape felt equally uncomfortable, since I'd be called a coward, or worse, when this narrative became public. My phone rested on my bed, out of reach and useless, while we inched closer to the front door.

His clothes smelled like mowed grass and peanut butter, so ordinary, the antithesis of dankness and rot thought to emanate from evil. I spotted a pimple developing on his chin. He didn't look like a monster, but they never did, these men so bent on causing harm. I kept the gun trained on him, my heartbeat thumping in my ears.

He continued to slink out of my house, saying nothing, his feet almost crossing the threshold of my front door. As he backed out onto the stoop, he stopped, sensing the steps behind him. He was almost out of the apartment, and I was nearly safe. My heartbeat slowed, confident in the power I possessed. I was the hunter, I was the one he should fear, and I wanted him trapped.

"I'll come back for you," he promised, his slitted eyes threatening. "One way or another." His voice was high-pitched, almost squeaky, the opposite of the Batman undertone I'd envisioned. "You weren't meant to survive this day." He leered, his words drumming into my mind, with his jaw made of his stone, his mouth creased and furious.

I responded by slamming the door in his face and locking it closed. I dropped the weapon, and my arms burned, my muscles drained completely. I was Gumby, a mix of useless appendages, made of rubber and shock. I wanted to collapse on the floor into a puddle of withheld emotion, but I needed to make sure he was gone.

From the window, I watched him jog down the road at a lackluster pace, which baffled me. If I were him, I'd be sprinting, but he seemed almost lazy, his pace affable. He turned left, shuffling onto the next turn in the road.

I raced to the bedroom, tearing at the bedspread, my hands dropping and grabbing my cell phone, the numbers of 911 already under my fingertips. I ran back to the window to continue my watch, certain he'd return before the police arrived. The gun remained where I left it, discarded next to the front door.

"911, what's your emergency?"

"HELP! Oh God, please help me. My name is Charlotte Winder."

"Ma'am please, we need to gather some—"

"I live at 301 McMasters Street in Chapel Hill, NC. Apartment four, ground level. I need the police out here right away."

"Okay, Charlotte, slow down, let's start—" Her voice remained calm and collected, so tolerant it seemed fake.

"I was almost the victim of a home robbery and assault. I think he's the Co-Ed Killer. Oh God. I need help, right now. He said he'd be back." My voice crackled into the phone, tears threatening to block my words.

A pause, then the sound of someone typing, the clickety-clack rhythm sounding too loud in the phone, a long break in the rushed conversation.

"Charlotte. Is the perpetrator still on the premises?"

"He walked down the street. He's the one who hurt those girls, I know it. If you hurry, you can catch him. You c-c-an," I stuttered. "He also said I was meant to die." His words replayed on a loop, and a moan escaped my throat.

"Please, he said he'd be back," I clarified in case she didn't hear, and I really needed her to listen. "I need some help; I can't keep him away by myself. Not again." My breath changed, coming out in short bursts, fright blurring the edges of my vision.

My eyes were glued to my window, watching for any sign of his return. I reached for the gun, my torso elongating to grab it off the floor. I let it rest on the counter, while the 911 operator fired off rapid questions.

"What was he wearing? Tell me the details. Tell me what you remember," she instructed, her voice steady. But she seemed far away, her voice muffled. I could barely hear her, and I couldn't think straight.

"Hello? Charlotte? Are you there?"

"Yes," I whispered, "I'm here. Please, send help."

I continued to gaze out at the street. She asked me more orienting questions, and I knew she was trying to ward off shock. She used my name too much, her voice trained to sound safe, security bleeding from her honeyed tones. I peered out the window, my fingers gridlocked against the blinds. He could be circling the block, letting me rest before doubling back for his second try. Another minute and I'd hear a window breaking, the soft thud of feet connecting with the floor.

"Please," I begged, my voice bordering on hysterical. "I'm so scared. Where are the police? When will they be here?"

She told me that help was on the way, but it sounded like a lie. I remembered the way he looked at me, all dark eyes and determination, then the wash of disappointment. A serial killer had been privy to all my private things, not just my name but my surroundings. He knew me intimately, and it made me feel like no place would ever be safe again, now that he had me in his sights, a bloodhound with my fragrance in his nose.

A rainbow of blue lights reflected off my living room wall, the screech of sirens blaring in the darkness, heading my way.

I hung up with the operator, though I thought I heard her protest, and dialed another number quickly, one I was certain would provide the help I required.

"Dad. It's me. I need you," I began.

He breathed into the phone. "Charlotte? Honey?"

"Someone broke in. I'm okay, listen I'm okay. But I… I need you."

My driver's license indicated that I was an adult. The lamination showed all the regular facts, that I was twenty-one years old, brown-haired, capable of deciding upon organ donation and my place in the world. I paid my bills on time, I watered my plants, and yet knew in five seconds I'd no longer be able to stand without reinforcements. I may be a full-fledged person but right then, I needed my daddy.

"Hang on, Char. Coming to you. Should I bring anything?"

That could be code for more weapons, which he had plenty of, or food. But there was just one thing I needed.

"I need you, Dad. Fast as you can get here. Police are already on their way."

"I'm on it, honey. See you soon." He could make the drive in thirty minutes, but I was counting on him to speed.

His voice steadied me, providing me an extra dose of strength. A double knock rapped against my front door, matched with the welcome sound of sirens. I dropped the phone and rushed ahead, flinging open the door. Four policemen blinked at me, their faces taut and severe under my entryway light. Darkness shone over their shoulders, because night had descended while I was locked in battle for my life. They asked to search my home, their badges shining like fools' gold.

"You can come in, take whatever you need. My gun is in the kitchen. I didn't use it but I have a license for it."

Numbness descended while the two officers bombarded me with questions. The others cleared the rooms, yelling directions to each other, their voices firm, making my head spin.

I asked if I could sit down, eyeing the nearby stool, certain I'd collapse if I had to stand up a moment longer. The two cops nodded, pens at the ready, and I gave them as many details as I could remember. I told them about his height and the way he carried himself. I described his outfit, his long black hair, and the way his voice seemed too high to be real. I told them about how he had surprised me but likely staked me out, since he knew I lived alone and seemed comfortable in my apartment, taking his time, pausing to gawk at me from head to toe. He wasn't concerned about a roommate barreling through and interrupting what he had planned. Only my weapon made him change course.

"That's notable, too, that he didn't seem to know his way around a gun."

"What makes you say that?" The officer closest to me sat poised, his shoulders tilted slightly in my direction, his notebook small in his hearty hand.

"He made no attempt to disarm me or call my bluff." I'd expected a fight, but he'd promised a do-over. I shivered, remembering his last words. "But maybe that means he's got unfinished business." My voice cracked, my shoulders rattling beyond my control, threatening to knock me off-balance.

"He said he'd come back for me," I quoted him, his last warning stuck in my throat. I needed to move, so I showed them his last location and pointed at the spot where he rounded the corner.

Then I spied my dad's car in the driveway, the loud stomping of his boots crossing the threshold.

They let me go to him, and he hugged me tight. I breathed in his usual mixture of Marlboro cigarettes and peppermint aftershave. It took all my remaining strength not to sink into the safety of my dad, to let him lead me to the couch and cover me with blankets while he stood vigil over me all night. But I wanted to finish up the interview, to ensure that whoever else was on this man's hit list stood a good chance of being saved. Dad stayed by my side, shoulder to shoulder, not an edge of space between us, while the cops continued their questioning.

A rush of excitement reverberated down the hall when a junior deputy dangled the ski mask in his latex-covered hands.

The swarm of officers were ecstatic, greedy for fingerprints and saliva, provoking a tweezing frenzy and multiple evidence bags. They black-lighted my room, finding some hair follicles near the doorway, their combined joy wafting through the apartment. A sergeant took my fingerprints and a hair sample, navigating around the blanket that covered my shoulders, the soft cotton no match for my shivering.

The police offered me gratitude, which I took, and sympathy, which I rejected. I wasn't interested in anyone's perception since I barely understood my own. I couldn't find a way to take in the scene, the barrage of police swarming my tiny kitchen. They looked over my permit to follow protocol, but I saw their glazed-over eyes, their work here almost done and dusted.

"Good one, sir, training this one to carry." The youngest officer congratulated my father, like the gun was my dowry, his little girl safe because of his quick thinking.

"Heck, I can't take any credit, officer," Dad corrected the policeman, and I loved him even more for setting the record straight. "She's a better shot than me when she wants to be. I'm happy she came out of this best-case scenario."

My previous good will deflated. I wanted to correct him, to tell Dad and these officers that the best-case scenario was that this never happened to me. If this trauma had been avoided, then I would've believed the lie that my world was full of safe people and harm only lived in paperback novels, with no direct experience, no proof, of wickedness. I could never get that back, that feeling that terrible things happened to someone else, and I felt crushed under the weight of my current circumstance.

A sob escaped, another one followed. I knew there was no way

I could stay in this apartment because he'd tainted it, the killer's presence removing every semblance of security. I wouldn't be able to sit on my back porch or daydream out the kitchen window while I did the dishes by hand. Instead, I would think of him standing in the doorway, the horror movie version of a welcoming party, my heart hammering posthaste.

Even if he was caught, my sanctity had been violated, my house scarred with someone who wanted me dead. I wouldn't be able to stay without locking every door or curating an armory. But even with the gun, I still couldn't breathe, the seriousness of the encounter threatening to pull me under, to lock me into a life of fear and regret.

The injustice of it all made me sick. I knew I should be grateful that I'd escaped. But this apartment was the first place that was completely mine. My neighbor Amanda was more family than friend, and she and I had a long-standing *Bachelor*-watching date where we'd judge the contestants harshly over cheap beer and snide remarks. Giving up this place was more than an address change. It made me wish I'd shot the bastard, but then my home would be tainted and unlivable, the carpet full of bloodstains, the walls smeared with evidence.

While the police gathered their kits, I laid my head in my hands, fending off the tears. Because I wasn't hurt, raped, or wounded, I didn't know how to conceptualize these feelings, to say I was still scared even though I'd avoided the worst outcomes. The police and my father offered handshakes, the mood serious but not fatal, their faces reflecting a job well done.

I wanted to beg them to stay outside, to keep assault rifles trained on my door, an army waiting for another attack. I couldn't believe they were leaving, onto their next task of surveying and canvassing the neighbors. Anger curdled inside of me, the swiftness of my emotions threatening to knock me over, the unfairness creating a continual mood swing.

Then I thought about the legions of women who likely carried this same dark mark, a wound unseen, and how the world was full of people like me, who were drinking their coffee or lacing up tennis shoes when their lives turned upside down, forever altered, by a riptide of fright.

Not a mortal wound, but not nothing.

I didn't confide in my father. A flash of guilt blazed and extinguished. No matter how close we were, my dad wouldn't understand this. He was older, and wiser, but for him the worst part was over. But for me, I focused on the second act, the future where I dealt with what happened, the remnants of the break-in long lasting.

Instead, I let Dad take care of me, like I was a little girl, home sick from school, in need of chicken noodle soup. We found a western on TV and turned the sound off, my head leaning against his firm shoulder. Sleep flitted around me, and he assured me he'd take the night watch, his rifle beside him, his attention on the locked doors and windows. I dozed, my mind turning, cycling through jittery sleep, flashes of the day knocking against my subconscious.

My last thought was that I wished I'd killed him. Instead, the dark curtain of sleep descended, safe but not content, calm but not rested, the final pinprick of fear settling down to roost.

Chapter 8
Sherry Taylor
Date: October 20th, 2007, 5:30 p.m.

I liked Noah on my couch, the manly bulk of him contrasted against my pink cushions and sequined tassels. I imagined his woodsy scent of pine needles and lake water seeping into the fabric, marking my home with his rugged presence. I longed to make our relationship permanent, to be branded with something I couldn't wash off. Kisses were appreciated, but I wanted tattoos and wedding bands, signs of infinity and commitment, more than a lingering whiff on a discarded throw pillow.

I smiled over at him with a grin I couldn't undo. There are a million reasons why I shouldn't get my hopes up, but when this floppy-haired Adonis beamed back at me, my insides went mushy. I was bursting with puppy love, content to sing in the shower and skip to class, my neck marked with hickeys, my heart swollen to twice its size.

A pretty boy with a brain was a whole new level of easy intoxication, and Noah kissed like he was going off to war.

I tried not to swoon or mistake a maybe for a sure thing. It was foolhardy to claim a future not yet written, but Noah made me want to linger, to write promises in permanent ink and share a last name, to book a church, invite our families, make everything official in a sexy white dress with a dollop of cleavage.

Pull it back, I told myself as I slipped out of his embrace. Men must take it slow, to ease into the idea of commitment. I'd remain behind the scenes, the marionette expert, not the main character, pulling strings to make this relationship remain in his best interest.

It was addicting, the manic pace of making out, the whirl of his hands on my body, our legs intertwined. I didn't want to stop. Which, of course, was the definition of an addiction, and I was in the throes of it. My head preached caution while my body yearned for the head rush of another sultry kiss.

My mom joked that I came to UNC Chapel Hill to find a man, not a degree. She wasn't wrong. Here, the college men were polished, so unlike the boys back home that were holler born and bred, the kind who considered the rodeo a fitting first date. These students were top tier, the type that could tie a Windsor knot with their eyes closed, their fingers cloaked in graduation rings, thick as knuckles. I salivated over the dangling suffixes and ballooning bank accounts, certain that one of these well-postured fellows was my perfect match, an American Prince William intent on show-ering me with crown jewels and prenups.

We'd dream over coffee and textbooks, sharing meals together in the student union, while playing games of footsy under the table, a sly smile perched on my ruby lips. He'd take me to his summer home, where his family would challenge me to a round of croquet, their pastel cashmere sweaters draped across firm shoulder blades, awash in good health and luxury. The life I deserved reached out in front of me, a grasp away, close enough to get high off the scent of crisp one-hundred-dollar bills.

I'd made quite a splash at student orientation, a regular Dolly Parton, branding myself a sweet-tea-swilling Southern marvel in a room full of buttoned-up bourbon. Most of the girls at Chapel Hill were the studious type, with glasses aimed like daggers, their heads bobbing between textbooks, their nails needing a good French manicure. When the boys saw my sky-high updo and low-cut sweater vest, it was all biology, just moth to flame. Heads swiveled and boom, we were off to the races. I could have my pick.

The XY set at UNC didn't stand a chance, especially when I opened my mouth and all those South Carolina manners slipped out, the accent pure magnolia. Hook, line, and sinker, I knocked that first impression outta the park.

Honestly, it was some of my best work.

I encouraged the men to label me, to project what they thought I should be. I wasn't nearly as innocent as they assumed, but I dropped all the right breadcrumbs, leading Noah, the best of the bunch, to another smooching Saturday. He settled into my couch, my socked feet cupped in his sizeable hands, everything just right.

Call me Goldilocks, 'cause I played my cards precisely, not too clingy, not too aloof, with Noah engorged like a tick on the entirety of my affection. Rounding out at a handsome six foot two with a strong cleft chin and a brown mop of hair, Noah McClarty was perfect, the kind of boyfriend I'd begged for on every childhood game of M-A-S-H. I twirled my hair, my heart ticking, allowing him to drink me in, his eyes brimming with lust and need.

He was a looker, but also polite, sprinkling in enough "yes ma'ams" to prove he was the take home type. His parents were country clubbers who played polo, the sky-high membership dues no issue for those steeped in generational wealth. "Put it on my tab," I imagined them saying, with barely a glance at the dinner balance, the check whisked away by uniformed waiters, money so ubiquitous Monopoly could make it.

The only complication was Noah's tendency to monologue about political science, working his major into every single conversation. It was obvious Noah wanted to be taken seriously because he, too, had a mold to break.

A blush crept up the back of his neck, spreading like a heat rash.

"Most of the pledges in my frat think I'm some kind of trust-fund playboy," he confessed, his eyes skimming the couch, feeling so *very* misunderstood.

"I'm much more than that, you know. I've got plans that extend past my family's name, with goals of my own, geared up for the taking. I can make them a reality; I know I can."

I bit the inside of my cheek hard to keep some sarcasm from escaping, curbing an eye roll on the horizon. Noah was born rich and entitled, with monogrammed baby pillows and gated entrances, plus a brand-new silver Mercedes on his sweet sixteenth. I had no idea why anyone would work to remove that label. Given half the chance, I'd embrace it, take a bath in all that gold, a la Scrooge McDuck, and never look back. I could make a career of flaunting furs, with diamonds as big as dinner plates, letting the peasants garner a glance before I jet-setted off to the Caribbean in a Pucci bathing suit. *Put me in, Coach*, I wanted to say, *I'll spend that cash lickety-split.*

But maybe I assumed it was easy because I'd never had money. It was a rite of passage for the prosperous to grumble about their millions, to complain about the ability to buy their way out of everything. Affluence wasn't a genuine hindrance, and Noah sounded naïve, his words a script made for those with silver spoons and Tiffany baby rattles, no struggle to be had.

Don't flinch, I reminded myself. *Don't show disgust, not now, not ever.* But my mind wound up, his words too privileged for real-world concerns like mortgages and student loans. I kept quiet, but my judgments banged against my brain, wanting release.

"You have to intern for a while, and that's how you pay your dues," Noah lectured on, soaking in his own soliloquy. "Skip a salary, start from scratch, do the time. Even someone like me must be humbled. But if I do a respectable job, then it's a straight path toward clerkships. After that, the future should line up easy, and Washington can become ours, a place in politics secured."

He clasped my hands and gave me a warm squeeze, his words so earnest they'd hurt if they weren't also steeped in nepotism. His smile widened, gleaming so bright it looked lethal.

I wasn't sure I'd ever want to leave the South. To me, security consisted of humid summers and double-decker porches, evenings spent languishing on acres of land, with a dip in the pool to beat the heat. But I played along, murmuring in all the right places. I guided his hand, bringing it to rest on my neck, giving him my best '40s pinup look complete with a breathy whisper.

"Do you really have to go, Noah?" I maintained eye contact as I moved closer, giving him a hearty glimpse of my push-up bra, my bosom barely contained by the underwire. "I get so lonely when you aren't around."

"Yes, baby. I gotta go. For real this time."

He mumbled a list of to-dos about a group project and a term paper that was due. I pouted, but I was ready to be alone, since a phone date with my best friend Jenny was already on the books. I looked forward to lounging and letting my TV soaps run in the background while I decompressed and painted my nails a dainty pink color. That was my ideal weekend night, full of pampering and gossip, and maybe a new face mask, no males in sight.

Men liked it when you ceased to exist without them, so I pressed my lips and whined, giving my best vaudeville disappointment. I over-did it, pairing bedroom eyes with an audible grumble, letting him know my life crumbled once he walked out the door. Really, I craved the alone time, to stretch and tone these muscles, to do crunches until my abs tingled. My nightly routine was my own and not available for a live audience, but I kept with the theatrics, my curtain call a locked door.

"Please don't go." I curved my face into his neck, my nails weaving slow circles on his lower back.

"It's only for a bit, Sher. Then I'll be back, and we can continue what we started." He leaned in, providing a shower of kisses, my hand winding through his hair, tugging softly. Then I pumped the breaks on the passion, letting my hands fall to my sides. He responded by dropping his arms, reducing the rating from PG-13 to G, a chaste backdrop, Disney appropriate.

Our intimacy appropriately paused, I pulled him to the door, our hands still linked. He wrapped himself around me, his lips mushy, his tongue playful.

Dreamy. But he still needed to leave.

"I'll see you soon, sugar." He stalled, giving me another deep kiss, our lips melting together while I balanced on my tippy toes.

We broke apart, and I wiggled my nails at him, offering up my best see-ya-later smile, a study in Shirley Temple innocence.

Then I deadbolted the door, eager to connect with Jenny and remove all this makeup. The mental gymnastics of our date kept my head full of cotton balls, devoid of any meaningful thought. Noah was auditioning for a role I'd already curated, but his chatter made my head hurt, and the vestiges of a migraine bloomed in my brain.

It might be a new millennium, but I still needed a man. I'd witnessed firsthand my mom's wrong relationship choices, and I wasn't going to end up with two black eyes and no grocery money, dependent on Uncle Sam and the WIC office to meet my needs. No, I wanted to land the *right* man, the antithesis of my mother's exes with their hard hearts and heavy fists. I'd vet them, wed them, and leave nothing to chance, an Ivy-educated gold digger, going in with both eyes open.

Jenny understood everything. She'd witnessed my mother's lame efforts at covering up bruises under drugstore foundation, the purple bleeding through her chalky, mismatched attempts. She'd watched as my mom dreamed big, only to be crushed under another jerk's iron fist and bullshit. With each relationship disappointment, and every stepdad wannabe, Jenny offered me a place to stay, a refuge from the broken bottles in the kitchen and the sea of glass that became a breakfast landmine after yet another midnight fight.

A friend like that, who knew the details of my messy home-life, yet withheld judgment, was worth everything to me. Jenny's name was a refuge, and her home was the reason I survived high school. I spent hours crisscrossing the well-worn path to Jenny's house, when Mom and her men got to be too much. My best friend was always waiting for me with a tight hug, enveloped by porch light, my head resting on her sturdy shoulder.

But Jenny hadn't gotten the grades to attend a top-tier college, so instead we'd settled for a phone call before bed, her voice my last good night. It felt strange to work at our friendship, to devote time to talk when before everything was instantaneous. In high school, her parents were my surrogate family, my status secured with my own place setting at their dinner table, an approved bonus sister, with the option to adopt.

Hell, Jenny's mother, Mary, still sent me letters, packing my campus mailbox with double-wrapped packages and extra stamps. Seeing Mary's curvy cursive on the packages was bittersweet since my own mom hadn't asked for my address. Our contact was limited to rushed phone calls in between her shifts at the restaurant. Mom sounded clipped, the dinnertime rush flowing in the background, the clink of silverware overpowering her voice. Each time, the dial tone came too early, the sound associated with another weak attempt at improving the mother-daughter relationship. It usually ended with me staring at the phone, all my whispered words coming up short, my mouth full of failure.

Instead of exploring our fault lines and fissures, I preferred to lie to myself, to explain away my mom's flaws with overtime work and minimum wage. But on bad days, when it rained, and my mascara wilted along with my mood, I could see the glimmer of truth beneath the surface. Mary exerted more effort and reflected more comfort. My best friend's mother cared for me better than my own blood, and my heart ached with a familiar wound long carried. I worked to store the truth in a secret place, deep in my heart where it wouldn't sting. It refused to be contained. Mother's Day, parents, or my hometown were triggering verbal minefields that could terrorize me for days.

If I was honest, my mom only had enough energy to carry herself from one unhealthy relationship to the next, half-dragging a kid into her domestic-violence wake. She made it clear my presence did her no favors, that the existence of a child kept her from more coveted relationships, forcing her to play with a handicap.

I could almost hear her voice, smoke-scented and scratchy, that pushy rasp ringing in my ear.

"I coulda done better, but I had a child. And the kind of man I wanted didn't yearn for some ready-made family. So don't judge me for settling for what we got." She tapped her cigarette. "You made it so that we had no other choice."

I frowned at the memory and dialed Jenny's number, sinking deep into the couch cushions. There were days I ached for Jenny and the shorthand we'd created. This apartment was spacious in square footage, which further increased my loneliness. I longed to prop my best friend beside me, our popcorn topped with Molly McButter, the *Days of Our Lives* music blaring in the background, the shared blanket of friendship tucking us in tight. I wasn't homesick for home, but I was homesick for her. Life without Jenny felt tedious, her absence a bruise not yet healed.

I fiddled with the pillow tassels, allowing my emotions to circulate, praying the mean-reds were thwarted. Noah had no idea I was more Audrey than Marilyn, more bookish than sexpot. Dumbing down every conversation was an art form, but it left invisible scars and a sour mood that could last too long.

Jenny answered on the second ring.

"Soooooooo, how'd it go?" The soft tremor of her voice soothed me. Jenny jumped right in, asking all the right questions about my steamy third date.

"Oh, Jenny. He's the whole package. Maybe this time I found somethin' that can last."

"What's different about him?" I heard the familiar crunch of rice cakes. Jenny chewed her way through most conversations. I smiled, imagining her in her favorite faded sweatshirt, her toes Barbie pink, her hair pulled into a high ponytail.

"Well, I think he still wants all the things other men do." I giggled. "That was obvious during our make-out session. But he's sweet, too, a real gentleman, following through on what he said he'd do, right on time." I reached down to turn off the television and brought the blanket up to my chin. "No large red flags found so far. A conversationalist he is not, but I'll let that one slide. I realize I can't have it all, so I'll settle for a sturdy, steady, rich boy, even if it means feigning interest. I'm holding him off, keeping him interested while I wait to be sure. I wish you could meet him, to let me know your thoughts."

"Me, too," she said, her voice thick and serious. "Plus, Sher, I worry. The news here in Columbia keeps droning on about the

Co-Ed Killer at Chapel Hill and I just… It all seems so dangerous. My mom called, too, sick with worry about you. I spent thirty minutes calming her down. She wants to get you, and it's not the worst idea."

I laughed, the sound getting caught in the back of my throat, so it came out hollow.

"That's the news for ya. Nothin' to worry about Jenny, I promise. We've been over this. There's certainly no need to leave campus. It's all overblown, for real. They require somethin' to sensationalize that nightly schedule. Please reassure Mary that I'm fine and that I live in an apartment crammed with students. This place is anything but desolate."

"But, Sher, it's all anyone can talk about. Aren't you worried? Even a little bit?" Jenny pressed on, her voice climbing high into another octave.

"Listen, I paid extra for the deadbolt, plus I got Noah to keep me company." I glanced back over my shoulder, the lock still firmly in place, the apartment hallway silent, no footsteps to be found.

"But there were two victims right? Chrissy? Sheena? They completed the interviews with their families on Five-Alive last night. I watched the whole episode. Their families cried through the whole thing, and everyone was scared. It was terrible to watch."

"Totally different area of campus and they've added security to every building. I can't walk to class without spotting three campus police officers. The campus feels like a war zone, I'm telling you. You'd have to be crazy to attack someone now, with everyone on high alert." I paused, ready to add a detail I knew she'd enjoy.

"Also, I haven't been slacking with the weights. Every night, just like back in high school, no cheat days, I promise. I'm fully following the program, Jenny."

She paused, likely remembering those early days when we learned to pack a punch. I had Jenny to thank for keeping me strong, her mind working double time to recognize a threat before it surfaced, her plan introduced during our junior year of high school.

I'd dumped my bookbag on her bed, ready to tackle my algebra calculations, when an expression crept across my best friend's face that I couldn't place. Jenny was perched on her bed, her mouth a straight line, her face full of unwelcome news.

"Listen, Sher," she said, in her PowerPoint of hard truths. "I've been thinking. If your mother's boyfriends are cruel to her, it's only a matter of time before they come for you. We can't let that happen, so we need to plan ahead."

The room creaked, the serious topic sucking up all the air, the subject far from extracurriculars and school transcripts, football games and cozy fall sweaters. My life was harder than most high-schoolers since fairness and decency got traded for my mom's tawdry lipstick and first-date jitters. Jenny let me marinate on her words, her jaw set tight.

Then she stroked my hand and gifted me a backup plan full of dead lifts, squats, and bicep curls. We traded friendship bracelets for triceps kickbacks, spring break for gym visits, and we never again discussed why our routine was essential. Instead, Jenny matched me rep for rep, my favorite training partner and forever friend, each of us stronger by working together.

"Okay, okay. You're right, I'll stop peppering you with questions." Her voice brought me back into the present. "It's tough, being so far away. It feels so weird not copying your math homework or going cruising on Saturdays." Jenny sighed, a touch too long.

I didn't want to ruin my third-date butterflies, but she was right. The distance between Columbia and Chapel Hill, between Jenny and me, felt heavy, the mile markers a stretched rubber band, too taut for comfort.

That's something my mom *was* right about, that friends were more loyal than lovers. Mom was always supportive of Jenny's friendship, her crooked smile lingering on Jenny's face, her eyes full of thankfulness. In a way, Mom taught me all the valuable lessons I needed to know; she just did it by broadcasting the errors first. I got the lessons but in reverse, the knowledge only available in retrospect. But she always made it a point to mention Jenny, her voice sad and far-off sounding whenever my best friend was discussed.

"Having Jenny in your corner is gonna serve you well, so hang onto her, if you can," Mom would say, tapping her cigarette against the living room table, scattering the ashes to the wind. She brought the cigarette to her lips, deeply inhaling. "She's a wonderful friend." Her prophecy concluded with the swish of her windbreaker, in search of a nightly stiff drink. Even Mom in her intoxicated fog understood what Jenny meant to me.

My home phone crackled, reminding me of my nightly timeline and the work still draped across my desk, in need of review.

"Well, I best get going, Jenny. If I keep spending all my time with Noah, I'm not gonna be in college much longer. Especially since he may be back for round two. And hey," I added, "I miss you, Jenny. You know I do. Girls here aren't like girls back home. And no one is like you." My voice fractured on the syllables. "My BFF, for life, you know."

I didn't want to elaborate about the university girls in their tight pastel Polo shirts, their mouths puckered into continual frowns. With a campus devoted to the upper echelon, these females dripped pique, all bitten fingernails and stick-thin bodies. I gravitated to the outskirts of group outings, the social equivalent of treading water. I yearned for a female confidante, but so far all I'd gotten were cold shoulders and raised eyebrows. These co-eds shouted with their eyes, their cutting stares marking me with a modern scarlet letter. My self-esteem shattered a bit with every lingering glance, even though they never said a word.

"I know, Sher, and same, of course. I miss you every day. And please, stay safe. You know you can always come here if you get scared. Just say the word and I'll pack up the Camry and come."

I laughed. "That car's on its last legs and you know it."

She chuckled. "Yeah, true. But I love you. And I'd drive that clunker through Hell if you needed me to."

I smiled, picturing her speeding this way in her gas guzzler.

"Love you, too, Jenny. Always."

The dial tone blasted into my ear, and I debated throwing the phone against the wall, suddenly full of anger and regret. Since I started at UNC Chapel Hill, I worried about Jenny and me, that our connection would slip through my fingers. I imagined us drifting, our calls flatlining and sparse, until I'd only see her at high school reunions, the ghost of what we were drained to friendship dust.

I wouldn't let that happen. I grabbed my good paper palate,

the one stacked with yellowed archival paper, fit for a king's portrait. I slid into my pint-size desk, preparing the charcoal and blowing on it for luck.

Hoping for snake eyes, I chuckled to myself while my fingers smudged the page. Most of the time I drew for others, but Jenny made me want to get creative. I watched as hair snagged across the page, resting on toned shoulders. I'd hang Jenny's portrait on my fridge, a gentle reminder to not leave someone vital behind.

While shading her eyes, I remembered how Jenny would sneak out to come check on me, her fingers ghostly on my windowsill. One tap from me meant everything was normal, but two taps signaled danger, a morse code for get the hell out. On those nights, Jenny would help me shimmy out the window, our hands clasped, weaving our way back to her silent house.

It always hurt to leave my mom behind, the upper range of her voice echoing in my ears while I escaped. But Jenny assured me I wasn't responsible for my mom's bad choices. I let my best friend envelop me with her down comforter, and I drank up Jenny's reassurances like they could save me. Sometimes they did, her whispered words washing away my guilt. I slept well, snug and smug beside her, while my mom shrieked in the darkness too far away to hear.

I glanced at the clock, surprised that I'd been drawing for two hours. I could lose time like that easily, my fingers content to shade and scratch across the page, safety found in symmetry.

But I needed to complete this week's assignment, a residential re-design that I'd neglected, its due date creeping up on me. My scholarship depended upon my interior design work and my ability to create something out of nothing, pulling pretty things out of thin air.

That pressure of perfection would sink some students. But I had my mom to thank for my future career. I dreamed about leaving home so much that I made it into a vocation. I drew commercial and residential spaces, all open floor plans, with enough square footage to drown in. My drawings looked nothing like my childhood two-bedroom ranch, with its cramped, second-hand furniture, the surfaces tainted with knicks and scratches, the smell of smoke thick in the air.

With each project in my portfolio, I drew my mom a beautiful cage, with built-in bookshelves and floating staircases, grand enough that she'd never want to leave. I imagined her in a different life, certain that if I could get it right, my mom would be free. In the house of our dreams, Mom would twirl with open arms, a modern Julie Andrews in *The Sound of Music*, securing a happy ending where no one got hurt.

My stomach rumbled a complaint since I'd skipped dinner. The kitchen offered scant supplies, limited to stale crackers and past-due milk. I washed the charcoal off my hands, wondering if Domino's would deliver once they knew my zip code. Chapel Hill was under a curfew, with curtains drawn and doors double locked, proactive measures guarding against the Co-Ed Killer. I'd call, soon as I was done cleaning, the sensation a salve for my troubled mind and hungry belly. I scrubbed each finger twice, sterile as a surgeon's, my eyes on the phone, which threatened to tip off the couch cushion.

A brief knock rapped against my door, the sound of it muted over the running water. I peeked at the clock. Eight p.m.

Noah had kept his promise.

My brain buzzed a warning about my unfinished homework, but my heart pitter-pattered, eager for another good-night kiss. Maybe a brief touch and go was in order, a way to keep me enrolled in school but also a reward for Noah's good behavior. I tiptoed to the door, my head resting against the frame, an excuse forming on my lips. I unlocked the deadbolt, creaking the door open an inch, expecting his blue eyes to meet mine.

Standing on my doorstep was not Noah. This man was taller, the top of his head almost even with the doorframe. He leaned in casually, a bored postman delivering a package. I glanced down, but he kept his spindly fingers behind his back, no mail in hand.

"Um, can I help you?" I gripped the doorknob, a second away from shutting it completely. But sometimes neighbors got the wrong apartment number, and a quick clarification could send them in the right direction. He was maybe a little older than the average student but still certainly young enough to belong on campus, his unlined face hidden underneath a baseball cap.

"Sherry? Sherry Taylor?" He peered down at me, his voice mundane, his lack of interest flattening his features.

"Yes?" I replied, the words barely registering before he pushed completely against my door, knocking me backward, my feet fighting to remain upright. The stranger barreled into my apartment, dressed in black, and he hurried to lock the deadbolt behind him. His fingers were concealed in thick black gloves that crept up and covered his wrists in puffy fabric.

My heart sank, the whole of me melted onto the apartment floor. A man, in black, an apartment break in, gloves because of fingerprints. My mind connected each dot, urging me to scream.

But my throat forgot how to make a sound, clogged and stunted, useful no more. I became uncommunicative, my mind flatlined at the worst possible time.

"You should always look through the peephole first, you know. Especially during these dangerous times. But you thought lover boy was on his way back." His voice was squeaky, reminiscent of males in puberty with their creaks and peeps, halting and not fully formed.

I shook my head. He spoke English, but I couldn't connect with what he was saying, my eyes instead focusing on the bulk of his body, which blocked my only escape.

He glared at me, his shoulders no longer hunched. His spine locked into place and his height seemed to keep going, inches that turned into feet, less of a man, more of a giant. He grew like monsters do, his measurements bigger than I expected.

"He's not coming back, by the way. I watched him leave, and he didn't go where you think he went." His smile went wide, gleeful with secrets, taunting me.

"What?" I asked, my eyebrows furrowed. "What do you mean?"

"I mean, your sweet boy toy isn't such a good boy after all."

"You're wrong. Noah is coming back," I bluffed. I looked right at him, knowing this narrative full and well. The easiest way to rebuff a man was to tell him you're taken, a lesson all women know. I leaned into my story while also broadcasting a SOS message in my mind for Jenny, Noah, or someone to save me.

"He's on his way. We already agreed on it. He'll be back at any moment."

Help me, help me please, I thought urgently, my plea aimed at the locked door.

"No, he isn't. In fact, he's with someone else already, a pretty little co-ed in the freshmen dorm. Her name is Jennifer. Tsk-tsk, Sherry, you picked a lemon again." He released a high-pitched chuckle, his voice sick with satisfaction.

His words hurt, but I swatted them away. Noah didn't matter with danger front and center, though a piece of my heart crumpled softly, our future timeline reduced to mist.

Think, Sherry, think!

I debated throwing the first punch. His height was a problem, but I had the element of surprise. I could strike his midline, come out swinging. I pulled my fingers into a tight fist, my nails cutting into my palm.

"I wouldn't do that if I were you." His voice was all sing-song storybook villain. It made me nervous how relaxed he seemed, this stranger deposited on my doorstep, maskless and ready to wound.

I scanned the kitchen for weapons, but they were behind me, tucked neatly into their knife block home. I'd never reach them in time.

My whirlwind thoughts distracted me. When I looked up, his body was closer, the sweat on his hairline shimmering under my kitchen's low lighting.

There was nothing on the dining room table I could use. I'd wiped it clean of crumbs, a nod to the precise housewife I'd become, my apartment tidy in anticipation of Noah's return. The stranger studied me, amused, my agitation evident and overflowing.

From his back pocket, he unsheathed a serrated knife slowly, a strip-show of power, each flickering inch spreading his grin further. I reminded myself to breathe as my eyes widened, taking in the whole of his weapon.

"Look what I have here for you," he mocked, licking his chapped lips.

I could run to the bathroom. It was the closest door with a lock. It wasn't sturdy, but it would put some space between us and buy me some time.

He gripped the knife, the blade luminescent, winking in the light.

This son of a bitch thought he'd waltz in and do what he wished without a hint of resistance. *Not today*, I thought, my shoes sprinting to the bathroom, the thunder of footsteps deafening. I jumped past the couch, turned, and made for the bathroom door. He caught me quickly, his hand grabbing my arm, spinning me into his chest, with the ease of a choreographed dance move.

I screamed, loudly, my throat finally remembering its only job. I gulped air, ready for round two, but he clamped his hand over my mouth roughly. He pulled me closer, my back resting against his stomach, his arms curled around my belly.

"Now, now, none of that," he whispered, the hotness of his breath tickling my cheek, his gloved fingers mashing into my mouth. "We don't want to ruin the fun, do we?"

I tried to bite his hand, my teeth clenching together, but they couldn't cut through the gloves.

He laughed, then slipped his tongue in my ear, the surprise wetness making my insides churn. I squirmed, but he continued, lapping into my ear, leaving a nasty slug trail to dribble down my neck.

I shoved him, finding an inch of release. I sped to my bedroom door, my fingers finding the doorknob and holding it tight.

"Bitch!" he uttered while I slammed the door against his gloved hand. I put all my weight into holding the door steady, my feet braced for contact, my palms taut against the plywood.

He pushed with his shoulders, both of us arguing for control of the door. I held firm, adjusting my stance, pressing every inch of my body against the door with both hands burning.

He stopped pushing, my body sagging in the absence of tension. Confusion bounced in my head until he levied a kick, splintering the door panel, pieces of wood flying in all directions.

I screamed again, but it was wispy and less confident, the door continuing to splinter down the middle, no match for his strong front kicks. He thrust into the room, his shoulders bouncing against my body, my head morphing into a basketball that bounced against the carpeted floor.

The impact of his tackle caused my mind to swim. He levied a kick to my ribs, the forceful crack paired with rebounding pain. He kneeled, stuffing a bandana in my mouth, the taste of it sour, slick with someone else's sweat. I gagged against the binding, while he shoved it deeper down my throat, farther than I thought possible.

Stand up, I ordered myself, wiggling against his sturdy frame. *This is the fight of your life.*

For years I'd promised myself I would never curl into a fetal position like my mom, who took every blow, her passive stance resulting in broken ribs, hospital stays, and deductibles we couldn't afford. I wouldn't let punches rain down on me without rebuttal. In the darkest parts of my soul, where hatred was housed, I knew that's what I despised most about my mother. It wasn't that she put me in dangerous situations, or her complete lack of self-respect.

I loathed that she never once fought back, never said, "Come hell or high water, I'll never be treated like this again."

Well, I wasn't my mother's daughter.

By fighting back, I was Jenny's sister, and I wanted to be worthy of that title.

I slithered away from him, ignoring the cloth wedged between my teeth. I had no time to plan, only a second to enter a boxing stance, arms at the ready, feet shoulder-width apart, abdomen locked, posture straight.

He eyed me, charmed, his stringy dark hair half covering his face. But I held my ground and pulled myself into the orthodox stance, fists clenched and ready.

He stepped forward, and I hit him with a brisk jab, one that he deflected. I lodged an uppercut, then added a hook, each punch paying homage to Jenny. We'd practiced against the worn-down boxing bag in her basement, taking turns naming a foe, then going to town. I recalled the smell of chalk and the gloves two sizes too big for us, the satisfying sensory experience of a good fight. I channeled that rage, even as my arms tired, threatening to collapse and quit.

A left-handed jab connected with his cheek, his gloved hand curving to protect his stomach.

I imagined that Jenny and I were twins, hands linked, two girls facing a broken world. And I fought for all I was worth. I darted out of his way and eked out a right cross. I contacted his jaw, and it felt glorious, the crunch of his bones all the motivation I needed.

I tugged his hair, pulling him downward, his long strands winding around my fingers. My knee connected with his stomach, and he moaned, crouching closer to the ground. I stalled, unsure, straddling the line between fighting and fleeing. I was upright, and he was waylaid, the bedroom door a tempting beacon of escape. I delivered another jab, then sprinted to freedom.

I rushed toward the door, the handle within my reach, but he rebounded too quickly, his left leg blocking my path. I ducked, side-stepping his foot.

We eyed each other, both out of breath, and I dove forward, trading a strike for a getaway, escape my only goal. My teeth felt the force of his assault before the rest of me did, their warning rattle heralding the mountain of molars I'd find on my bedroom floor. I'd made a mistake, my face paying for the greed of liberty, the door a distraction from the battle at hand.

He'd outmaneuvered me. While I broke for the door, he slung a stray backhanded punch, the movement similar to a slap but with more power.

My forehead scraped against the carpeted floor, my face full of flames, agony devouring my intent. Blood doused into my mouth and onto the binding, the rush of moisture harsh against my burning esophagus.

I stayed on my side, winded, a squashed bug set for slaughter. I winced when he turned me over. He mounted me, his hard bottom resting on my belly.

"You bitch, you stupid bitch," he muttered. I moved to evade his grasp, searching for leeway, but felt plastic securing my hands.

I didn't know how to escape being tied. That was supposed to be addressed two weeks ago in the YMCA self-defense class, the one I'd enrolled in after studying the flyer at the gym. I'd paid forty dollars to attend but skipped the last one, safety neglected in favor of eating ice cream with Noah. Instead of learning how to protect myself, my tongue made suggestive swirls into my double chocolate fudge, the cone a phallic substitute. I'd skipped out on self-preservation for a second date.

The things I'd forsaken for a man might cost me my life.

Maybe I belonged on my family tree after all.

I continued to squirm, but he hit me so forcefully that my body forgot how to function. My neck ached a damaged reply, my bones moving in ways they shouldn't. I wheezed, trepidation darkening my thoughts, the cinch around my wrists rubbing the skin raw.

I tasted blood in my mouth. I winced while his eyes claimed a victory. He peered at me in triumph, his expression exalted, pupils dilated in ecstasy. A dot of blood danced in the corner of his mouth, and I focused on that. I'd harmed him, if only a little, and it felt like a badge of honor.

In his hand was the knife, the blade stretched longer, the dagger growing like Pinocchio's nose into an impossible length. I shook my head, my scream a pitter-patter, the bandana muffling all my alarm.

"Hold on now." He paused, his hands massaging down my leg, until another restraint chafed against my ankle. I flexed my feet in his direction, aiming for any contact.

"A fighter, I like that. But I am taking no precautions with you." He placed his hand on my hip, pressing down hard. I jerked on the bedroom floor, taut as a fish on a line.

He swayed above me, the light highlighting his side profile, same as a camera flash.

He hovered, his fingers softly stroking my soggy hair. There was tenderness there, and I hated it, the way he caressed me, his touch gentle in the aftermath of our fight.

I saw the knife rise in the air, the nurturing expression replaced with rage and tightened lips. The blade bit into my bicep, my flesh offering no resistance. Voltaic currents of anguish radiated down my arm, vibrations I couldn't stop. I urged myself to fight against the blackness that threatened to pull me away, my vision polka-dotted with dark splotches.

He craned lower, his nose touching mine, a flesh-colored cloud, a maze of beige, erasing everything else.

"Look at me," he instructed.

The swish of the knife rammed in my chest, front and center, where all the major body systems are housed. A blood-spatter rainbow flung against my pale beige wall, dripping into uneven, zigzag dashes.

It's abstract art, a study in Kusama, I thought, while the room faded in and out, my mind powering down, drained of all energy.

"Look at me," he repeated.

He cleaned the blade against his pant leg. In the brief reprieve, I commanded my body to obey me, and I pleaded for the calvary to come. It hurt to stay aware, the edges of my vision turning a muted silver.

I prayed my screams attracted a nosy neighbor, a 911 call already initiated, squad cars circling the parking lot. Maybe the police were on the other side of my front door, a second away from saving the day. If I could hold on, I could write a different ending. I'd register the heave ho of the front door breaking, my apartment awash with walkie talkies and SWAT teams.

I waited. I hoped, bargained, and swore, making it through all the five stages of grief in a minute.

No one came, and finally, my wounds wound down, my body conceding defeat. I thought of Jenny, her hand against her mouth, the neon nail polish at odds with her sorrow. Her parents would surround her, and they'd mourn me proper; I was certain of it. I longed to say goodbye, to thank them for the family they'd given me, for the only sister I'd ever known. I'd give anything to hug her one last time, to give her the goodbye she deserved.

My mind rang the boxers bell, signaling the end of the match, blackness covering the horizon. My eyes flickered, my thoughts slowed, and my chest refused to rise.

I succumbed to the fight, my fingers uncurling from a dead-locked fist, the whole of me deflated. I imagined a referee shaking his head, clothed in domino colors, eons away from my crimson-soaked floor, blowing the final whistle, the sharpness piercing through the burgeoning crowd.

My adversary held his arm aloft, fully extended over his head, preparing another victory stab, my body his desired championship trophy.

The numbness of defeat outstretched its hand, and I took it, the final knockout complete, acknowledging my removal from the winner's circle, my floor no longer where I belonged.

Chapter 9
Sheena Board
Date: September 26th, 2007, 09:30 a.m.

I jangled the bottle of pills, debating, straddling the line between cautious optimism and logical pessimism. Doctor Williams promised these antidepressants would be different. He swore upon the bible of Lexapro that these pills were dissimilar to Prozac, which had caused me to stay awake for two days straight. He'd witnessed the aftermath of that, my body tight and power charged, refusing to be limited by tables, chairs, or gravity. I buzzed and paced back and forth, a human Energizer Bunny, and he'd quickly changed course once he saw my bloodshot eyes.

"I'm a campus doctor, not a psychiatrist," he clarified, "but this time, maybe we'll get lucky. Depression is a treatable illness, Sheena, though sometimes it only works through trial and error."

I shook the piñata of pills, listening to them rattle, wondering if contentment was found in pharmacologic solutions. The doctors preached better living through chemistry. But all I'd known was side effects and try again, the jangle of medication synonymous with faith abdicating. I kept my reply to a brief nod. I didn't want to infect the good doctor with my cynicism, to cover him with words like treatment failure and rebound symptoms. He believed in me, not knowing that was a surefire way to become disappointed. The doc believed I was a witty college student, a ruminative sophomore with too many feelings and too much time on her hands.

Those who knew me better thought less of me. I wasn't eager to change his opinion.

Despite his prognosis, my odds of recovery weren't good, not that I deserved them to be. My cloak of sadness hadn't come out of nowhere, and I didn't expect to be spared. This disease of sadness wasn't bestowed on me arbitrarily. I wasn't a good person.

My depression diagnosis arose as a punishment because of my own sins, the lies that leeched out of me, cloaking every contact with my personal brand of discontent. This mental illness was just another way for karma to pay it forward, and I was doing hard time. I prayed it wasn't a life sentence.

I eyed Dr. Williams, wondering if he suspected as much. He jotted barely legible letters onto his dwindling script pad, his feet tapping a distracted rhythm across the laminate floor, too energetic for the early morning hours. I kicked my Converse tennis shoes against the examination bed, liking the echo it made in the small room, the thuds an antithesis to his cheerful pitter-patter.

If Dr. Williams knew the kind of person I was, he wouldn't work so hard to heal me. Hell, this university wouldn't have let me in, not if I hadn't worked to keep my darker side corralled and controlled. Maybe the depression was because I concealed my true self, to keep the wicked girl inside shackled and silent. Sometimes I wondered about the effort it required to snuff out the other me, the one who wanted to gain control and wreck it all.

Sad me wanted to start a wildfire and watch the world burn. And she's not some other personality, either, no id, ego, or any of the above. Depressed me saw the world logically. That's true for all psychiatric sufferers. They even did a study on it and found that those who were apathetic saw the world as it was, a doomed universe, often absurd, dictated by little more than luck. Nietzsche, Beckett, Kafka, they all got it right. Earth's a ruined rock, set to spoil.

Spoiler alert, the world's terminal. It's the positive ones who're delusional, who regarded the planet as a box of could-bes, immersed in butterflies and rainbows, a folie à deux spread across the universe. The blond Barbies and their slick-haired Kens were suffering from perceptual inaccuracies, but they're popular and outnumbered the glass-half-empty set. No one wanted to bang an Eeyore. So now it's me that had to be medicated, even though I saw life accurately.

There's no pill or booze strong enough to tempt me away from a warm bed, carbohydrates, and the thick cover of apathy. I'd accepted my fate, my layers of sadness a comfortable winter coat, worn in and waiting to embrace me. But sometimes that little whisper of promise alighted, a small match strike, encouraging me from the depths of a pitch-black cave. I couldn't release the sadness, or surrender completely, even when my grief clawed and screeched. Her rattled cries were all foul susurrations, causing another round of retracted insomnia, and still, like a disheveled phoenix, I rose.

Too sick to be happy, to well to pull the plug. Limbo was frustrating in its indecisiveness.

I rattled the pills again, contemplating one more round of medication Russian Roulette, and settled for a shrug.

Dr. Williams cut his eyes to the door, his schedule packed with patients to see and ailments to cure. He tore the blue script from the pad, a pesky frown overpowering his lips.

"The samples will be good for the week but go ahead and drop this off at the Walgreens by the quad." He rolled his chair next to me, stopping short of hitting my leg.

I nodded and collected my beat-up leather purse. At least I could still read a room accurately. We'd come to the diagnose-and-adios portion of our meeting.

"So you will try them, Sheena? And report back in two weeks? These will help you feel better if you take them consistently."

I hesitated, unsure if I was ready for another cycle of side effects lassoing through my digestive tract, the push-pull of bloating and diarrhea. But then Dr. Williams adjusted his eyeglasses, and a smile shone through, the look of enthusiasm redolent of sunny days and beach towels. He raised his eyebrows, and the smile flourished, florescent and reaching the corners of his eyes.

Only an asshole would say no.

"Yeah, Doc. I'll give this one a try." Maybe I could give it a go for him, a subtle reward for his never-ending patience with me and his willingness to swat my sarcasm away.

He beamed at me like I'd authored a dissertation in psychotropics.

See, it really was easy to make nice people happy. I should try to do it more often.

I scooted to the door, doubling my pace, since I knew the waiting room was swollen with patients he could actually help. Dr. Williams would usher in the students, with their sniffles or sinus infections, their menial maladies requiring only a one-and-done trip to the pharmacy and some R&R. I was jealous of those students, whose problems were simple, their cures over the counter and accessible. Maybe it wasn't even envy that I felt, but hate, their problems solved in fifteen-minute intervals. Easy, breezy, beautiful.

I was much more malignant, the core of me a hairball, covered in grime and trash.

"Hey, and be careful out there, Sheena." He swiveled his stool in my direction, his white lab coat too large, puddled against the glossy floor. "The break-ins on campus, and the, um, student. Chrissy Brown." He bowed his head in respect, her name evoking a moment of silence. "It's been a year since that horrible day, which is hard to believe. Promise to keep your head on a swivel. No risks, okay?" He studied my face, fatherly advice rendered, before turning back to his computer with fingers already on the home keys.

I wasn't afraid of things that went bump in the night, but I gave him my best atta-girl smile anyway. I shut the office door without fanfare, leaving him to his notes.

"I need a school excuse," I murmured to the front desk lady, an optimist rocking too much foundation. I purposefully didn't make eye contact and studied the business cards instead.

She cleared her throat and tapped her manicured nails in my direction.

"It was only a thirty-minute session. You sure you need an excuse for that?"

I rolled my eyes, hating the effort it took to converse, to play at politeness, especially with someone I already disliked. This woman was such a waste of words, the uptick of her voice equivalent with nails on a chalkboard, her mouth sounding polite, cloaked in a snobby veneer.

I looked up, observing her stupid blue headband, her adult braces, her fake smile glinting through all that metal.

Don't scoff, I thought. *Play Nice, do better.*

"Yes, I'm sure," I stated, then added, "Please," as an afterthought.

My manners were rewarded with the requested note, the ink still wet on the paper.

She looked like she wanted to say more, her teeth clacking together, the thin metal scraping against bloody gums. But I didn't give her the opportunity. I heaved up my belongings and scooted quickly for the stairwell.

I hated the elevator here, which brimmed with students nursing poor hygiene and hangovers, threatening to make me hurl and add to their combined depravity. To choose to be saddled together in the coffin-size space amongst strange body odors was appalling, especially when the stairs were right there, a sanctuary of space, ripe for the taking.

I liked the sound of my footsteps on the steps, the heavy thumps reminding me that I was alive. I clomped extra, enjoying the resonance it made on the concrete floor. It was childlike, the way the stairs morphed into mud puddles and days meant for umbrellas. But for me, a brush of levity was an accomplishment, so I let myself be easily amused.

I trekked to the student union for my daily brunch of a Mountain Dew and a candy bar. My mom would freak if she knew how badly I ate here, how the vending machines called to me, their florescent offerings on display. She was always urging me to eat vegetables, no matter how many times I told her I was a prefertarian.

"I only eat what I prefer, Mom."

Then I'd watch her cheeks heat up, the fury initiated, her words stacking together like Tetris blocks but her body language working overtime to smooth out her aggression. I'd study her, the way she melted her rage into a small nod, with pursed lips, ever polite and predictable. She swallowed every harsh word I hurled at her and kept asking for more.

Her eyes gave her away. It took effort not to despise me, and she glared over the untouched casseroles and burned broccoli. I'd rejected all her attempts to feed me, to bolster me with vitamins and minerals, and save me from myself.

I almost missed the way she fought to keep me healthy. My mother was a worthy opponent in the battle waged to keep me alive. She cared about me way too much, and I gave it back to her in spades. I force-fed Mom a mountain of willfulness to combat her over-protectiveness, until our homelife was deadlocked, neither willing to budge. The more she fought for my well-being, the less I tried, and my stubbornness waged its war, the nights ending with my mother sobbing into her damp pillow. It made her sick that she couldn't rescue her only daughter, her kitten cries the result of my indifference.

I'd feign recovery for a time, conjuring some manufactured desire at self-care. I'd go through the motions of brushing my hair, waking up early, and running a toothbrush over my shellacked, yellow-tinged teeth. But I'd always revert to my laziest self. Mom would be disappointed, those glimpses of health a temporary slingshot before the inevitable setback. She should've known better than to bet on me, though each time she vowed I'd be different.

The only thing I got good at was breaking her heart.

The student union was a mid-week ghost town, the trays scattered haphazardly, with plates towering too high beside overflowing trash cans. The vacant chairs bothered me, as if the zombie apocalypse had started on campus and everyone forgot to tell me. Maybe the students were as spooked as Dr. Williams, limiting their studies to cramped dorm rooms and walking only in pairs, a newfound caution awash in their veins.

I was meant to be alone, and if it made me a target, so be it. I was often overlooked, so even a murderer wouldn't consider me a viable option. I was not the stalkable type, with my chipped, secondhand bike and dog-eared library books bouncing in time, full of ho-hum and humbug. I wouldn't make his top ten list, secure instead in my bystander role as Extra #2. Not everyone's a leading lady, and that's fine by me.

I scanned the lunchroom offerings and grabbed an apple, in addition to my chocolate and caffeine staples. I glanced at the hair-netted lunch lady, her attention diverted onto a *Cosmopolitan* quiz, her pale polish creasing her cuticles. Her watery eyes glanced at my student card before turning another glossy page. I blushed, feeling forgettable even to a minimum-wage worker in an empty cafeteria, like I'd evaporated under the harsh glare of the fluorescent beams. I could steal half of the food on my tray, and she still couldn't place me in a lineup. I watched the lights flicker, but she remained a statue, immersed in "101 Ways to Please a Man."

I bit into my apple, the liquid sweet in my mouth, the runoff dribbling down my chin. That was good fiber, plus I'd get my exercise in today, since my room was on the other side of the quad, a good mile and a half from campus proper, with enough hills to make my bike ride formidable.

I got stuck in Old-East, the janky dorm that everyone wished they'd tear down. It was musty, a brick antique throwback from the late 1800s, with crumbling walls and questionable foundation. Some of the fussier students complained it messed with their asthma, the rooms infected with black mold and bad luck. It was no one's first choice, and most took umbrage with the registrar's office, demanding a reassignment.

But I liked the history it exuded. It was the initial building to house America's first state university back in 1795. I'd read there were underground tunnels that ran between the buildings, a connected labyrinth that begged for further exploration. I hadn't convinced my roommate Tessa to come with me yet, but she was on the verge of agreeing. Her curiosity was circling the drain, contemplative, a maybe turned into a wary yes. She'd been close, until I'd made my most recent drastic error.

I'd been thankful to be paired with Type-A Tessa, I mused, whirling across the sidewalk, my shoes tight against my bike pedals. Her class override ensured our interactions were constrained, her schedule toppling the university's glass ceiling for aptitude. Tessa's straight-A aspirations offered me some down time but also kept me entertained by her relentless pursuit of scholastic excellence. Watching Tessa balance her tower of textbooks was better than prime television, her frustration punctuated with unhappy huffs, knee deep in her academic obstacle course.

Tessa herself was an antidote to sorrow, a shining example of roommate perfection. She was never too clingy, and her smile was liquid, never forced. She earned relationship bonus points for stocking our closet with upscale snack options, and she bought me extra Red Bulls during finals week without asking for reimbursement. We chugged and studied through our anxious feelings, until the caffeine crash pulled us into an uneasy sleep, somewhere around two a.m.

The thoughtful types were difficult to discard, and I felt a camaraderie listening to Tessa's diminutive snores, close to calling her my only friend on campus. She kept her blanket coiled under her chin, an innocent bunny cradled in the family burrow.

Tessa didn't know the real me, though I was tempted to drop hints when we spoke in the dark, the lack of light encouraging an atmosphere of unfiltered opinions.

Underserved kindness was always my Achilles heel. And Tessa was Starburst sweet, an owner of pink boat shoes, the kind of person Tom Petty sang about. A patriotic American who loved family, horses, Fourth of July fireworks, and a good potluck dinner. Her needs were simple: a new highlighter, spacious libraries, and the purr of her childhood tabby cat, Whiskers. Predictable Tessa, the roomie version of a pedestrian crossing guard, dripping in good will, her earnestness a visible Girl Scout badge. She carried her skin well, all her truths evident in her crooked smile, the definition of what you see is what you get.

I'd tested the waters, which accounted for our current frosty standoff. I'd made the mistake of experimenting with some autobiographical content. Last Wednesday night, Tessa had been pensive, propped up against her purple overstuffed pillows, blowing on her freshly polished fingernails.

"What's the worst thing you've done, Sheena?" she asked, lobbing a doozy of a question in my direction. I skipped over the top five immediate hits and settled on one I regretted but could at least speak about, aiming for a story that was only unsavory.

For the first time, I showed her a glimpse of the real me.

I flipped back to my senior year of high school. It was New Year's Eve, and I'd bought a sequined dress from Express, ready to party with thirty acquaintances in a rented mountain house, the location unknown to parents and undesirables. My younger brother Jerry was a sophomore, and he begged to tag along. He'd aced his licensing test, and wanted to flaunt our parents' hand-me-down vehicle, the old maroon Subaru, in front of the partygoers. It would've been his first legitimate kegger, and with his keys in hand, he wanted to pull up and puff out, displaying the scratched car like it was a red Lamborghini.

"He'd dressed up, choosing some dark-wash jeans, paired with two popped collars." I laughed, recalling Jerry with his boyish grin, his hair parted exactly in the middle, the droplets of water still clinging to the back of his neck.

"I told him no, but he wouldn't leave me alone, like brothers do, asking and re-asking until I finally gave in." Tessa giggled at the old trope, all too familiar with firstborn troubles.

There wasn't anything wrong with Jerry. In a way, he was the boy version of Tessa, calm and well-rounded, the brother equivalent of a Golden Retriever. That's what made it worse. I had no reason to be cruel to him, yet I did what spiders do, weaving a web around my brother made of silk and lies, waiting to sink in my teeth.

"He was late to the party, and it was edging close to eleven, but he still wasn't there." The party was at its pinnacle, and I had to step outside to answer my flip phone. I dodged the drunks on the porch, hiking into the backyard for better cell service.

"He was on his way. He wanted to know where to turn," I began, remembering the excitement in his voice, paired with the rumble of the car engine in the background and the whiny voices of Blink-182 pulsing through his speakers. "He was close, minutes away, and would make it in time to watch the ball drop on TV."

And then I gave him the wrong directions. Out of my mouth came something completely implausible, a mish mash of lefts and rights, which kept him lost until he almost ran out of gas. He spent New Years of 2006 alone in his car with no holiday kiss or swig from a red Solo cup, the radio his only companion.

"But I gave him wrong directions on purpose, leading him away from the party and my friends, causing Jerry to get hella lost, his car almost sinking into a roadside ditch."

I laughed like I was in on the joke, but the sound came out feeble, dying in the silence that followed.

The next day Jerry sulked a sad circle around me, wondering what he'd done to warrant my wrath. He didn't even complain, because Jerry was too pleasant for aggression, so the deserved confrontation perished before it began. He crossed his arms and sighed, and I shut the door to my room, leaning against the frame, debating on whether I should wash the makeup off my face.

Tessa was quiet after my story concluded. The next morning, she said she'd fallen asleep, but I knew she was lying. She wouldn't make eye contact, and she grabbed the closest clothes within reach, settling for a ketchup-stained sweatshirt. For precise Tessa, the harried pace and soiled clothing said it all. Before she scurried out, she uttered a flippant goodbye over her shoulder, rushing to leave my presence. I'd contaminated our shared air, my evil deed contagious, or at least she wasn't taking any chances.

After that, it was the same old story. Tessa created a list of easy excuses, trilling from her mouth double time, about dinner plans, long study sessions, anything to avoid me. Her perfect ponytail, and her wall calendar featuring a different puppy of the month, belonged galaxies away from me.

The sting of Tessa's withdrawal was welcome-mat familiar. My confession kept her gone for two whole days, with dust collecting on her Dell laptop. When she returned, our room resembled a nursing home, formalities circulating in recycled air. She refused to look at me, our closeness fading without a proper fight. I shrugged it off, though I switched from Red Bull to Mountain Dew to avoid another queasy reminder of a rejected relationship.

I was welcomed back to an empty room. Tessa's twin bed was made immaculately, her quilt tucked into flawless corners. I dropped my bookbag on my bed and placed my prescription script on my nightstand, my fingers jittery with too much free time. I didn't have a class until four thirty, and my English essay on British Gothic writers was already complete, ready for red ink and peer edits.

I turned, eyeing my disheveled covers, content to let sleep fine tune all my worst moments. The escape hatch of unconsciousness was bittersweet. I slept too much because I enjoyed the anonymity of rest, the way it could blot out a day, a month, hell, even a whole year. Sinking beneath my satin pillow was my favorite pastime, allowing my world to shrivel into one continuous night.

But I wasn't tired, my mind whirling fast with unwanted details of Tessa and loneliness. Instead, I grabbed my purse, stuffing it with the essentials: my student ID, the unfinished apple, and my dorm keys.

In order to get better, I needed to do something different. I drafted a plan, certain I could keep myself occupied until my class in Greenlaw Hall.

Nikki, my therapist from back home, told me when in doubt, find some water. She instructed that everyone needed something to orient them, and water was soothing, the tides coming full circle and responding to the earth.

"It's a handy metaphor for life," she said, tugging on the ends of her vintage cardigan, her fingernails bitten to the quick.

I wasn't sure I bought into all that, but I'd liked Nikki. Her voice morphed into a soft purr, creating space for my worries to land. She was therapist number three, and I was charmed by her simplistic grace, her head slightly cocked, her office awash with lavender incense. She reminded me of a housecat, never rushing, her half-shuttered eyes far from the session clock. We had found a groove, where I rambled and she listened, and some days I felt like she understood my troubled mind, putting me back together, one puzzle piece at a time.

Other times her feet turned blue, and it distracted me, her poor circulation evidence of a flaw she didn't hide. Maybe that made her a good counselor, that ability to take each day through hell, highwater, or cobalt feet. Somedays I'd look forward to her faded green couch, focusing on little details like her skinned knee or the sound machine's death rattle. I'd learned to trust Nikki enough to take her advice, which for me was almost miraculous.

I grabbed my bike, my hands pulling it closer. It was a typical mountain bike, but it was mine, and that counted for something. My mom had gifted it to me right before I left home, her present propped in our driveway, wrapped in a bright yellow bow.

I smiled, remembering how the seat fit my frame like it was custom fitted, my mother squealing while I turned slow circles in the cul-de-sac. It was a necessary gift because the campus at UNC Chapel Hill was sprawling enough to require a mode of transportation. But I enjoyed the feeling of my feet on top of the pedals, my hands steady against the textured handlebar. On days when the wind blew through my hair, my mood responded in kind, a windmill of happiness cycling through my heels and my head. I was a knight in a colorful bike helmet, with an asphalt kingdom of bike trails ahead of me, ready for the taking.

Battle Park, which connected to the eastern campus of UNC, boasted a stone amphitheater, but I was more interested in the brook and the bench that overlooked the winding stream. The manmade pond separated the larger walking trails, winding through ninety-three acres of protected forest land, a favorite of students and professors alike. I'd found a bucolic spot far from the walking track, where a family of ducks swam by, their quacks providing a welcoming soundtrack. Even I had a tough time not smiling at that. Watching the babies sink under water, and rise back up, their beaks full of excited chatter, was often the highlight of my day. The momma ducks would cluck at them, and all would seem right with the world, if only for a moment. I would ride there to consider counseling and medicine, the tranquility clearing my head before my last class of the day. It was a Nikki-approved decision, mature and right by the water.

I rode there at a moderate pace, the droplets of sweat creating a headband on my hairline. Most students were cool with bikers and knew when to yield the right of way. Necessity dictated that most of my peers were cyclists themselves, so it was easy to ride and drift, allow muscle memory to do its job, and go where the road took me.

There wasn't much traffic, and the sun shined through the puffy clouds. Every so often a beam would catch me straight on, but I didn't mind. It was perfect weather, hot enough for shorts, but cooling down fast. For once, I had no complaints.

I slowed on the gravel path, waiting for it to curve. A tall man sauntered into the middle of the path, blocking my way. I slowed down, creeping almost to a stop, waiting for him to yield. When he didn't, I felt that old angry impulse rise for a retort. I wished for a bell or horn, a sound reserved for assholes to alert them to their idiocy.

He continued to prance along, eyes straight ahead, packed to the gills with his own self-centeredness. He stretched his arms out wide, his wingspan, and limited braincells, evoking a farm scarecrow.

I pedaled slow and sighed dramatically. He didn't move, continuing to amble smack dab in the center of the path. I had tried patience, my speed decreasing to a walk, then a crawl. Anger started in my belly but quickly jumped to my vocal cords. After my pedaling stopped completely, I'd had enough.

"Yo! Lurch! Move outta the way!" My voice carried, and his head turned to meet the opposition.

He paused, and I scrutinized him, his starched jeans, their creases too stiff for the outdoors. His jaw tightened; his teeth clenched into a sideways snarl. He didn't look remorseful, but he did yield, and I took that as a sign to sprint by. I gave him a hard look, eyes rolled skyward, conveying the appropriate amount of annoyance, though I still wanted to send him off with the hint of a horn. Maybe I'd ask Mom for a bicycle bell for Christmas. That would make her happy, knowing her gift had proved beneficial.

I whizzed through the rest of the path, breaking through the small gap in the woods, the bench vacant and waiting for me. I'd brought my journal, though I hardly ever wrote in it. I was a reluctant writer, since my thoughts continued to swish-swash in my head, too wispy to put on paper. Still, I'd kept this diary, and that was progress. Usually, I'd toss the pages before I even wrote a syllable, but this one continued to live in the bottom of my bag, amongst discarded pens and potato chips, its continued existence proof of a brighter future.

I tossed my bag on the bench, bending down to secure my bike against the iron armrest. It was quiet, and I breathed in the forest sounds, the quick chirp of the crickets, the soft hum of insects. I watched the small wake ripple in the water and longed to see the ducks, but they were hiding. I belly-breathed, summoning Nikki's words.

"Focus on the present moment. Lean into it, feel your back against the chair, fill your lungs, allowing them to open and drink in the air."

I closed my eyes and attempted to clear my mind, to listen only to the hum of the brook and the swaying trees.

Nikki said that if I focused on my senses, I'd learn to soothe my emotions. It hadn't worked yet, but I felt more content, my back resting against the sun-warmed bench, its bulk stable and toasty against my T-shirt.

I felt the sting of the sun on my bare shoulders, akin to preheating an oven. I relaxed and breathed in again, wishing for enough optimism to power through the rest of the day.

I heard a twig break behind me. I jerked my eyes open, my ponytail whipping around fast. The pedestrian from the path was there, gripping the edge of the bench, his giant knuckles peppered with black hair.

Lurch had invaded my serene place or followed me to it. His hand massaged the back of my bench, his lengthy fingers summoning images of the Stretch Armstrong toy, with appendages that kept growing.

"Well, look who I found," he said, his voice high pitched and ringing over the water.

I peered behind him, looking for a pedestrian savior but knowing the path was empty. The bench was off the main path, closer to the water and the quacking ducks, tucked away on a steep incline. That was the appeal, but now it felt ominous, the location far from the park boundaries.

I stiffened. "What do you want?" I asked, my voice all sharp edges. Often that's enough to shut people down. It was a practiced pitch, the way I could make my voice cut, drawing first blood. My intonation declared get lost, even if my words were innocent.

"Well, first off, I think you need some manners." He enunciated his words, stiffening his arms against the bench, lengthening them, his muscles slick with sweat and on display.

He flexed, and he watched me, his toned arms a threat in this deserted space.

I stretched my legs, preparing to duck and run. This creeper needed a good solid punch, but I remembered his height, his shadow sprawling on the pavement, two sizes too big. Sprinting to the safety of the path was preferable, and I ground my tennis shoes into the ground. Thank God they were worn in and ready to put distance between me and this asshole.

"It's funny," he continued. "Normally, there're so many people here. You know the outdoorsy types—hikers, walkers, and the in-betweens. Even bikers like you. But you know what today is, I guess. Why there's no one here." He paused and smiled, showing all his teeth, glancing from left to right, indicating how alone we were.

I wasn't sure what he was referring to, but I didn't want to give him the satisfaction of scaring me.

"Whatever, dude. This conversation is done."

I stood up, placing my hands on my hips, matching his rigid posture. I came up to his chest, but I remained firm, contracting my leg muscles, warming them up.

He smiled again, but it looked wrong, the opposite of welcoming.

"Today's the memorial? For that dead chick, Chrissy Brown, the candlelight vigil, the wailing wounded. A shitty excuse for everyone to wear black and get drunk afterward." He raised his eyebrows. "It's morbid to celebrate the day her body was found, and all that messy aftermath. I thought of going, of course, but then I wondered. Maybe there's a better way to pay my respects."

He chuckled, his excitement out of place with his somber story.

"That leaves the park wide open for people like *you* and people like *me*." He turned his head over his shoulder, making a point. "In fact, I think we might have the place to ourselves."

He flung his arms out wide, a sinister Jesus without remorse.

"Just me and you, Sheena. Look at the two of us!" he yelled, creeping closer to me, his head tilted sideways.

He knew my name, and that jump-started my escape. I barreled toward the left, leaving nothing to chance, finding my footing fast. I rounded past the bench, my shoes connecting with the solid ground. He rushed forward, his reach farther than I'd anticipated, his branchlike arms colliding with my chest, the force of his push knocking me backward.

I struggled to remain standing, my brain a high-pitched buzz. I course-corrected, angling away from him, but he rammed into me, the impact causing my feet to buckle and my balance to shift. The force of his blow caught me on the chin and cheek, my mouth overflowing with tepid, iron-laced blood. It occurred to me that a fight had begun.

I stumbled, falling down into the ravine. He jumped across the rocks with ease, his elongated fingers grabbing my ankle.

He pulled, drawing me closer, as if my body was a rope. He added a swift kick above my hip bone, his foot connecting with my soft stomach.

I flinched, then coughed, surprised by his sudden violence. I felt plastic wrap surrounding my feet, and then I remembered to scream.

"Help!" I cried, while I separated my legs, kicking them to the side, angling them in opposite directions. He placed a heavy foot on my thigh, the thick leather of his boot muddy and wet. I geared up to yell again, the words tumbling in my throat.

"Ah!" I got out, barely a windswept sound, before he stomped down on my leg, and I felt my knee hum. A quick glance registered that it looked crooked. My leg flashed an emergency signal, and my head swam, my brain ricocheting too fast.

"Oooooooo!" The sound I made wasn't human, it was feral, right as he delivered another blow, a stomp to my shin. Tears sprang from my eyes, and I imagined myself a magician's assistant, separated by halves, my torso and bottom parts no longer connected. I tried to lift my head, but the movement was too much. He grabbed my hands, locking them together tight, secured with a cable tie.

"Ouff!" I cried, my words no longer English, pushed through terrified breaths. My sputtered gasps couldn't find a rhythm, and I convinced myself that his shoe had been left in my body, a monument to the worst of my injuries. The pain swelled to a fever pitch, while vomit swished in the back of my mouth, a rancid, concentrated liquid.

My mind warned me something important was broken, but I

couldn't focus, because hazy stars burst in my brain, disconnecting all reason.

He let me yell once more before he stuffed fabric in my mouth, sticking it too far down. I gagged against the material, which tasted like old leaves and bread mold, the texture an itchy wool.

My eyes widened. Currently they were the only body part I could move. I was restrained, with aching legs and a stomach on fire, combating the resurgence of the nausea that threatened release. I heaved again, with vomit soaking the cotton binding, a sickening mouthwash against my teeth.

"I've done this before, you know, in the forest, and I quite prefer it." My nemesis voiced a carefree monologue while he dragged me toward the river. "It allows me to take my time, and soak it all in."

He wasn't careful, his movements harsh and haphazard. He allowed my head to smash into a boulder without even shrugging, while my brain scrambled and short-circuited.

I thought of my mother, willing her to intervene, to realize when I needed help most. I conjured up her smell of lavender lotion and Tiger Balm that she rubbed into her skin to soothe her aching muscles. I pictured her in the kitchen, the silver kettle on and boiling, her mint tea hot in her favorite flowered mug. I summoned her image, the afternoon light lining our kitchen, the beige house phone close to her left hand. If I could call her, I'd be saved, her mom sense homed to my livelihood and location. She'd devoted her life to keeping me alive, surely she'd know I was in trouble.

My disconnected mind spoke of teleporting, and in the moment I believed that, with the strength of a mother's love, anything was possible.

"Mom," I murmured. "I need you. I'm hurt, and I'm so sorry. Help me."

A stream of blood poured down my shirt from the gash on my chin that was cavernous. The smell made me lightheaded.

Please not drowning, I pleaded, since that was always my go-to for worst ways to die. I'd contemplated suicide many times, had spent hours reviewing all my choices, certain that I'd explored the macabre checklist in detail. I'd take an overdose or a gunshot wound, no problem, but the thought of the water blocking my lungs, the struggle to exhale before the slow fade to black, made me hysterical. I panicked when my hands reached the chilly water. A warm spew of liquid ran down my shorts, my urine combating the icy rush. I was too terrified to care that I'd soiled myself.

I shook my legs, trying to loosen his grip. His reply was all punishment, banging the back of my head against another river rock. The wound throbbed and turned into an all-encompassing whooshing sound.

For a moment, the world went out. All sensation stopped, as if I'd been powered down. Then I returned to salty tears dripping at the edge of my mouth.

My head leaked, but not from the river. He'd stopped before we got to the current, pausing at a small inlet, beneath a curved rock structure.

He kept me half upright, discarded by the damp wall. I couldn't move, and he draped me haphazardly, a mannequin positioned all wrong. Only my eyes could move; the rest of me was slack, morphed into a Raggedy Ann doll.

"Mom," I tried, the noise muffled against the binding. "Oh my God, Mom, Mom, please, Mom." I focused on her face, the swath of wrinkles on her forehead, the patch of gray hair tucked behind her ears, peeking through her dark locks. I cried for her, because I was scared, back to being a child in need of rescue. She was the strongest person I knew, her love for me never-ending, even when I didn't deserve it.

I watched him remove a knife from his backpack and saw the tilted curve of the blade, the gleam of it vivid against the muted brown forest.

My pounding head and broken body did nothing to respond. I could only observe his macabre theater, my victim role secured. There were no more moves to play, no speedy getaway or edited ending. I strained against the cotton in my mouth, showing him all my terror and hating myself for it.

He crouched next to me, his green eyes glistening. His cheeks were pink, flushed from exertion or excitement. This time his smile was genuine, the crinkle in his eyes evident. For him, it was Christmas morning, and he'd waited all day to unwrap his present.

"Now, now. Let's not take the fun out of it." He kneeled next to my abdomen, running the end of the knife across my exposed skin, creating goose bumps on my belly.

"Lurch, was it?" he queried, tickling the blade near my belly button. "I've been called worse, to be honest. Really, Lisa, you ought to know better."

My eyes locked into his. That's not my name, not even close.

He'd used my name before, frightening me with the familiarity. I watched his wild eyes blur. I tried to speak, straining against the rotten ball of cotton, eager to convey his mistake. An inaudible sound was all I could muster. Desperately, I used my tongue to move the dank material around.

"Mmmm," I muttered, willing my mouth to work.

The possibility of this being a misunderstanding flooded me with energy, a horrible case of mistaken identity. My wished for escape hatch dangled in front of me, enough to spit out a sentence.

"Mnnemw, it not my, me, name. Not name."

"What was that?" he whispered, his forehead swimming close to mine.

Concentrate, I urged.

"That not me, my name."

I said it again, straining to enunciate, ignoring the chunks of vomit that swished in my mouth.

"That's not your name?" he queried, his eyebrows sky-high.

I used all my strength to nod vigorously. I became a bobble-head, convincing him he got the wrong girl. He'd regret the violence, but I'd ensure I wouldn't tell a soul, would take it to my grave. He'd knock me out but let me go, searching for the original source of his vendetta.

I waited for recognition to slide over his features.

Instead, he crawled closer and licked my cheek. I retched and flexed against the restraints, his saliva leaving a stain on my face.

"It doesn't matter," he murmured in my ear. "You'll do just fine; you resemble her anyway."

I was only a substitute for the woman who'd hurt him, an

understudy for him to control and torture. I hated her, this Lisa, her sins written on my skin, her iniquities carved into my body.

I squirmed, but that did nothing to combat the knife sinking into my abdomen. I pitched forward, trying to untie my hands, to plug the wound with my body. They remained clasped behind my back, and I saw what I looked like on the inside. He hovered above me, studying the details of my face, his eyes dilated, with globe-size pupils.

Doctors say that most suicidal patients decide to live only when they've chosen to die. That's not what happened to me. After all the pills, and pharmacies, the copays, and hourly sessions, I didn't see a collage of Tessa, Jerry, of a life yet lived. I felt my resolve leave, my motivation sink into the riverbed, the runoff mixing with my blood and bodily fluids.

I felt myself let go, drifting into nothingness, flitting away from my body and my wounds. The peace Nikki described encircled me, even as designs were carved on my skin.

It was the ending I deserved, my comeuppance for being a deadbeat daughter, for not loving my mother enough to try harder. This was for all the little letdowns I committed every day, like lying to my coworker Marge at Claire's. We'd become friendly, and she was kind, a pudgy brunette in a too-tight tank top. But I'd taken advantage of her good will, calling out sick, when I really was watching *Jeopardy!* and eating chocolate ice cream straight from the carton. She'd work overtime and clock me in, calling every other day to wish me well. But I'd continue, first declaring I had the flu, then mono, then never bothering to call in anymore. I cashed my checks but quit by default, my gratitude to her never acknowledged.

This was for stealing the beaded bracelet from Bloomingdale's, though I had the money to pay for it, or how I scooped up the thick envelope from the high school floor, knowing full well it wasn't mine, happy to pocket the money inside. Later, I read the attached note, the writer proud of Tom's graduation. I promptly spent his money on earrings and movie tickets, laughing that I'd put my night out on Tom's tab.

Finally, this was for Jerry, and my casual cruelty, and for my broken-down DNA, for every wrong I'd caused, and all the ways I made his world worse.

I was remorseful then, my mind littered with apologies, of words I should've said, of reparations I could've made. But I was never a good person. And if depressed people really saw the world accurately, then I'd known it all along. There were those like Jerry, Nikki, and Tessa who tried to believe the best of me, but they were delusional.

This was always going to be my end, Karma secure and satisfied. The culmination neared, with sinking eyelids, my brain drained of complex thought.

"Look at me," he roared. I stared, watching my fluids leaking onto the riverbank, the water red with my runoff. I sank further still, arriving at the final act I'd once desired.

I had feared death, but not anymore, the way my surroundings locked into focus. The silver rocks shined, while a wave of water surged, wetting my hair, the taste of it entering my mouth. I accepted it, allowed my mouth to contain it, one with nature at last.

I thought of nothing, and then nothing came, a tingling sound, then a curtain of black.

It was better this way, to embrace the emptiness. I was one with the bank, the current tangling my hair, braiding it with sticks, the blood and tears drifting from my body into the river, the tributary, and beyond, to the ocean, myself mixed into the sea, the final push to arrive full circle, beautiful, as I never was before or would be again.

Chapter 10
Lisa White
Date: March 1st, 2007, 4:00 p.m.

The fog rolled in, bringing with it a downpour of rain, which had soaked my hair, frizzing up the ends into an ugly poof, with droplets weeping on my shoulders. I hated that feeling, that burst of wetness, and it made me squirm. I didn't have time to leave the library before my next class, no opportunity to rid myself of this dampness. I rocked back and forth in my seat, like I had a UTI infection, immune to the disruption I caused the other students. I avoided theme parks most of my life because of that sensation, the clamminess stinging my skin, enough to make me itch. Log flume rides were out and forget sitting in damp bikini bottoms. That's my version of torture, the mugginess a hot poker, causing all kinds of discomfort.

I twisted in my chair, trying to shake my hair loose, dying for a ponytail holder, when I caught his eye. A tall student, stretched almost to the ceiling, stared at me, his black hair resting on his shoulders, reminiscent of a vintage Gavin Rossdale. His locks remained dry and voluminous, like he'd stepped out of a Pantene ad, not a strand out of place. He watched me wiggle and shot me a smile, nothing flashy, lightly flirty. His smirk made me want to lean in, the way he didn't overdo, his lack of winks or cheesy pickup lines a win for originality.

I was used to men spoiling it. You couldn't run in the pageant circles without being introduced to the type that wanted to trophy-wife you, lickety-split. My momma had shimmering eyes at the thought, her ideal June wedding already vision boarded, complete with a reception at the country club where my daddy played golf. She'd kept her wedding dress on display in the cedar closet, primed and ready at a moment's notice. Hell, at this point, she'd take a shotgun wedding, anything to get some grandkids on the family tree. Every time I visited she got more and more antsy, flitting about like she'd taken too much gas station speed, stamping anxious circles around the kitchen table, a snippety sermon from her overdone lips about how I was spoiling my prime. She dropped names like breadcrumbs of debutantes already engaged, of peers six months pregnant and showing.

I took her ire in stride because I had bigger dreams than church receptions and husbands. Though recently I worried that I'd levered my future on a pipedream. I returned to my chemistry homework, which resembled hieroglyphics. I copied the blackboard in its entirety, but it was gibberish, with a professor that didn't care whether I passed or failed. His eyes glazed over my raised hand in the front row, labeling me another disposable freshman, not worthy of a second glance or extra help. He was tenured, but I was toast since I'd failed every quiz so far.

In fact, the whole campus was ignoring me, with students walking briskly between classes, their nods crisp and unwelcoming, their bespectacled faces flashing critical glares. I thought UNC Chapel Hill was hospitable, its brochures sparkling with Southern manners and money, exposing a culture of education and opportunity. Thomas Wolfe had hung in these hallowed walls, a pencil in between his teeth, crafting literary marvels before breakfast.

But I'd purchased a lemon, cause so far I'd spent a hell of a lot of money to be disregarded. The most attention I'd received was from my roommate Beth who blanketed me with snippets of the macabre. She lobbed veiled warnings at me, about a student named Chrissy who was mangled in her home after a night of booze and wanderlust. Beth practically force-fed me a panic attack with all the gory details, her eyes blazing, a poor man's Stephen King. Her story succeeded in keeping me bound to the library with a healthy dose of paranoia. Someone evil lurked behind these brick-backed walls, drunk on ill intent and desire. It had all the makings of a Gothic ghost story, but I had no interest in securing a starring role.

I'd faced my fears and gone to my TA's office hours to pester him about my chemistry homework, but the swirl of information only created a confusion tornado, with compounds and molecules too difficult to pronounce. I went to recoup in the only quiet place I could find, but the library only provided space to review everything I didn't understand. The equations remained unsolved, paired with storm-cloud thoughts, casting a cloak of pessimism over my work.

This kind of day made me feel low down, like every hurdle

was so high that even lunch was insurmountable. I longed for the comfort of my four-poster bed, and the smell of the horse stable, the feel of galoshes stuck in fresh mud. The homesickness churned in my belly, and my eyesight blurred. I searched for a crumpled tissue, frustration and tears spilling onto my composition notebook.

"What are you studying?" the long-locked student stage-whispered, his books resting next to mine, the screech of his chair breaking the silence of the library, causing some students to turn their heads. His posture was erect, his spindly fingers creased around his mouth, cupping his cleft chin. Apparently no introduction was needed since he'd already entered my space, choosing not to acknowledge my mini mental breakdown.

I sniffed in reply. He looked familiar, his presence close enough to cling to. I debated it, leaning into him, wanting that hit of reassurance, even a lovely lie, that everything would be okay.

"Well, I'm attempting to study," I replied, surveying my table crammed with books and crumpled notes. "But it's not exactly working." I bit the inside of my lip, willing myself not to cry again, though my emotions were unstable atoms themselves, all negatively charged.

"One of those days, huh?" he replied, like he understood the flurry of my repetitive destructive thoughts, aware of the stress that flattened my dreams.

And he was there, snug in his green V-neck, which matched his emerald eyes, cozy as could be, with a sharpened pencil in his right hand. It was inappropriate, but I longed for a hug, to steady myself against someone and borrow their strength.

When he scooted closer, I was thankful.

"You ever feel it's all a bit much?" I asked, focusing on the slow twirl of my fountain pen, instructing myself to calm down. As a freshman, I yearned for a mentor to set me straight, to reassure me through college's steep learning curve and mold me into the perfect student.

"No, never," he answered, not an ounce of sarcasm in his reply. He continued to stare at me, his serious gaze devoid of any frivolity, the golden irises of his eyes twinkling in the low lighting.

I tensed. What kind of person hadn't felt the heaviness of life, the weighed-down drudgery that made days dreary? Half of my life was spent in the rut of over-committing and clawing back out, and it reflected in my grades, and deeper, weaving into my heart. Almost perfect but not quite, the old Mary Poppins conundrum. Full of good intentions but also hot air, never one to top any list, break any curve.

"I don't feel stressed because I break things down into parts. You know, what's that joke?" He watched me, his arm knocking against the table, bridging the gap between us, the curve of his fingernails buffed with no ragged edges. "About eating an elephant? You've got to do it one bite at a time." He said it all offhandedly, the words curling from his confident mouth, despite a squeaky voice.

And while he wasn't traditionally handsome, it created a pleasing effect, the way he was able to hit the mark just right, the goldilocks version of a male specimen. Polite but not dramatic, interested but not eager, causing a rush of desire bounding through my bloodstream. I felt myself gravitating toward his subtle self-assurance. Maybe he was something I could study instead.

"Take for instance… you." He smiled again, advertising bright-white teeth. "What is it that has you so agitated?"

"Well. At the moment, chemistry." It came out confessional, humbling to admit the subject was fraying my last nerve.

"Oh." He shrugged. "Well, chemistry is math in another form."

"Math? No, this…" I gestured at the papers, quick to clarify it was no ordinary class. "This is about compounds and other stuff I can't comprehend. I know algebra. But this, it's diabolical."

"No. You see, chemistry is about a balance. If you can achieve that, you can understand it."

He reached for my notebook, without my permission, and proceeded to draw an equation. His penmanship was masculine and block lettered, so different from my comely calligraphy.

"Well, I'm getting my Master of Science degree here at Chapel Hill. Chemistry is my specialty area, the focus of all my research hours. And what I can tell you is this: chemistry, at its heart, is about all things being equal. It's fair, you see, and always perfect."

His eyes held mine, and I could tell he was patient, the opposite of my professor's terse replies and my TA's rushed explanations. My cardigan brushed against his well-muscled arm. He didn't pull away. I let my hand linger.

He repeated the same words from class, his voice soft, catching on words like "electronic" and "steric effects," but his cadence sounded like high-pitched poetry, the rhythm in his words all love. He drew diagrams and went slow, checking in to make sure I understood, weaving a rhythm I could follow.

"I'm Jason, by the way," he added, after thirty minutes had passed.

"I'm Lisa. Pleasure…"

"Is all mine." He blushed, with a grin delivered straight from Cupid's bow. I bit my lip and returned his gaze. Smart and sweet, that's a balance I could pursue with fervor.

"Thanks for taking the time to explain it all to me. I feel so much better, you're a wonderful teacher." Relief gushed in my words, but I meant them, he really had clarified all the loose ends I was lacking.

"I didn't mind. In fact, I would love to help you. They say the best way to learn is to teach, so you'd be doing me a favor too."

We agreed to meet in the library every night that week under the guise of studying, our relationship developing over neutrons and protons, our knees colliding under library tables. Jason loved science because it was flawless, a singular devotion to one right answer. He said it like a proposal, his tutelage connecting between my head and his. He double-checked my homework, and he never ridiculed my questions. Instead, he would smile and start over again, patient in his expertise. By the end of our study sessions, chemistry made more sense, and my crush on Jason flourished in return.

He wasn't from Chapel Hill and had no trace of accent, his voice a geographical chameleon. I noticed he rarely talked about himself, content instead to ask questions about me, with detailed follow-ups that were never reciprocated. I didn't mind; it was nice to be asked my opinions, the discussion far from my rounded hips or bra size. In the safety of the library, I was able to relax, to prop my feet up against a stray chair, while strategically dropping my pencil to scoot closer to Jason, an inch away from sharing a seat.

He smiled, but stiffened, my touch briefly unwelcome. I wondered if he was a virgin, but at his age, that would've been insulting. He continued to bristle when my fingernails traced the length of his arm. He was quick to soothe his nerves, but I noticed a flash of fear before he wiped it clean.

I vowed to take things slow, to worm my way in, until I was as comfortable to him as the periodic table. I wanted him to be fluent in me, to speak Lisa, his world and desires mirroring my own.

Jason could ease my rough edges, whittle me into something known and valued. He was secure about what he wanted, in life and in love. He said he was getting his master's in chemistry because he wanted to be an expert and devote his life to one area of study.

"And one woman, too. A life in a lab, a family, one strong foundation. That's all logic, but it's what love is, too, a formula to follow."

He didn't look at me when he said it, but he didn't have to. I knew his words were meant for me, and I blushed, turning the tips of my ears blood red.

My mom would frown if they were introduced. He was a far cry from my father, who preached the virtues of hard work and golf, his summers spent with a farmer's tan peeking through his Polo shirt. His strong work ethic fused with the country club par 4's allowed my mother the freedom to redecorate the house at will, no permission necessary. She had her doctorate in spending Dad's hard-earned cash.

Jason was the bookish sort, and not one to spend frivolously, a sweet and certain spendthrift. He loved spreadsheets and calculators, his predictability a panacea for the waves of worry that washed me out. My mom might object, but he became my respite at UNC Chapel Hill. The ying and yang of insomnia and night terrors withered under our daily routine. Jason's punctuality, his good posture, his certainty with life became my anchor, shaping me with his capable hands into someone brand new.

I desired that. I didn't mind bending to his subtle corrections, curbing my opinions to match his whims. My plans were written in breadcrumbs, my trail adaptable to wherever he chose to lead us, piggy-backed and happy to be included, no questions asked. My only goal was college, so there was nothing to alter.

Over pencils, sundresses, and books, I fell in love with Jason LeDown, letting him lead me into green pastures where I could finally rest, free from my mother's monogrammed expectations. Jason instructed me not only in my studies but to his presence, the clearing of his throat a punishment for eyes that drifted. I replaced my yawns with feigned zeal, fueling energy into glances that lingered. Jason wanted to be listened to, and I was eager to be his ingénue.

For me, it was an easy trade-off; I could be malleable if he could love me. My chemistry average became a ninety-eight, clear proof of the progress Jason offered.

Each night, I slept easy under my patterned floral sheets, my thoughts a beautiful baseline, because Jason could fix whatever I wronged. It was appealing, having an ace in my back pocket, an academic handyman who gave out free tutoring and life lessons. He'd drawn a map of who I should be, and I acquiesced willingly.

"You must like this boy," Beth said, sending me an exaggerated, knowing wink. "You're hardly here anymore except to sleep."

"I do really like him," I demurred. I'd been loose-lipped about the easy-breezy men who'd come before, the revolving door of frat boys and ball players, their passion found in video games and hit-and-run hookups. But I found it difficult to talk about Jason, preferring to keep him squirreled away, our first kisses secured like childhood daisy chains. Our other attempts at affection had stopped prematurely, the rush of lust interrupted by Jason's chastity belt. He doled out kisses, under duress, like he had a quota to maintain. Our make out sessions were stale and disconnected, so opposite of the passion I had for him.

I was embarrassed to tell Beth about our lack of physicality. While our futures seemed intertwined, our bodies were not. We'd yet to move past making out, even after months of dinner dates and late-night movies, limiting ourselves to squashed kisses upon my squeaking futon. He never slept over or invited me to spend the night. I'd barely seen the inside of his off-campus apartment.

I told myself he was being respectful, that he didn't want to ruin a good thing. He was serious, his hands eons from the edge of my bra. His stiff fingers never found my jean buttons, even when I enticed him. Here was a man who appreciated order, not a boy built for strip clubs or hunch punch. After each daytime date, my optimism rebounded, and I brushed off any lingering concerns. My sleep improved, pulled under a languid undercurrent of good fortune, my previous anxiety replaced with love.

We'd switched our weekly library date to Thursday, because of his rigorous lab schedule. Afterward, we'd grab dinner, either at the Chinese buffet or the quaint Italian place two blocks over, bonding over fettucine and focaccia, ignoring the garlic aftertaste of stolen kisses. Our commitment was secured, reaching past the confines of college, stopping short of a formal proposal.

"I love how you need me," Jason murmured, his grip on my arm a touch too tight.

"I do, Jason. You're all I want or need. I always feel safe with you because you know exactly what you want."

While I did admire his perseverance, what I really adored was his expression when he noticed me. His face exclaimed that life started when I appeared. Lately we'd lingered over our parking lot goodbye kisses, his hips pressed into mine, moving in a slow circle, my fingers winding through his long hair. Eventually he'd pull away, with a look of longing so intense it turned grief stricken.

I'd return to my dorm, horny and confused, but I was in too deep to quit. He obviously was attracted to me, I'd felt the evidence through his pressed dark wash jeans. Sometimes moans would escape during our kisses, his enjoyment evident and observable. I remained sexually frustrated, concerned he'd walled off his affection so tightly I wouldn't be included.

THE CLOCK TICKED ANNOYINGLY, CHIMING PAST THIRTY minutes, then forty-five, each minute escalating my concern with Jason's increasing tardiness. An hour passed and still, nothing.

Another semester loomed, and with it the promise of Chemistry II. I'd enrolled at Jason's insistence, signing up for another long year of equations. He'd purchased a workbook, complete with one-on-one tutoring time to jump start my learning curve. I'd skimmed the material, already bewildered before the class officially began. My success depended on Jason showing up, and he was nowhere to be found.

We'd both taken summer classes, eager to strengthen our bond and our grade point averages. Jason's work required intensive lab hours, with little time left over for romance. His schedule was exhausting, and I ended up color coding our dinner dates on his dry erase board so he knew I existed. I saw less of him than promised, settling for quick kisses and take out options squeezed between his research requirements. It was disappointing to be sidelined in his life, and the relationship wound from the summer remained raw.

I peered at the bookstacks in the front, then stood, nervously slurping from the fountain water. I paced a worried circle while watching for his mane of dark hair. I tried his cell, but it went straight to voicemail, the sound of his greeting angering me. I didn't want to hear his voice; I wanted his presence, especially since I had my initial chemistry lab tomorrow. My TA offered extra sessions before the semester started, and I needed all the assistance offered.

I flicked my pencil, slowly packing up my supplies. It wasn't like him to miss our date, and I wasn't the type of girl who accepted being stood up. I dialed his number again; no response. Disappointment burned in my chest, and I glowered at the other students, leaning back in their chairs, faces cheery and unconcerned. I wanted to knock them over like flimsy dominos, to make a scene that matched my ruinous mood.

I considered dropping by his apartment but didn't want to

appear clingy. We'd been monogamous since the spring, amping up our commitment through the summer, and in four weeks, September 1st would mark our six-month anniversary. I'd already gift wrapped his present, a cashmere sweater that matched his eyes, stowed safely in my dorm closet.

A note of caution pinged in the back of my head, the quick shadow of doubt rearing up before I shoved it back into my subconscious. I settled on a simple excuse, hypothesizing that Jason was caught up by an inquisitive undergraduate and lost track of time. He was allowed a mistake, having never been late before.

When it turned nine p.m. and he still hadn't called, my temper was no longer controllable. Beth withstood the worst of my mood swing, frowning while I slammed my dresser drawer, the blameless furniture bearing the brunt of my frustration.

"It's such a mess in here. I can't find anything! Look at all this!" I motioned to the makeup on the counter, the pair of strewn jeans on the floor. In truth, it wasn't all that dirty, and I watched a flare of hurt settle in Beth's eyes.

"Calm down, Lisa. I'll clean it up," she muttered, throwing me a scowl, and then another.

I crossed my arms and pouted, every inch a disgruntled toddler, and it did nothing to relieve my irritation.

I slept poorly and dreamed of numbers that floated above my head, italicized equations that couldn't be solved. I woke up early, encouraged that Jason might be downstairs with a whirlwind of apologies or fresh-cut flowers. I stretched out my tight muscles, careful not to wake Beth, and snatched my closest clean shirt. If he'd surprise me with an extra-large coffee and a side of regret, I could forgive his venial sin.

I was used to male disappointment, familiar enough with the general script. Invent an excuse, vow to do better, give a couple of compliments, then all was forgotten. A thoughtful gift could fast forward through this hiccup, smooth out all my lingering resentment. A heavy dose of optimism and new shampoo cheered up my shower, anticipation warming me better than hot water. It was only a miscommunication, no need for hysterics.

Jason wasn't in the breakfast line in the cafeteria. He wasn't waiting by my dorm's double door, hat in hand, ready to take ownership of his oversight. On better days, he'd walk me to class, holding my hand and my books, making sure every part of me was taken care of.

I glanced at my watch, giving him another ten minutes to make his appearance. I stayed until I was in danger of being late to my lab, then I pulled my hair in a ponytail and stomped off to the science building. Halfway there, I saw Jason strolling through campus, with his shirt untucked and his hair cowlicked. His appearance took me by surprise, shabby in his stained clothing paired with bloodshot eyes. My boyfriend had morphed into an insomnia-ridden homeless person.

"Um, hello?" I started, much too loud, lobbing a furrowed brow and a glare his way. Jason looked aggrieved, my presence unwelcome and unwanted. He huffed, hands on his hips, his mouth yanked into a grimace.

He looked mad at me, which was intolerable.

"Excuse you! Why do *you* look angry with *me*? And where *were* you last night, Jason?" I queried, playing into a familiar trope, the irate girlfriend, and yet I couldn't keep the ache out of my voice.

"It's nothing," he dismissed me with an eye roll. "I got caught up with something important. No biggie."

"More important than meeting me?" My voice tilted, his words stinging poison darts directed at my heart.

"I'm really busy, Lisa, that's all. So I didn't show one time. Whatever. Like I said, no big deal." He glanced over his shoulder, already writing me off. His eyes glazed over, milky white, the stony stare of cataracts or apathy.

"There's a lot I have to do," he murmured, but I turned my tennis shoe in response. I upgraded to a jog since I was now officially late and two blocks away from the chemistry building. I was no longer interested in any excuse he provided. While I sidestepped other sleepy students, their pace languid and unconcerned, genuine tears pooled behind my eyes. His reaction was cruel, the opposite of the apology I was owed. I ground my teeth and stomped up the classroom stairs, my face red with exertion and hurt.

Two broken pencils and halfway through my pre-test, I realized most of my calculations were wrong. Everything I learned last year had been eviscerated by my heartache. I wanted to lay my head on the desk and sob, admit defeat publicly, ready to accept failure. My cluttered mind couldn't find a consensus, and I sat for ten minutes staring at last year's study guide, erasing most of my incorrect answers. The TA let loose a polite cough, and I realized I was the only student left in the room.

"You shouldn't be so hard on yourself. You have all year to catch back up," he encouraged. I didn't share his optimism. I feared I was headed to the low-grade gallows, my failure achieved before class began. The culmination of my hard work disintegrated in my hands, those study hours turned into academic dust.

I checked off the rest of my tedious to-do list, my concentration fully drained. The day was wasted once I ran into Jason, his indifference on replay in my mind, creating incessant ripples of worry. I panted, an inch away from the no-man's-land of catastrophizing and frequent trips to the bathroom.

I scarfed down a dry granola bar for dinner, my mood fully thunderous. No way I could sleep before I confronted him for some closure. I'd been to Jason's diminutive apartment, had woken up twice in his blindless bedroom. His place was tidy and monotone, his bed made militant, the vacuum lines etched deep in his carpet. He lived alone in a ground-floor studio, with no busty swimsuit posters on the wall, no lusty cars tacked with cheap putty. It looked like a fully furnished rental, the kind of place portly businessmen rented on weeklong trips. But I saw it as a tabula rasa, blank and waiting for a woman's touch.

Invigorated with righteous rage, I hurried to his apartment. I knocked, my feet firm against his generic welcome mat, the nylon edges worn and fraying. I heard shuffling from behind the door and replied with a more insistent knock. I would not be ignored.

"Jason?" I asked, certain he was home since a light flickered underneath his doorframe.

I increased my thumps to SWAT status, pounding with urgency that stung. I would not relent, I needed reassurance for the bouncing internal questions that tormented me.

The door creaked a reply, and with it the outline of his face. He didn't swing it open, keeping his welcome tentative. I was awarded a glimpse of his nose and long eyelashes, my entry reduced to a swatch of skin.

"Aren't you going to let me in?" I stalled, wondering why he was acting so strange. Our fight coincided with the new school semester, but he was too old for back-to-school jitters.

"It's not a good time, Lisa, I told you." His voice was sharp, labeling me a trespasser. He kept his shoulders squared, blocking my view.

"What is going on with you?" I stamped my foot, a rush of annoyance simmering to the surface. "First you stood me up, now you're keeping me outside like a stranger. What are you doing in there?" I made myself taller to peek behind him, my shoulder blade connecting with the curve of his door.

Jason stopped my foot with his oversize tennis shoe, creating a barrier, paired with a shaking head.

"No. Stop, just stop, will you! Listen, I told you, I have work to do. Now, please, Lisa, I need you to… go. I want you to leave."

He'd dismissed me, reducing what we had to an inconvenience.

My lip wobbled.

"Why are you doing this? I don't understand, Jason," I pleaded, hating the way it sounded, almost groveling. I rested my hand against his door, wanting him to reach for me, to soothe me.

"Lisa. You need to leave. I'm not joking." He narrowed his eyes, no regard for my red nose and watery eyes. "Get gone. Right now."

He didn't give me another option, the door hinges jangling against my crumpled face. I was left to decay on his doorstep, my label of emotional roadkill complete.

I waited for him to change his mind, counting to one hundred, then again. It took five minutes to regain my composure, fighting against the humidity and his callousness, until I could delay no more.

I made it to the dorm elevator before the weeping started. I was in complete hysterics by the time I reached my dorm room, ready to collapse into a puddle on the floor.

"Lisa?" Beth opened the door, and I fell into her waiting hug. The story spilled out, about how Jason wasn't who I thought he was, how I'd cast my expectations onto a good-for-nothing man, another caustic castoff on his doorstep. Beth soothed me, stroking my hair, motherly in her kindness. I could feel the dampness of her shirt, ashamed my snot was ruining her new clothes. But I couldn't stop, and despite my earlier tirade, Beth held me, being a better friend than I deserved. After an hour of bubbling half sentences and discarded Kleenexes, I crawled into bed, wrung out, with nothing left to do but sleep.

OLD HABITS DIE HARD. I RESERVED OUR TABLE IN THE library every Thursday for two weeks, longing for a glimpse of Jason. I cried through two voicemails that went unreturned, and I restrained the urge to continue. My dignity was dangling; almost non-existent. I'd do anything to get him back but he remained uninterested.

My eyes got teary when I completed chemistry equations, and I kept a box of Kleenexes within reach, the cotton mountain sky high by the end of the night. I'd survey the scene afterward, the tissue graveyard, mimicking my sorrow. The other students gave me a wide berth, their curious stares remaining at their end of the library table.

By the third week, I got a clue and started going to the library on Wednesday mornings. I checked out a chemistry textbook for beginners and started over. I made notes and cross-referenced, highlighted and memorized, my stack of required reading increasing. My ruled notebook overflowed with facts and page numbers to review. It took more time, scratching out each equation, and I went through a pile of erasers. I couldn't take any shortcuts since there was no one to save me this time.

I squeaked out a B minus on my next chemistry test, and the rush of pride took days to decline. If there had been a fridge in our dorm, I would've put my test on it. I kept it within eyesight, my accolade a reminder that I didn't need Jason to do well. This progress was all mine, and the pleasure of a job well done made me wonder what else I could master.

I attended all the review sessions and joined a study group, who broke up the molecules and monotony with greasy pizza nights in the student union. Before long, I was deep into my notecards, my confidence nearly restored.

I poured over my study guide in the library, my hair held back with a pencil, when I heard a cough behind me. I looked up to familiar dark hair against sturdy shoulders, his green eyes twinkling at me.

"Lisa. Hey. I've been looking for you."

I stared at him, my face flat, no reply offered. He didn't deserve my energy or my words, not after weeks of silence.

"I see you picked a different library time."

I nodded, keeping it brief. I'd practiced running into Jason, had prepped a script, with words stored for safekeeping. But now that it was happening, I was tongue-tied. He'd reappeared a week shy of our six-month anniversary, my lover replaced by a stranger in similar clothing.

"Listen," he began, sinking into the chair beside me.

"Umm," I started, angry at his presumption. "Sorry, I'm… I'm not staying." I grabbed my textbook and held it to my chest, shielding myself from whatever excuse was coming.

"Lisa, I'm sorry. I was going through so much back then. I shouldn't have treated you that way. It was the wrong choice, especially since I enjoyed our time together, and I regret that other things got in the way."

His tone sounded clipped, but his eyes scanned my face, eager for his apology to work.

His explanation was too little too late. I'd slogged through most of my chemistry studies, without his admonitions and sneaky asides about habits I should change. He'd knocked me off balance, leaving me in a puddle of anxiety and poor judgment. Now I saw his flaws up close, this flighty Icarus of a relationship that burned prematurely.

"Thank you for the apology," I replied curtly, my voice formal. "Now, if you'll excuse me, I have more studying to do." I purposefully looked away, my eyes on the title of my textbook. I let silence take over so my words wouldn't warble. "See you around, Jason."

I was done crying over him, so past the need for a postmortem breakup chat.

He continued to sit beside me, his stare making my cheeks go from white, to pink, to crimson. I didn't provide any more details, not trusting myself to speak. Jason wedged himself closer, almost stroking my leg.

"Come on, Lisa. I said I'm sorry. What more do you want from me?" He spoke urgently, his knuckles rapping against the wooden table.

I flinched, angry at his presence. I was over his censorship, his useless, controlling soliloquies.

"Listen, Jason, it's been weeks. You don't get to come to me now and pour out all these apologies." I huffed and stood up, the sound of my chair echoing in the quiet space. "I don't want to be with you anymore, and I'm no longer interested in what you have to say." I stuffed my books and pencils into my backpack, scooping up handfuls for a fast getaway.

He exited his chair, the bulk of him blocking my exit, with fists clenched.

"Excuse me, bitch?" He lowered his voice, closing the gap between us. I caught a whiff of body odor, his sweater spotted with dark stains. Jason pushed back his shoulders, his jaw tightening into a manmade wall.

"Say it again, I dare you, Lisa. Give me a reason." He clutched my arm, knocking my books to the floor, the sound ricocheting down the library stacks. He clenched my forearm, squeezing too tight, the look in his eyes murderous.

I remained frozen, throwing panicked eyes around the room, looking for a wayward hero. I wheezed, unsure of what to do since Jason's death grip circled my bicep.

"Excuse me, ma'am, are you all right?"

We'd attracted the attention of a varsity lacrosse player, his bowl-cut hairstyle and letterman's jacket secure on Jason's right-hand side. I thought I recognized him, the cut of his body athletic, his face pinched in concern. The stranger flexed his arms, registering Jason's grip but keeping a cautious distance.

I nodded, breaking Jason's clutch, and ducked to retrieve my fallen items. The athlete moved closer, creating a barrier between us, watching me shake while I gathered my belongings.

"It's fine, thank you. We're done here. Right, Jason?" My voice crept higher, my hands stuffed with personal effects. I wrapped myself into a tight hug, the top of my arm still burning from his grasp. I held my ground and raised my chin, my eyes issuing Jason a challenge in the form of a raised eyebrow.

He stomped off, throwing a quick "bitch" over his shoulder, escaping fast into the drizzling rain. I watched him slam the library door for good measure, his final tantrum parting shot.

I felt nothing but relief.

"You sure you are okay? That guy seemed really mad." The boy looked earnest, his light blue eyes radiating concern. "I'm Seth, by the way. You sit behind me in Anthropology class with Dr. Smith."

Then he smiled at me, and I noticed a dimple, then its twin.

"Right, thank you. I'm Lisa." I jostled my heavy bag onto my shoulder. "My ex decided today was the perfect time to act like a psycho. So thanks, Seth, for coming to my rescue." I said it breathily, and he responded exactly how I thought he would.

"Mind if I walk you back to your dorm? Between that dude and Chrissy, well, you can't be too careful. Plus, I brought my golf umbrella, and it's big enough for us both."

He held out one chivalrous arm, and I passed him my bag, the weight minimal in his capable hands.

"So what were you studying before you were interrupted?" he asked, routing us closer to the front door.

I sighed. "Chemistry II. It's my hardest class, and while I've studied hard, it takes extra work to understand it." I watched the rain fog up the library windows, dreading another lone study session spent writing notes until my hands cramped.

"Oh, that's my major! I took that class two years ago."

I grinned at Seth, matching him stride per stride, allowing him to lead me into the pouring rain. Maybe another tutor was exactly what I needed.

Things were looking up. Seth held open the library door, and I sauntered through it, the lampposts guiding us toward the dorm, our words connecting, forming a covalent bond, combustible and bright, two heads pressed together to avoid the rain, a new relationship teetering in the old one's wake.

Under Seth's golf umbrella, I learned that heartache was temporary, and Jason was replaceable. There's no shortage of men who were good at chemistry. This one earned bonus points for keeping my hair dry and avoiding the damp sensation I despised.

Maybe I was destined for the Dean's list after all.

Chapter 11
Chrissy Brown
Date: September 22nd, 2006, 10:05 a.m.

My head burned, the remnants of last night pounding an unremittent drumbeat into my forehead. The marching band in my brain reminded me of all the Yaeger bombs I gulped down at Downtime bar last night. I knew it was a bad idea then, but now the regret was twofold, my mouth brimming with stale spit. My teeth were covered in a sweater of something foul, my breath certainly lethal, the taste of rotten cheese molded against my gums. My tongue scoured the inside of my mouth, noting buildup of plaque and old liquor. Gross. Pretty soon I'd add cavities to the list of my college calamities, along with my side hobby of blooming alcoholism and financial stressors. UNC Chapel Hill was giving me a reverse education, with credit hours found in receipts for Tylenol and Gatorade.

I turned my head slowly, assessing my bedsheets, touching the dampness from my feet to my throbbing head. I sniffed, relieved to smell no traces of urine. The nighttime wetness had become an unwanted side effect of my binge drinking, soaking me in shame and extra quarters for the basement laundromat. I stuffed my sheets into the machines at night, to prevent my peers from noticing the stains.

It hurt to move, my headache proof of how detrimental the pursuit of fun could be. The good times could kill you, or so I'd been told, counting myself among the walking wounded who fell for well drinks and last call shots.

This was all Joanna's fault. I told her I needed to slow down, that my bank account and my health couldn't take another night out. She laughed off my complaints and shoved a cute tube top in my direction. That's all it took, my motivation pummeled by free covers and loud music. Chapel Hill was hella hard to get into, and even harder to stay enrolled. I traded high SAT scores for Alabama Slammers and a DJ blasting Nelly Furtado.

My eyes weaved circles on the popcorn ceiling, wondering how bad it would hurt to sit up all the way. I tested it first, resting lightly on one elbow, before lowering myself against my bed pillow. My stomach churned, warning me it was too soon for that much movement.

I remembered some of last night: the pounding of Fergie and the Black Eyed Peas, of Joanna rapping the words off-key, the sweat glistening on my shoulders while I writhed against someone's back. I bounced beside a boy who said he was in my Intro to Psych class, but he didn't look familiar. Everyone looked tinted under the glow of the spotlights, the bass drowning out anything serious.

A spiral of nausea recapped the nightcap wine, paired with

glass tumbler tipped on its side, dripping Pinot on the floor. My alarm clock was covered under capri pants, but I knew I'd missed my eight-a.m. class by hours, not minutes. I glared at the bright windows, the midday sun evidence that I'd slept in again.

I groaned. Professor DeWitt would kill me. I'd promised him I'd extend more effort, but I'd reverted to my status quo, hungover and regretful, college making a liar out of me. Soon I'd run out of his good graces, and then I'd really be screwed. My advisor was my last advocate before academic suspension or worse.

It's time to try to pull it together, to stumble into a warm shower, and assess how much of the day I'd wasted. I debated sinking further into my bed, calling it a Friday mulligan, claiming victim to another Thirsty Thursday. My covers and sleep could wash my bad mood away and give my head time to recover.

No, I wouldn't be that statistic, another stupid sophomore turned college dropout. My parents would rage at me, after I'd pled for a second chance after my lackluster freshman year. They advocated for a community college experience, offering a cheap semester devoted to maturity and academic review. Mom had kept her eyes on the ground, but still, disappointment came off her in waves. I'd rejected their brochures and their logic, convincing them to bet on me again, to stretch their budget once more in search of my scholastic happiness. My mom sighed and pulled extra nursing shifts to cover the cost of my textbooks. My dad crinkled the brochure in his working-man hands, his cuticles tough from years of manual labor.

I'd levered the last of my parents' good will on promises that this year would be better. If they knew the truth, they'd disown me, shocked by my overflowing trash can and the traces of vomit grazing my toilet seat.

I sat up, my head swimming, and grabbed the side of my bed like a life raft. One of the perks of living off campus was that I didn't have to suffer in a twin-size bed, having paid my freshmen dues in crumbling dorm rooms. I'd blamed my previous lack of progress on the hustle and bustle of a shared living space, with loud music and moans erasing my stellar study habits. My parents, and their shaky signatures, cosigned on my independence. Today, though, my solitary bedroom did little to improve my hangover or mood. I navigated to the bathroom, avoiding the heaps of soiled clothes.

The overhead florescent light was way too bright. I debated turning it off and showering in the dark, but there was no way my balance could be trusted in my half-drunk state. I leaned against the acrylic wall, scaling it an inch at a time, all blind man without a walking stick. I flipped the hot water knob to one level below scalding. I stepped inside, bracing for the initial burst of icy water.

The water pressure threatened to relieve me of last night's liquids. I deserved that hit of responsibility. Those cheap, sugary daquiris never treated me right, but I slurped them down anyway, prioritizing tequila sunrise over probiotics. Gut health was the least of my worries.

I knew my scholarship was in jeopardy, all those long essays circling the educational drain, threatening a free fall. All I'd wished and worked for was in danger, one mistake away from losing it all.

I should be more anxious.

All I currently felt was sick, my sour stomach deciding to

come out and play. I leaped from the shower, my tummy rumbling somersaults. I made it to the toilet, my naked body hurling, the smell foul and decaying. I waited for more, then decided to clear out my insides completely. I rested my knees against the tile floor, stung by their coldness, and gripped the sides of the porcelain toilet cover. I stuck two fingers deep into my throat, gagging on the mountain of vomit chunks. More volume filled the commode, colored ribbons of waste floating to the top. Tears formed in my eyes, and I wondered if I should add bulimia to my growing list of concerns.

I anticipated another round, but I'd emptied all of last night's evidence into the soiled bowl. I flushed and crawled back in the shower, letting the water rinse off the puke that clung to my hair and chest. At last, I turned off the water and searched for cleanish clothes, in need of some grease to keep the nausea at bay.

Chapel Hill was my reach school, the pinnacle of progress, but it sold me a baby-blue disappointment for $20k a year. None of my core classes were interesting, and the TAs who taught them faced the blackboard, not bothering to learn our names or majors. The students prioritized studying, a boring row of pencil pushers, contrary to the rowdy frat parties I'd envisioned.

I'd dreamed of picnics on the quad, with professors creating a salon-type atmosphere where ideas were debated, and futures discussed, over expensive red wine and vintage smoking pipes. They'd twinkle in their tweed blazers, amused at our naivete, underneath a cyclopean sky.

Instead, the tenured teachers barely held office hours, their enthusiasm aligned with a high school guidance counselor. Their resumes were long, but the professors rested in their own laurels and accolades, their investment in students decreasing annually. Maybe they were more attuned to the graduate students who could assist with their research. As a lowly underclassman, all I received were monotone explanations and recycled tests. I remained an anonymous face in the campus game of Guess Who, unremarkable to anyone except the local bartenders.

Almost Ivy League, my ass, I surmised. UNC Chapel Hill was a school for rich kids, who double parked their Range Rovers in the staff parking lot, adorned with conservative political bumper stickers and vacations to St. Simmons. Those audacious wealth displays made me cringe, the population akin to what Creedence Clearwater Revival sang about, all senators' sons and fortunate ones. The benefaction skipped over the rest of us, but to complain was bad form. My middle Tennessee upbringing was a paycheck away from being blue collar. Most of my peers had never struggled, and it was hard not to hate their ignorance.

The only thing that had matched my expectations was mentioning I was a Tarheel student. Strangers would award me a grin of approval. I finally understood what it meant to be special. I soaked in their envy, and I courted it.

I dried my hair, making promises to the mirror. This was a blip, a momentary adjustment to life living alone while my frontal lobe developed and stretched into place. My high AP test scores declared my aptitude, as did my inflated SAT scores. I belonged here, safe in the realm of the academically gifted with a scholarship to prove it.

But the meager money awarded to me didn't cover everything college required. My parents had beamed and taken too many pictures until we realized the cost of living in Chapel Hill. My dad had sulked when he received the itemized bill, his eyes re-reading the amounts. He brandished a calculator, his fingers pressing into every indented line. He totaled the amounts twice, certain there was a typo. I'd felt guilty then, and that was before all the regulars knew my drink order.

I finger-combed my hair into place and brushed my teeth twice, officially joining the land of the living. A quick glance at my watch, which was hidden under my duvet cover, revealed it was eleven a.m. on Friday morning. I'd missed bio and half of statistics, but if I hustled, I could still make my twelve thirty Intro to Psych class. I could find the student from the bar and beg to borrow his notes, securing the information I'd missed last week.

The campus wasn't crowded, too early for the burgeoning lunch crowd. I still marveled at the antique brick buildings, serving as a visual reminder that this university stood the test of time. The Bell Tower, at an impressive height of one hundred seventy-two feet, also reflected the university's statuesque potential. My disappointment continued but I couldn't ignore the beautiful commute to class.

I should call Joanna from my Palm Pixie to check in, but I had to jog to make it to the science building on time. I picked up the pace, but the acid in my stomach intensified. I slowed down into a brisk walk, offering my insides a compromise. I breathed in deeply, urging myself not to vomit in front of my professor. I hoped wherever Joanna was, she was in better shape than me.

I took the steps two at a time, making it to room 103 with six minutes to spare. The room was sparsely attended, the present students looking queasy and unkempt. A nod of acknowledge-ment came from the hangover crew, before leaning on their desk for support. I considered what it meant to be part of their brethren.

A redhead with a wide-brimmed hat slumped in the front row, his hands forming a flesh-colored pillow on the desk. Beside him, a girl in a green sweatshirt drew on her notebook, chewing heavily on a piece of gum. I took a seat in the third row, next to the exit, in case another bathroom trip proved necessary. The dizziness that lingered gave me a 50/50 shot I'd have to duck out of the ninety-minute class early. A handful of students struggled in, and a wave of displeasure murmured through the room when the graduate student approached the board. He gazed at us, daring anyone to voice discontent in words rather than whispered groans. No one took the bait, so he answered with a shrug and a crumpled attendance sheet.

I debated signing my name and sneaking out. I wasn't enthused to hear a twenty-two-year-old monologue about how the DSM IV-TR was a Dewey Decimal System for cataloging mental illness. These wannabe professors all suffered from the same illness, desperate with the desire to be taken seriously. I glanced around, assessing if I could make a quick escape, before deciding to join the rest of the class in pretending to pay attention.

This graduate student was trying to capture his audience, his voice struggling to reach the back of the auditorium with cat-scratch enthusiasm. Absolutely no one was listening to him. Half the class was dozy, corralling their puffy jackets into makeshift pillows. The TA kept at it, pacing back and forth, trying to put a dent in the collective apathy but not succeeding. I couldn't locate the boy from the bar. Then again, his details were blurred by the copious amounts of consumed alcohol.

I stretched, twisted, and forced myself to stay awake through the end of class. I barely made it, with my head promising to pay me back twofold unless I procured some Tylenol. I shuffled out with my classmates, dreading the walk back home, my body eager for water and rest.

My phone buzzed in my pocket. Joanna. Perfect timing.

"Hey there," I said, the noise of the hallway blocking out my words.

"Hey yourself," she wheezed, her voice thick with sleep.

"Ha-ha, you too, huh? You slacker, are you still in bed?"

"How are you awake right now? I'm dyingggggg. I don't even remember getting home." She whispered into the phone, not trusting herself to elaborate.

"Same. I missed my first two classes but dragged myself to the third. For nothing, as it turns out, cause the TA taught it. I'm not far from your place. Hair of the dog?"

"Oh God, Chrissy, no. We promised last night we'd take it easy, remember? We both swore on it. You got all teary about your scholarship, and I told you how worried my parents were about those break-ins and how they bought me that keychain pepper spray. We said last night was it. After we got tipsy we made a done-deal-pinky-promise not to get drunk again. Don't you remember?"

A hazy image appeared, akin to looking through the lens of a dusty telescope. The stickiness of the bar was slippery under my fingertips, the taste of mucus and salt slick in my throat. Joanna was beside me, her lips contorted into a scowl, her tube top streaked with sweat. It was a fuzzy snapshot, with no words attached, the ghost of her palm on my shoulder, the spotlight of the bar flickering above. The gaps in my memory removed any serious dialogue or alarm.

"I do, sort of, remember that," I lied. "But seriously, some grease and some Bloody Marys today can smooth out all this hurt. My treat."

I felt her hesitation, the swift activation of sucked-in breath. I didn't press her; I let her consider her options before adding, "And I promise we can talk about curbing our habits over lunch. Honest, Jo, for real this time. We will be sober sisters. No kidding."

"But, Chrissy, you said you were totally broke last night! You told me you've skipped loads of work study. I totally remember you saying that."

My cheeks registered her words, a sunburn of embarrassment. Apparently I'd been in a truth-telling mood last night, the drinks causing me to spill every concern into Joanna's lap.

"Okay, look, we'll compromise. Let's settle this at lunchtime. We do have to eat to take the edge off. Then we will hold each other accountable. We will refuel, then we will chill for the rest of the day before hitting the books. Deal?"

She paused, trying to mount a defense but crumbling. In the silence, Jo took a mental inventory of her hurting head, her tummy rumbling with a combination of missed breakfast and carbohydrate cravings.

"Okay. You win. But seriously, Chrissy. We gotta stick to this, okay?"

"Yes," I replied adamantly, and I meant it, too. She was right;

our status quo wasn't doing either of us any good. We'd get some sustenance and sun and then head back onto the straight and narrow, with limited damage done.

"Where do you want to meet?"

"Lestrange's is close to your place, and I'm halfway there. If I hurry, I can snag us a table outside. Meet ya there soon. And Joanna—no primping, I'm serious. I'm decked out in a campus T and sweats, so don't you dare get cute."

She laughed her reply and hung up.

I entered the parking lot right as the outside crowd began to swarm. The tables adjacent to the outside bar were already reserved, marked with hoodies and textbooks, place savers for the early birds who got the best seats. Tight circles yelled for pitchers of beer, the overflow spilling against knocked knees and sunglasses.

I knew the bartender, Mick, who was already working the lunch rush, his apron smudged with grease and grime. I signaled to him, with a wave and a smile, while I grabbed the last two-top in the sun. I placed an order of Bloody Marys with the server while I waited for Jo to show. That could barely be called a cocktail, its low alcohol content suitable for brunches everywhere. It was enough to lift our spirits without causing a drunken repeat.

People-watching on campus never failed to disappoint. From my umbrellaed table, I observed the sororities gather alphabetically with their Greek letters, Tri-Delta claiming the long table next to mine, and Phi Mu securing the largest indoor corner booth. Joanna called them sorostitutes, since they were more invested in securing a frat boy roster than engaging in academic studies.

Sorority row blazed their privilege like Christmas lights, with sets straight out of the *Legally Blonde* movie, complete with a harried-looking room mom working overtime to maintain their purity.

I had no interest in all that drama. I was content to study them from afar, those identical blondes and their bobs mushing together, duplicates with one-syllable names. I wondered if I shouted "Amy!" how many of them would turn around.

"Yo, Chrissy, order up!" Mick interrupted my daydream, swinging by the table to hand me a pitcher of Bloody Marys and four frosted mugs. "These are all for you, right?" He grinned, his yellow teeth dingy under the midday glare.

"Ha. Joanna's on her way." I felt a tinge of humiliation since I couldn't tell if he was joking. He handed me the generous glasses one by one, complete with wilting sticks of celery that were mostly for show.

"The troublesome twosome. Awesome. Well, have a good one. You know what I always say—be good or be good at it!" He departed, dodging the half-full tables, his pants baggy and beltless, in danger of dipping past the appropriate level.

"Wait!" I added, summoning him back. "I promised her I'd get us some food, too. We want the special, Mick, whenever you have time." I shot him a wink, earning myself some bartender goodwill. He nodded and collected my menu, tucking the laminated copy under his armpit.

I resumed eavesdropping on the sorority girls, having completed all my required ordering duties. I sipped the tomato juice slow, the crushed ice a sweet-and-salty combo. The girls would provide good gossip until Jo arrived. I paced myself, taking small sips from the cocktail, letting my mind focus on anything except my own mistakes.

"I heard he only likes blondes, so you'll be fine, Whitney," the headbanded sister to my right opined, a touch too loud, her voice taking on a caustic edge.

"Bitchhhhh, you know I never sleep alone. He only targets those girls that sleep solitary, and that hasn't been me since I got on this campus," she crowed complete with shimmied shoulders. The first girl retreated, slumping down into her chair, losing the battle of words.

A chorus of laughs echoed, and the girls leaned in, creating a swath of pin-straight, shoulder-length hair. I took another drink, wanting them to continue.

"No, but seriously, should we be worried?" A tall brunette in Tar Heel attire dipped her chin to her ample chest. "I heard a girl's apartment on Rosemary Street was broken into, but nothing was taken. The police kept it hush hush, not wanting to incite paranoia."

"Too late," muttered her friend with the dark Ray-Ban aviator glasses. "My parents keep calling me on repeat, begging me to come home for the weekend. I reminded them that we have that mixer with Sig Ep, but they are frantic and told me to skip it. Which I won't. But still…"

Nods rebounded from the co-eds, but my attention swerved onto Jo, her three-quarter-length shirt and tight bootcut jeans stopped directly at the table. Her dirty-blond hair was tied in a low bun at the nape of her long neck, and her lips were slicked with pink gloss. Her eyes were secure behind huge sunglasses, which shielded any hint of a late night, making her resemble a low-budget Jackie Kennedy. She dragged out the chair, unceremoniously dropping herself and her purse into it.

"This one mine?" she asked, already reaching for the closest Bloody Mary.

"You know it." I grinned, elbowing her slightly.

"Did you have to pick a table right on sorority row? My head can't take it," she mumbled, glancing at our noisy neighbors with distaste.

"Listen, Rumpelstiltskin, we are lucky I snagged this table at all! Look around. The place is jamming. And Mick is coming over with our burgers and fries, complete with extra cheese and no ketchup. So the correct response, I believe," I paused dramatically, "is thank you to my best friend, Chrissy."

"Thank you, Chrissy," she relented, sucking her drink through her straw like it could bring her back to life. I drained my drink, too, letting the tomato juice drip on my chin. We both began drink number two at the same time, clinking our glasses together, the buzz erasing our midmorning slump.

Two burgers, fries, and two more Bloody Marys led to a pitcher of Bud Light beer. My shoulders turned pink, then a threatening red, while Joanna and I set about getting sloshy. One drink turned into too many, the sunburn making us thirstier, our laughs turning unruly. Mick shot us a side-eye after another round of refills but kept his opinion to himself. Joanna got giggly, and then she got fun, her body bouncing to the cover band, who chose to open with Tom Petty. I tried to keep up but took a tumble, my red Solo cup flying onto one of the sorority sisters beside us. The contents stained her crisp collared shirt with a urine-colored streak.

"Who *is* this mess?" she rebuked, her words competing with the loud guitar solos in the next cover, Journey's "Don't Stop Believing."

"Eww, day drinker. Get the hell off of her. Look what you did!" chimed her friend, and she pushed me, her manicured nails connecting with my cherry-red shoulders. I winced and stumbled before Joanna caught me.

"Shut up, you nasty slut. I don't need advice from a Greek Letter Barbie." My voice pitched, and I saw their whole table cock their collective head. I doubled down, too drunk to care. "I didn't do shit to you, so yeah, shut it. Shut your trapppppp," I screeched, curbing the slur of my syllables, the beer slackening my train of thought.

I felt Joanna wrap her hands around my waist, pulling me back to the band. The sorority girls regrouped, ready to rumble.

"Time to go," Jo advised, juggling a ballpoint pen and our receipts.

I resisted, ready to continue my altercation, but Jo held strong, weaving me toward the door, away from the crowd and liquid temptation.

She ushered me down the crooked steps of the porch, while the roar of sorority sisters clapped and wolf-whistled, mocking our progress.

"Ya should have let me take them," I muttered, my feet concrete heavy, with one shoelace untied.

She laughed in my ear and handed our receipts to Mick, while we struggled to navigate the throng of rabblerousers outside in the parking lot. The dinner crew was arriving, confirmation that we way overstayed our welcome.

Jo and I stumbled back to her shared quad room since it was the closer of the two. She turned the fan on high and shut the door, crawling under the covers of her twin bed. I collapsed on the floor, curled into a ball on the itchy carpet, my head a spinning top. I closed my eyes, sinking into the refreshing dark, feeling the twirl of the overhead fan soothe my sunburned skin.

I woke up disoriented, my neck stiff and achy. It was dark, and I shivered, my skin prickled with goose bumps. I touched the floor, unsure of my bearings until I heard Joanna snoring loudly above me. I glanced at her nightstand, the red clock lights blinking 10:34 p.m. We'd passed out and slept away the day, our good intentions lasting as long as it took to order another drink.

I remained on my side, my head throbbing and my throat desperate for water. I tried to ignore the desire, but the pounding in my brain would not relent. I tiptoed to her shared kitchen, careful to not alert her bitchy suitemates. Joanna lived in a four-bedroom apartment and her roommates were not my biggest fans. She attempted to insulate me from the worst of their critiques, but she wasn't that good at running interference. I could feel their condemnation, even if I made a simple mistake, such as placing my glass on the table without a coaster. They protested, obvious in their displeasure, with heads pressed together before I left the room. I was the stray their roommate had picked up, the unwelcome rogue who spent too many nights on Jo's floor.

The kitchen night light led the way, and thankfully no one intercepted my water run. I grabbed a glass for Joanna, too, before sneaking back to her room, shutting the door with the tip of my toe.

The water helped me fade back to sleep, a cursory refreshment before the hangover hell I'd face in the morning.

I dozed until the sunlight felt hot on my face. The room was humid, and Joanna's snores had ceased. I opened one eye like a dragon awaiting treasure hunters and saw Jo glowering at me, her hair matted across her forehead.

"*That* was not the plan, Chrissy." Her voice was firm but winded, releasing in tight gasps.

She couldn't blame me for this one. We'd both gotten caught up in the thick of lunch that turned into something a little boozier, a little more lighthearted. It wasn't that heavy, just another afternoon spent living the college lifestyle. I hoped she wasn't preparing for another lecture because the drumbeat in my head couldn't take it.

"Hey, okay, so it turned into a bit more than we bargained for. But that's—"

"What? *No*. You were trying to singlehandedly take down Tri-Delta."

I laughed. "No, I mean that girl deserved it. She—"

Her eyes narrowed. "No, Chrissy, you spilled your beer on *her*. Drenched her in fact—down her hair, neck, and her whole shirt."

I scrunched my forehead, trying to remember the order of events.

"I don't really recall that, but even so, I mean, who cares? We got out of there, we came here. No biggie."

"I care," she replied, her voice a touch too calm. "I can't keep doing this, Chrissy. We promised, and then we did it again. I worked so hard to get here. We both did. And we promised we'd take it easy." Her voice cracked, with vulnerability and shame.

"I know," I reassured her, ready to make more promises, to assuage the guilt gurgling in my stomach. "And we can be good. We still have so much time ahead of us, and now it's the weekend. A new day ahead of us to do it better."

"You said that exact same thing yesterday." She looked me in the eye, her face tight with concern. "Then when I got there, you were already deep into the Bloody Marys." She paused, letting her words hang heavy in the air. "Chrissy, my roommates are right. We can't keep hanging out with each other. We are not good for each other. This kind of pace, with the drinking and the bars, it's not sustainable." She blew out a breath, trying to move the hair on her forehead. It remained stuck. "It's got to end."

"What do you mean?" I asked, though I shouldn't need clarification. The answer was in the depth of her frown, and the ache in my lower back, paired with a head that refused to stop swaying.

"It's too much alcohol and poor choices. I wake up feeling like death, and I've hit my limit." She leaned over the side of her bed, momentarily creating twin Joanna's in my blurry vision. "And you, Chrissy. I don't know. Maybe you have a problem. You keep saying you'll stop, that you want to, then you don't. Maybe you… have like… a disorder or something. Perhaps you need to get it checked out." She concluded with practiced indifference, her last word held aloft in casual cruelty.

My anger triumphed over my headache, looking for a reason to change the subject and let loose.

"Yeah, all right, Joanna," I replied, paired with a dramatic eye roll. "Now you sound exactly like those uppity roommates of yours." I grabbed my purse, spying it under a pile of dirty clothes, and began stuffing items inside. I held an unwrapped tampon in my hand, and lip gloss missing a top. My phone's black screen lay beside me, the battery fully depleted. I snatched it with my free hand, ready to storm off with my head held high.

"I'm not trying to be mean to you, Chrissy. You're my friend, and I care about you. But I need a friendship break. Too much of a good thing, you know…" She trailed off, watching me heap my possessions in my purse with no help given.

"Right, well, I wasn't alone in this. This is not my fault. You were there, drinking on my dime, not a care in the world until this morning." I stood, gripping the edge of her bed in case I wobbled. I'd planned on leaving in a histrionic huff, but I required a moment to steady myself. I debated slamming the door and waking up the whole household. But each step closer to the door felt like walking the plank, so I departed angry but without fanfare. Joanna and her hypocritical ways didn't deserve my ire, and I required extra concentration to walk without tripping.

I trudged back to my apartment low down and abandoned, my head muddled, not registering the other Saturday stragglers. Joanna was the most recent friend to highlight my drinking, but she was far from the first. Various acquaintances learned to approach it gingerly, soft and offhand, before turning forceful. The worst was when they sounded defeated, their voice breaking with sadness, admitting failure with their parting shots. All that was left after that was goodbye.

The first time was on Steph's birthday in high school, during our preplanned hella-secret junior camping trip. We'd secured a secondhand tent and told our parents about a church lock-in. We'd planned it for months and even made a contingency plan where nerdy Nancy would vouch for us. Me, Steph, Aaron, Linds, and Nathan crowed like lost boys in the nearby woods, happy for a night free of parental involvement.

I spiked the punch in celebration, downing a liter of it while the rest slipped politely on their Burnett's and orange Crush. I attempted to multi-task and build us a campfire while they caught up to my drunken level. In my sloppy state, I had let the fire drift, the sparks reaching onto our tent, backpacks, and random driftwood. My good intentions led to a seared tent and an almost wildfire.

Steph's camping celebration got ugly fast after that, with a damaged tent that leaked large raindrops, deflating our moods and sleeping arrangements. The group huddled together, whispering. I was outside, devoting most of the night to throwing up, my throat burning from sickness and guilt.

The next day, my core friendship group nicknamed me Neck of the Bottle Chrissy, since I'd gotten sloshed fast and furiously. They assembled themselves amongst the charred area, forming a gossipy oval, while I picked up the containers, shoulders hunched.

On Monday, I found Steph leaning against my blue top locker, her eyes downcast, sent to deliver the friendship final punch.

"Seriously, Chrissy, you really did damage the tent. And, like, we borrowed it, you know. It was expensive, and hard to explain why it came back with burn holes in it." She paused, and I remembered how her eyes looked, her job to put me down easy. One shot, straight to the heart. "You don't know when to stop."

I didn't take kindly to her intervention.

"I never asked you to watch over me!" My voice rose, and soon I was shouting, my complaints booming down the upperclassman hallway. "I don't need a babysitter, and I sure as shit don't need you, Steph, telling me what to do."

I should've stopped right there and not gone for the jugular. It wasn't a consciousness decision to hit her back hard. Her words were light, but when combined with watery eyes, her quivering hint of rebuke alighted a dormant volcano. I could handle her anger, but not her pity.

The words came out before I could hold them, or even realize their content. "Especially when everyone skirts around the fact that you don't eat. We got booze, not food, for your birthday celebration. You ever wonder about that?"

I stared her down, making each word hurt. "We all know; it's obvious in your size-zero pants and the food you push around your plate. So don't go feeling sorry for me, you anorexic bitch." I slammed my locker, the finale complete, waiting for her to hit me back or worse.

Steph didn't. She shook her head, wiped her eyes, and slid down the hallway. My prior clique waited by the double doors, forming a protective circle around her, four against one. Like a caged animal, I attacked first, to avoid looking at myself too closely, and that's how I lost all my friends in one day.

Well, to hell with them anyway. Girls like Steph and Joanna were fillers, steppingstones until someone better appeared. College was big and rowdy enough to find another sidekick quick. The place was brimming with those who needed to let loose, to take all that worry and drop it down for a while. I'd find my goodtime crew, the real ones who'd build me up instead of lecturing me.

My apartment looked like I felt. I scanned the front stoop, reviewing it through crusty eyes. The plants were long since saving, their leaves a sickly yellow. My welcome mat was cockeyed, with frayed edges that looked uninviting. I shrugged, promising a homemaker facelift another day, and unlocked the door. A blast of air conditioning hit my face. I'd left it on all night, and the place was an ice box, which helped mask the dirty dishes piled in the sink and the trash that needed tending. The bill would be my undoing, but it felt so right, the jet of cool air nestling my eyelashes.

I left the door cracked behind me while I trailed into the living room. I'd turned most of my makeshift home into a dump, with no energy to cook or clean. The couch remained free of clutter, except for my mother's handmade quilt, which hung lopsided on the end table. I curled underneath it, the frigid air cocooning me, the darkened windows masking the burgeoning sunlight. I let Joanna and all my troubles slink off my shoulders, the sweetness of sleep offering much-needed amnesia.

I awoke shivering, the blanket slipped far from my shoulders. It was dusk, and the apartment was black. The door had been shut, and it was somewhere between dinnertime and night. I reached for my phone but came up empty, assuming it was lost to couch cushions. It was dead anyway, and I didn't have the energy to locate a charger.

I stayed still, not wanting to move and fully enter wakefulness. I squinted, wondering where I'd put my purse. I peered over the couch, too far to spot the kitchen island. I thought I'd discarded it there, but my throbbing head was an unreliable narrator. I sat up, attempting to gaze through the shadows, the vestige of my hangover sensitive to sudden movements.

I squinted. There was something looming beside the kitchen

counter, but it was too tall to categorize. It looked like a coat hanger, but I didn't own one. I tilted my head. Nothing should be there, only a wall and two secondhand bar stools, but this shape looked person sized.

I jerked my head, a touch too quickly. My mind was playing tricks on me, the combined result of day drinking and low-level depression. My head pounded, and my sore legs agreed that I was in no shape for impulsive actions.

The shape didn't move. But I caught a better glimpse, one clear snapshot, and my heart sank.

In my kitchen was a man, with his lengthy back growing larger against the breakfast nook wall. He was statuesque, a giant when paired with my seated position. My hands searched for the remote, anything to distract the specter in the kitchen. But all I had was the tangled blanket.

"Hi." He tittered, his voice airy. I was not imagining this. He was speaking, walking closer, out of the shadows and moving fast.

He donned a black mask, the point of it tipped and ill fitting. The mask covered everything but his mouth and his eyes. My mind twisted, trying to grasp the events that led here. My stomach churned, a sickly spiral that needed release.

"I see you've woken up, Sleeping Beauty," he regaled, his voice too bright for the dim-lit room.

I didn't reply. My arms locked across my chest, keeping myself contained. I tracked his proximity, my thoughts veering into panic mode. There was no easy way of escaping, no back balcony to vault off, no windows to break. He'd blocked the front entry, meaning that to escape I'd have to face him head on.

"What do you want?" I asked, my voice gravelly with sleep. If I engaged him, I could buy myself some time.

"Now *that* is a good question," he stated, his presence fully formed in the center of the room.

He towered over me, less than six feet apart, his black hoodie and sweatpants a size too tight. He held his right hand behind his back, his other hand wiggling his fingers at me, the kind of wave you'd give a toddler in the supermarket. His strangeness frightened me, because his actions were jaunty, as if choreographed by a ventriloquist.

I looked to his right, judging the distance to see if I could squeeze between him and the hallway. It would be tight. Maybe on a good day I could close the gap, but after two days of heavy drinking, my coordination was suspect.

"You can't run," he whispered, telepathically. "There's nowhere to go, Chrissy. No one to ask for help."

He knew my name, his voice enunciating every syllable, drawing them out wide. I bent my hand into a fist. This would end badly. If he knew my name, then he knew I lived alone. He understood the layout of my place, not a simple intruder but a personal one.

"Let me go," I pleaded, appealing to reason. "There's no need to do anything crazy. I won't tell a soul you were here. Whatever this is, it can remain between us."

I hugged my knees together to keep myself from shaking. A wave of tremors began, my body already aware of the danger I was in.

"Now, now. Where's the fun in that?" He closed the distance

between us, his sizable feet grinding the corner of the rug, out of place beside the coffee table I'd purchased from Target.

I shook my head, trying to corral my busy brain, grasping for any leverage.

He leaned closer. In one hand, zip ties rocked languidly, the white plastic glowing in the dark. In the other hand, he angled a long knife, the hilt of it tight in his grasp.

"No! I'll scream!" I prepped. I zipped to the left, letting the frozen air ready my lungs. I didn't know my neighbors, but I'd seen them leaning against the mailboxes, backpacked and caffeinated, walking to class and back.

He pounced before I could plan. "Ufff," was all I spoke before he wound my wrists into tight circles, my belly itchy against the Berber carpet.

"Help!" I shouted, but the sound was muffled, my agony heard only by the crumb-dusted floor. He ground his knees into my back until they felt welded, marred into my body with steel and fury. I had limited movement from my prone position.

"Please," I begged, my chin rubbed ragged, with a carpet burn developing across my jawline.

He tossed me, his motions rough and indelicate, into a supine stance.

He traced my face with his fingers, which I took as a good sign. I could convince him to stop, with my tears and facial expressions, all my fear reflected underneath him.

He drooped over me, his eyes wild and unfocused. He pinned me with his knees, and his fingers reached for the edge of his mask.

"HELP!" I closed my eyes, not wanting to see his face, when a smack reverberated, bouncing my brain backwards, breaking all my synapses.

I knew if I saw his face, I'd never be left alive. That's a truth found in every thriller or Lifetime movie, a script written since movies were invented. I pressed my eyes together, my nose wrinkling with effort.

"Look at me," he directed, putting more of his weight onto my upper thighs.

I shook my head. He pressed his palm against my chest, bearing down hard.

"I do, I die. I know how this works." It was difficult to speak, my words puffs of air, too wispy, too flimsy to be sounds.

"Chrissy. That's going to happen no matter what you do." He spoke with the detached tone of a professor explaining historical events or a cashier at checkout.

I opened my eyes to study his face, expecting a joke, terrified I was wrong.

His eyes were green, and lips furred carnally. His knife was poised above me, the tip of it menacing in his grasp. His eyes flickered onto mine, and I caught my breath, before he plunged the knife deep into my chest.

I didn't register the blade or the blood. It was the hard and firm divide that hit squarely in my breastbone. I squirmed, watching his black hair swinging back and forth, a pendulum delivering all my pain.

I ached for a shot of fireball whisky, for the oblivion that came with another beer, another drink. Urine leaked in my underwear, the smell familiar from too many late nights and discarded sheets. A fire, not dissimilar to Everclear vodka, licked my throat.

Panic pooled in my veins. He shifted his weight, and I burned. My chest heaved, and I felt myself become smaller underneath his touch, a miniature girl, who called a dollhouse home.

Nothing flashed before my eyes, no camera-reel highlights, no last words ringing into the abyss. A pinhole of light crept smaller and smaller until the blackness rose, accompanied by shadows without texture or form. My finger tapped once, twice, a barely held morse code. I tried once more but nothing moved. My pain wrapped around me tighter, bubble-wrapped close to my skin. Another swish of the blade descended, paired with a cackle from above. My last moments contained his soundtrack, a mix of grunts and pleasure. I tilted my head to the right, my final conscious glance capturing a broken vodka bottle beside a shattered TV remote—fragments of my drunken narrative.

I died as a lived, next to the mess I made, my world reduced to nothing substantial, remarkable only for the potential I squandered. A tear I couldn't wipe away clouded my vision, a symbol of remorse and unfinished promises I'd never get a chance to fulfill.

Chapter 12
Professor Anthony Lennon, PhD
Date: March 15th, 2004, 07:30 a.m.

Not all students could survive graduate school. There's a reason it's called higher education, reserved for the best and brightest. The rigors increased when courseloads doubled, and natural selection would prove true. Professors functioned as the selected gatekeepers, to assess the caliber of students awarded accolades and honor cords.

In my own program, Professor Contour had begun our first class with the typical gloom and doom. "Look to your left, look to your right. Study the faces, because at least half won't make it to graduation." His methods were malicious but the facts remained indisputable. Most graduate students were left with student debt, not a diploma.

It was harder still to ferret out the brightest stars meant for donning doctorate hoods. Most of my current students were regressions toward the mean, suitable for academic discard, their report card crumpled in the trashcan like their dreams.

I retied my tie in the mirror, cursing my fumbling fingers. No matter how many times I fiddled with it, it was impossible to get it straight. Mondays were minefields recently, and I needed to look my best.

"Samantha!" I bellowed; our closest walls too thick to be heard through unless I grumbled at full volume.

I relocated from the closet to the top of the stairs, shouting to be heard over the television downstairs.

"Samantha! Need you!"

"Coming!" my wife called, ungluing herself from the living room couch and the morning news. 11 Alive broadcasted another attack on the North Carolina Central University campus, NCC for short. We lived five blocks from the campus proper, my tenure paying for our two-story Tudor, which had stood the test of time. The historic house plaque gleamed from our front porch, and sometimes I shined it with wax when no one was looking. I was proud my family had a claim on generational wealth, on an acre dated back to the 1800s. But the increasing violence caused a rash of for-sale signs to overtake the neighborhood, forsaking original colonial columns for increased security. Since 2001, the university had been plagued with rumors of break ins, which had culminated in an unsolved murder that rocked the Durham community.

Durham boasted a midsize city population, in which occasional violence and mayhem took hold. What made these crimes notable was the population selected. The killer had been targeting college females, which added another layer of uncertainty and calamity for my students and staff. The last homicide, still unsolved, was from 2003.

The television confirmed what I feared. The police had found another body. Another unidentified college female with fatal stab wounds, making this Monday worse than all the others.

My wife and daughter consumed the news for dinner and again at breakfast, dual companions on tiny barstools, glazed eyes drunk on readymade despair.

"Tony, did you hear?" Samantha pressed, halfway up the stairs, ready to fulfill her wifely duty of constant nagging. "There's an update on the campus killing. "

I wouldn't engage, stifling the urge to repeat myself. I'd informed Samantha that the North Carolina University Chairman, Dr. Smithson, had reassured the public of the university's intent to uphold justice and peace. I trusted my boss to speak the truth, even if his presentation lacked resolve. His receding hairline and wavering voice did little to calm the rising tide of hysteria. I wished I'd be given the PR reins. My timid superior was no orator; his cheeks, slick with sweat, seemed to confuse Vaseline for blush.

"Samantha, we've been over this before. It's under control. The press and the relators lean into the macabre to encourage people to short sell their homes."

It was practice, reassuring her. I pictured myself in a designer suit, poised in front of microphones. I'd remind the press that this wasn't a Ted Bundy at Florida State situation. There was no Jeffrey Dahmer luring male co-eds back to his apartment. This was Durham, NC, head of the research triangle.

We were in a new millennium, not the 1970s, armed with Palm Pilots and text messaging.

That was the problem, of course, the press a monster that

needed fresh kill for their nonstop news. But this perp would be caught because people were more connected, conjoined with the internet, a country all its own. The world wide web allowed mortals to touch down in Hong Kong and Dubai without ever buying a plane ticket, extending the bounds of imagination.

Just because I support innovation doesn't mean my daughter, Katrina, is getting text messaging. I told her she could call whoever she wanted but I wasn't paying good money for typing at twenty cents per message increments. That earned me an eye roll and a troll-under-the-bridge routine that lasted until dinnertime. Let her complain. My home and my classroom were ruled by an authority of one, despite interjections from disgruntled students or daughters.

My wife continued to summarize the daily news, her messy bun plopped on the side of her head, a twinge of body odor wafting from her pajamas.

"Help with the tie?" I cut her off, my patience for her solil-oquy wearing thin. She shot me a look that said I was too old to need help, which meant our ongoing argument would continue. We'd been at a standstill since Friday.

The weekend had started pleasantly with a mid-level Merlot and a movie from Blockbuster, but the mood soured quickly after Samantha pleaded for us to move further off campus.

"It's all overblown," I said in my calmest voice, reserved for stray dogs or anxiety-ridden students. "Remember last year when I oversaw security in the chem building? It's increased, and guards are patrolling campus every hour, plus it's statistically safe here in the outskirts of Durham. There's no evidence this is an ongoing problem."

"I'd say one murder and multiple break-ins are the definition of a chronic concern," Samantha countered, scooting further away, her socked feet moving underneath her, no truce found. We pretended to watch the movie, each not wanting to negotiate.

My claim was factually correct. The suburbs had been claimed by the wealthy and the educated (or a combination of both). Money provided insulation from life's adversities, and our neighborhood was gated and loaded with top-notch alarm systems. Whoever was hurting the students wouldn't be tempted by our tennis courts or lawnmowers. Our pruned gardenia hedges were designed to keep out undesirables, and for years it had worked without a glitch.

"There's no bogeyman hiding in the bushes," I'd concluded, gesticulating to prove my point. Samantha stood and turned off the television, mid-movie, confirming the terms of our impasse.

With the discovery of another body, I was losing the battle. I could feel it in her frown, and in the way she looped my tie tight. I let her stew, allowing her to release her anger on my clothing. No use broaching the subject now, not with the meetings that ballooned my schedule, my Monday loaded with conferences. There's no leftover time or energy to devote to marital negotiations, so my mirrored reflection chose to ignore my wife's scowl.

I topped off my coffee and juggled my caffeine and briefcase in one hand. My exercise bag dangled off my shoulder, and I shot off a goodbye to my family, who promptly disregarded it. Some days I felt the sting of rejection, the way my wife and daughter had pigeonholed me into a caricature who wrote checks, the befuddled middle-aged buffoon in a sitcom. On good days, I didn't let my family's apathy settle into my bones and set up shop. On bad ones, it's all I could see.

I balanced my coffee against my windshield, reviewing my current reality. My tenure pay afforded me financial leeway and job security. The summers were spent at my leisure, offering periods of rest and relaxation. NCC wasn't a top-tier school, which lessened the pressure to publish or attend expensive conferences. My wife and daughter longed to drip in diamonds and off-the-lot Land Rovers. But they'd modified their tastes, accepting pre-owned vehicles and trips to Trader Joe's. Their lack of appreciation was a flesh wound, but my chosen profession involved being overlooked, equivalent to a chronic civil servant but with less pay or recognition. Academia promised an ivy tower, but I'd settled for a scholastic knock-off brand.

The real disappointment, I mused, unlocking my Volvo, was the indolent student population. They were content to plug in their headphones and complain about being an American. My father used to say every generation got dumber, and I was previously offended by his wisdom. But maybe the old man was correct. This generation would rather rap and make out on the quad than complete any real work, and their dwindling grades reflected their lackluster motivation. Daily, another vapid daydreamer begged for an extension, citing laptop troubles or histrionic relationships dramas. These "scholars" were pot-smoking degenerates who napped and slacked, the whole of them offering nothing I could use in the lab or otherwise. Chemistry was in the details, and these pupils lacked basic insight.

Their collective entitlement sanded me down further, shaping me into a grouchy old man who grumbled and reeked of coffee breath. I'd had grand plans of inciting young minds with new ideas. However, rateaprof.com had flatlined my motivation, discouraging any sense of job satisfaction.

One night, drunk on one-and-a-half bottles of Murphy Goode merlot, I broke down and perused the site. It was a mistake, akin to reading someone's diary, with comments best ignored. Anonymous posts mentioned I was unattractive, a bore, a monotone geek, with a scratching, birdlike voice and chunky waistline. It hurt because I wasn't expecting their vitriol. I could be demanding, but only because I wanted them to reach their potential. Their complaints continued, permanent under the harsh computer glare, declaring I was the worst teacher in the building.

My snooping episode curated a newfound paranoia. My once confident professor presence was reduced to crippling insecurity. It made my midyear conferences a minefield. I used to deliver bad news to my pupils in stride. I pretended I was a divorce attorney, unfazed by those who left my office in tears. Now my reviews were liable to award me with another paragraph of foul language online. I was uncertain how to proceed, awash with indecision that I couldn't shake.

I reversed from the driveway, peering at my daily agenda. The first student was an initial coveted academic recruit turned nonstarter. He was his school's valedictorian, arising from the ashes of a tragedy. I remembered when I congratulated him on his accomplishment, he winced and elaborated that the girl in first place had died tragically at the hands of a vagrant.

"I was only ever salutatorian. I'm afraid I'm here by default," he explained, his voice tight and shrill. Jason kept his eyes on the floor, and I felt pity for the small-town boy on a scholarship, whose brush with trauma secured his academic placement. He told me he loved mental math and calculations, which for a chemistry professor was a fluent language. But Jason's performance was average during his subsequent semesters, his tardiness noticeable, paired with an unremarkable grade point average.

He'd asked for a reference to Chapel Hill's master's degree program, and I considered it in between the blinking taillights and stop signs, the traffic ever increasing due to university expansion. Jason had the brains, but I wondered if he'd ever be successful. LeDown was the back-of-the-class type, content to ride the tide of mediocrity. He'd sleep through class, then redeem himself with a random A on the final. His lab sheets were sloppy and difficult to read, though he performed well on pop quizzes. Chapel Hill was almost an Ivy League school, and currently out of his reach, considering his uneven performance.

Chemistry could be a lot like baseball. The rookies flamed out, too much too fast, making me second guess my roster, and our hopes for the next semester. *Goes to show statistics can't always predict the future.*

I decided it was essential to confront Jason's inadequate process, to cite my concerns before removing my recommendation.

I sipped my coffee, dreading how my words would stumble. Harsh news transformed me into a stuttering ignoramus, so different from my lectures or when I faced the chalkboard. Those moments were second nature, the ions and protons emerging from my brain to my tongue. Confrontation produced a flummoxed scatterbrain, far from the man I wanted to become. It wasn't the negative feedback that made me stammer. It was the remedial duties, using my advanced degree and reducing my skills to those of a guidance counselor. A PhD in chemistry used to mean distinction, but I felt demoted.

My bad mood soured further by the lack of street parking. The parking decks triggered my claustrophobia, the concrete tower akin to an aboveground mausoleum, a second away from toppling over. It'd be nice if the university would reserve spots for staff, but they kept kicking our requests down the line, more proof of continued disrespect.

I gritted my teeth and pulled into an empty space on the third floor. Being late increased the day's frustrations. I jogged inefficiently in my brown dress shoes, heading straight to the lab. I'd complete Jason's review and remove the dread in my stomach.

A brutal stench circulated in the chemistry lab, similar enough to sulfur that I checked the burners. Nothing was out of place. The only outlier was Jason, his head covered in a stained hoodie, his greasy hair tussled against his acne-lined face. He slumped in his stool, his shoulders curved, with eyes that looked itchy. It was a shock to see him disheveled.

When he'd arrived on campus, Jason looked like he'd stepped out of the 1950s. He wore shiny shoes, paired with retro glasses and starched pants. I'd labeled him a compatriot, the vintage type who enjoyed Nick at Night and quoted JFK. His appearance had been meticulous, but never modern, earning him stares from his peers who kept a wide berth. There was a hint of rigidness in Jason, a preciseness that never felt lived in. I respected his fastidiousness. He resembled a scholastic soldier, his outfits eschewing responsibility, checking all the boxes required to make an excellent chemist.

The student in front of me showcased a crusty, charred stain in the center of his shirt. Senior year could increase unease, grinding the students down before they left the collegiate nest. Instead of physical hazing, the professors waged academic warfare. I was trained that way, battling through tough mentors, Socratic questions, and educational torment that became a rite of passage. But Jason was hollowed, wearing yesterday's clothes, his skin shining like it'd been dipped in wax.

"Hello, Jason," I began, laying my briefcase open on the table. A wave of Jason's body odor infiltrated the lab. It was more than unwashed armpits, or the lack of a shower. This stench was rotten, launching an assault upon my nostrils. I needed to open a window but didn't want to add insult to injury, given the upcoming conversation. Jason was oblivious to the stench, his head still lowered while I stifled a gag. The ripe smell of dirt and refuse wafted from his pores.

"Let me open a window," I started, already opening the latch. I gulped the outside air and lingered, taking deep inhales. I kept my head tilted and breathed again.

Better now. Reluctantly, I pulled on my professional face, turning to him.

"Hello, Professor," Jason mumbled, not raising his head to look at me. His words weren't slurred. The window lessened the smell slightly, and at least there was no vestige of tequila or vodka in the stench. I kept close proximity to the window, doubting my empty stomach could go another round with his hygiene and win.

"Jason," I lowered my voice, attempting to sound collegial, "I called you here today to talk. You aren't in trouble, but I've noticed a change in you. You seem less... invested. In your studies, but also in your work." I watched him, but he didn't respond. His elbows formed a fleshy wall, blocking all his facial expressions.

"I couldn't help but notice you've been different." I cleared my throat, giving him a chance to explain his recent behavior. He stayed silent.

"And so I wanted to check in, especially in light of that letter you asked me to write. The recommendation letter."

My face burned. I looked for a gentle way to let him down, to ease this stray dog's suffering. I frowned, imitating fatherly concern, summoning my best platitude. I pressed my glasses further up my nose, stalling before I dashed his dreams completely.

"I understand, Professor." He kept his head cradled against the desk. "I didn't mean to disappoint you." His already high-pitched voice cracked, a second away from sobbing. My job description read "head chemist," but I had neither the inclination nor the bandwidth to deal with his mood lability.

"Jason, let's refocus," I began again, leaning into logic.

He raised his chin, the puffiness under his eyes reminiscent of large grapes.

"No, you're right. I've been distracted. I know I have. And you are kind to let me know it in person."

"So, Jason, you understand," I clarified, quick to ease the tension. "It's part of my job to know what's going on with my students. Is there anything I can do? To help you, I mean." I hoped a question would divert his tears, since we were still on shaky emotional ground.

He paused, opening his mouth like he would speak, then zipped it. He gathered his hands to hold himself erect, the poise of a toddler in trouble.

"I find, Jason," I continued, "that sometimes change is hard. Classwork is one thing, but it's more than that, right? It can be hard to connect with your peers. Great minds don't always lead to human interactions." I smiled. "I've walked that path, too. I was a late bloomer, and honestly I don't know what I would have done if my wife hadn't made the first move."

Samantha had been twenty years old, petite in her bright-pink dress, waving me over to her large group of friends. She puckered her lips into a shy smile, the sheen of her lip gloss lingering in the light. I was swollen with nerves, but my wife created her own luck that night, and I remained thankful for it. I filed that image away, an antidote to our recent marital troubles.

"Sometimes we all need a bit of help in that area," I concluded, half in my memories, half in the present.

"It's not that," Jason replied. "I know about you and Samantha, and your daughter, Katrina."

My nostalgia evaporated. I hadn't said their names, careful to never mention my daughter at work. My desk contained no pictures, myself a firm believer in keeping my homelife private.

Jason's voice took on an uneasy edge. "Look, it's not the work or the people, Professor. I'm so tired, and my thoughts don't let me rest. Do you know what that feels like? When your thoughts keep you awake, and you try and try not to listen, but sometimes they… well, they break through!"

His wily fingers combed through his hair, his voice agitated to the point of concern. He remained seated, his chin to his chest. I decided to handle him alone, eager to shut down any references to my family. It was time to politely push him aside by providing a new agenda.

"Whatever it is, Jason, we can work through it together. But I need you to show up on time this afternoon to start the titrations. There is no compromise there."

He stared, then nodded, happy to have a task to complete.

I cleared my throat. "You will also have to pull up your grade in my class if you want to apply to graduate school." I glowered at him, letting my line in the sand get drawn in permanent ink. "It will require exceptionally hard work on your part since you're already behind. I'm only saying this because I see some of myself in you. I want to help you but I need your commitment."

He scooted the chair back, creating a low hum. Another blast of his stench wafted, a mixture of rotten eggs and cabbage. I crinkled my nose before I could mind my manners.

He smiled, his mouth turning into a jack-o-lantern grin. "Sorry, Professor. I guess I need a shower, too. I've been so busy. There are certain activities that have captured my attention, and I've been careless. That's all this is."

I hesitated, wondering if a follow-up question was necessary.

"Well, Jason, if you can make your education a priority, I will consider writing you a letter of recommendation. But it all depends on your desire to turn things around. I need you to focus, to regain lost ground." I force-fed him a stern glare, showing I wasn't a pushover.

Jason grew to his full height, his former good posture renewed.

"Thank you, Professor. I won't let you down. I realize there's a change to be made, beginning with my appearance. I was just so distracted." He smiled crookedly at me.

"I've never been so busy I've neglected personal hygiene," I replied stiffly, shifting from mentor back to authority figure.

"Then you haven't lived, sir. Certain hobbies are always worth the interruption." He cackled, and the sound vibrated across the beakers and the funnels, his high notes threatening to jangle the equipment. He reached the door before hesitating.

"Thanks, Professor. While there are activities more pleasurable than the chemistry lab, I won't let them deter me." He shot me a carnivorous grin. "You're right. I am smart enough to do both. It takes more planning and studying. But you've been an immense help." Jason stepped into the hallway. "Give my best to the family," he called, letting the door swing behind him.

I shuddered. The lab was hot, but my blood chilled. I grabbed the edge of the desk, a swift dose of vertigo leaving me discombobulated. I stalled, allowing the fresh air to circulate, releasing the remnants of his smell and our awkward conversation.

I was left with uncertainty, something that lingered and looped in my brain after Jason left. His casual reference to my loved ones caught me off guard. Uncertainty remained in the empty lab, like the day after a funeral, complete with ghostly undertones. The oddness of his words kept flowing on repeat, my wife and child's names in his mouth.

I gathered up my folders, stacking them, then restacking, my mind replaying our dialogue.

Something was wrong with Jason. I couldn't clarify what; I had no proof to point out. He wasn't aggressive; nor was he rude. He wasn't failing, but he lacked the motivation to be an upper echelon student. He was different, a strange one indeed. What my mom would've called an Odd Duck. Another shiver ran up my spine, paired with a desire to run away.

I made no case notes; I issued no referrals. There wasn't enough said to be written or reported. But then and there I vowed to stay far from Jason's wake. The smell of rot, combined with his emotional dysregulation, was enough to keep my distance. I locked the door with a shaking hand, five minutes late for my first class of the day.

I clenched my jaw, debating whether a splash of bourbon in my coffee would get me through my classes. The merry-go-round of students twirled on throughout the day, placing Jason and his problems on the back burner. I left that Monday with a bitter taste in my mouth, my moment of panic lost in the chaos of class.

At the end of the semester, he'd completed every task provided, his final test securing an A-minus average. Jason's attendance improved, without us having to meet individually again. He reverted back to the student I knew, his hygiene and work ethic restored.

I rushed through his recommendation letter, summarizing his grade point average and affinity for chemistry. I scribbled my name, giving him enough stars to feel generous, but not enough to overstate his case.

I held the paper, pairing it with my earlier reservations. I considered crumpling it or creating a reason to change my mind. It seemed prudent to not anger him, having observed the way his moods vacillated, the name of my family members dropped intentionally. It was easier to acquiesce and let higher education weed him out, no need for me to dismiss him outright.

I wrote *Jason LeDown* on the envelope cover. My family was waiting at our favorite restaurant, and I'd devoted enough time to the underworking's of Jason LeDown. Whatever became of him would be as uninspiring as his undergraduate career.

I sealed the envelope and placed it in his desk, the imagined smell of fettuccine alfredo and hearty portion sizes putting a pep in my step. I locked the chemistry lab door, and what was left of my worries, behind it.

Chapter 13
Leslie Carton
Date: March 12th, 2004, 12:22 a.m.

Rush and Greek letters, exclusivity and sisterhood, I'd drunk the sorority Kool-Aid, full steam ahead, and now I regretted it. The snakes of pink-and-white streamers lay crumpled on the gym floor, and I was almost out of Hefty trash bags. The wreckage on the floor remained, awash with discarded Coke cans and beer caps. Friday's formal was fabulous, and my leopard sequin one-shoulder dress stole the show, but this cleanup was tedious, unbecoming of a sorority president. I'd signed up for the notoriety and glamour, never suspecting that my duties included mopping floors and guaranteeing security deposits, half janitor, half accountant, appreciated by no one, and always the last to leave.

I rested my head against the wooden broomstick, feeling fully sorry for myself, a regular Cinderella left to decompose. We'd established a committee to assist with this, but I'd lost them to Jell-O shots and cheap Burnett's vodka, their commitments dying in the hangover haze. They'd left for bedrooms and greener pastures before I could protest. I was the lone soldier in a cocktail dress, stone cold sober.

Delta Delta Delta promised me companionship, with friendships turning into future bridesmaids. Tri-Delt rolled out the university red carpet, billing itself as a shortcut to luxury, complete with access to the sorority mansion and monograms. They dropped words like legacy and term limit, cloaking me in purple, a true elected official, my royalty confirmed.

I ate it all up and asked for more. My VP bragged that I was securing a future for my daughter. Granted, I'd yet to find even a boyfriend who was slightly suitable, amidst the Marshall Mathers wannabes with their bleach-blond locks and frat-boy scorn. Hell, I didn't have time to date. My nonexistent free time was spent running ragged, tardy to every class, rush practice, and standards committee. I was the White Rabbit in *Alice in Wonderland*, my head threatening to fall off, my feet never moving fast enough, with one bloodshot eye on the ticking clock.

I'd fallen for the lofty adjectives, signing away my free time for fidelity, loyalty, and all that bullshit. I'd agreed to the terms of president half-drunk on Malibu coconut rum, pouring the last shot into my tumbler after bid day celebrations. The slur in my words created a memory filmed through cheesecloth. My first night as president was spent hovering over the toilet a la Princess Di, the tile cutting zigzag indentions into my kneecaps.

Self-deception covered some mistakes. At first, I bragged that my title was the university equivalent of an LV purse or whatever Christina Aguilera was rocking on *TRL*. I'd create a distinct heritage, a beloved end to my four years at NCC. Who needed good grades when I could put a crown on it and call it a day?

I enjoyed the popularity, and the way Settler Bar came to life when I walked in, a real-life version of the show *Cheers*. I played to the beaming smiles and the hometown crowd. My status vibrated across the room, gaining access to free drinks and quick nods of approval. Nights like these were my penance for that kind of name recognition.

The tasks piled up, taking a toll on my mental health and working memory. Contact this venue, pay this deposit, and oh your name's on the hook if this all goes bust. My parents had already had two serious living room discussions about my burgeoning credit card debt, my dad breathing heart-attack heavy while my mom bit her nails to the quick. I assuaged all their worries and promised to do better, knowing everything outta my mouth was false. I gave my family a filibuster, while I rushed down my to-do list, praying to get paid back later.

Things started to slip this semester, my manic pace no longer sustainable. My room was packed high with unfolded laundry, the décor dingy with unfinished pizza boxes and half-molded bread. My dusty graphing calculator, worth almost two hundred dollars, lay forgotten on my bookshelf, along with my dipping statistics grade. For weeks I swore on the bible of busyness to distract myself from report cards, parents, and the dean himself. I pushed past the warning signs in favor of the next night out, the next mixer, always ready to show up and show out.

I looked around the gym, gearing up for another all-nighter. One Republic crooned softly on the radio, singing about love found and lost. There wasn't enough coffee or rock 'n' roll to make this go faster. The only way out was through.

I hummed to kick up the energy, making sweeping motions and wiggling my hips. I twirled, giving into the song, because the Timberland verse kicked in and the band was playing my jam.

A flare of hunger interrupted my moves. Back at the mansion, my mini freezer was packed with starchy Lean Cuisines, one notch above cardboard, the mushiness in the middle enough to make me queasy. I prayed the Tex-Mex place down the street would still be open when I was done. The comfort food of chips and white queso could take the edge off a late night, offering a high-caloric lullaby before bed.

My rank hair draped over my face, confirming my need for a shower. The stress of planning and putting away all our décor for next year's formal stunk up my shift, leading to gross hair and armpits. It's not pretty, but there's no one to notice. A pimple bloomed on my chin, thick as a witch's wart, the result of forgetting to remove my makeup, my foundation leaving a tiger stripe on my silk pillow. My body carried the markers of loneliness and hard labor, while my peers splintered into dark corners, their bodies joyfully landlocked. I lived vicariously through their hookups, since I was left to collect the remnants of everyone else's good time.

I felt fully middle-aged, prepared to be a soccer mom with minivans and a packed schedule, dodging traffic in high-waisted designer jeans. Greek life and its string of over-commitments had tricked me, removing frivolity, training me to keep eagle eyes on my bank account, Diet Red Bull in hand, drowning in my forced maturity.

I secured a stray streamer, the harsh florescent lighting reflecting sticky bleachers and puddles of punch. I didn't belong on this river of smudged mascara, surrounded by other people's trash, with fading tan lines crisscrossing my strained shoulders.

I surveyed the scene and called it done. They could keep the money, or we'd raise some more, but I couldn't spend another minute as a discount custodian. I flicked off my heels, shook out my hair, and grabbed the handle of my purse. *To hell with it*, I thought, taking one last inventory of the room. The gym wasn't clean, not even in low lighting. Black skid marks zagged across the slick plywood floor, and the lingering smell of puke wafted from the boys' bathroom. I shrugged, deeming it no longer my problem, and heaved the last of the decorations into the container, with the borrowed master key dangling on top.

We still had the weekend to clean up the rest. I'd let them sleep before drafting the underclassman to finish the job. I wasn't wearing a watch, but I knew it was late. Maybe Jamie could spot me some of her Adderall, one pill could power a midnight study session. I outranked her and didn't want to force a power differential, but I'd debate the ethics of borrowing psychostimulants when I could think clearly.

I swiped at another crumbled party favor, securing my fingers around the stepstool, dragging it and myself to the double doors. I balanced the multitude of salvageable material on my hip, hoping it wouldn't bruise. My mutinous feet already betrayed me, requiring a mountain of effort to move an inch.

I nudged the outside door open with my ankle. I'd need to lock up, deposit the rest of the decorations to Amy, then brew up a pot of black coffee.

I glanced down at my Blackberry. Twelve forty-five a.m. Oh my God. All I wanted to do was sink into my tiredness, to admit, for once, it was all too much. Tears pricked at my eyes. I swatted them away and stepped under the streetlight, searching for the master key.

I couldn't forget the most important step. The janitor had drilled me on the importance of locking up. He was a known Tri-Delt hater, his male pattern baldness glinting in the sun while he scolded me preemptively for twenty minutes. I mortgaged a year's worth of sweet talk and shy grins to rent the gym, pairing every promise with a low-cut sweater and a peek of cleavage. He'd glared at me, his calloused hands tight against his chest, perturbed by my existence, a miser in a denim jumpsuit.

The key turned into the lock, clicking into place. Time to crank up the caffeine and get shit done, aided by Jamie's pills, providing better living through chemistry.

I heard a faint sound from the street. It wasn't a rush of traffic or the squeal of rubber tires. It might have been a whistle, breaking through the silence of the night. A shadow flickered across the gym door, while I steadied the bulky box. I squinted, but all I could make out was the glare of the streetlight. I pulled the key from the lock and heaved the box across my chest. It was doable to carry it the four blocks back to sorority row, but it would zap me of all my remaining strength. I debated calling for reinforcements, but that would take time I didn't have.

You can do this, I encouraged myself, prepared to huff and puff all the way home.

The box dropped first. Twisting tree trunk arms collided with my waist, a surprise lover's embrace from behind. I registered the muscles against my abdomen, tugging me backward, black sleeves encasing bulky biceps.

"What in the he—?" I stammered as a *thunk* collided against the back of my skull, rendering me speechless. My brain swung with the unexpected jolt, and I raised my hand to the back of my neck. It was slick, with red paint covering my fingers. No, not paint, it wasn't thick enough. I saw the uncoiled streamers reach the road, a colored rainbow against the blacktop. Where did they come from again?

Glitter exploded on the sidewalk, and I stumbled, concerned about the ruined decorations, laid bare on the dark concrete.

Green-and-gold banners tumbled at my feet. Red confetti blanketed the ground.

Not confetti. It was my blood. I looked at my hand again and squealed.

"HELP!" I cried, my knees crumpled beneath me. My attacker shoved me next to the outdoor silver bleachers, to the left of the gym entrance. He grabbed me by my hair, causing twinkling lights to erupt in my peripheral vision. The world rotated and spun, no longer on a predictable axis.

He smelled like fresh-cut grass and gasoline, his gloved hands stiff against my hips. I stomped my feet, but there was nothing to cling to, no orange life preserver to keep me afloat, no backup plan to initiate.

I heard it before I felt it. Another whack, the item candlestick heavy, inserted into the back of my brain.

I toppled and tasted metal and rust that stuck to the top of my mouth. My eyes swayed, searching for his weapon of choice. I tilted my head to spit, wishing I could cut the metallic taste from my tongue with scissors.

He forced me under the bleachers, dragging my limp body amongst the discarded trash on the ground. There were multiple moons in the sky, the night turning into a dream-colored backdrop. My head oozed, and blood wet my eyelids. A boiling magma of misery crashed against my neck. I tried to rid myself of the river of red across my forehead, but it soaked, clotted, and spun.

There was too much of it. No way to keep up with the flow. My arms stopped moving, succumbing to the deluge.

I faltered, with unfocused eyes, onto the man's face above me, the glint of a knife swinging from his right side.

I tried to tell him something, anything. I wanted to make myself known, but the words jumbled into a crossword puzzle, coming out in rickety spurts.

I choked on the blood and saliva as a flash of sickness leaked onto my shirt, soaking me in putrid liquid.

My mind said I was sorry for the mess, but my world was devoid of all sound. I couldn't hear his breathing or my own.

My eyes bulged, and I couldn't move, the vomit gurgling between clenched teeth.

My assailant leaned down, and I yearned to suffocate him with the whole of my insides, to drown him in bile.

But I gurgled. And I wheezed. I couldn't direct my puke, the last bit dripping languidly down my chin. A ring of fire alighted my throat, scorching all other sensations, a private volcano erupting within.

A swatch of pink used bubblegum dangled above my head, next to carved initials in a heart under the stacked bleachers.

I couldn't blink. My eyes burned.

"Look at me," he whispered, watching my blood mix with the dirt and candy bar wrappers. A half-eaten Twix bar intertwined with my curls, my final resting place amongst people's discards.

I wanted to crawl, to scream, to fight, to pray.

"There, there now." He spoke gently, slowly removing the knife, a finger against my cheek, feather soft. His kindness paired with the next plunge of the dagger, my chest burning like petrol at a bonfire.

I clenched the ground, clinging to a white Pepsi cap bottle, twisting it my hand like it could morph into a weapon.

I held it tight, focusing on the ridges, until I lost feeling in my hand. My eyes locked onto a faded Milky Way wrapper, an inch away from my nose, the soft scent of chocolate and blood, the taste of sweetness and sorrow combined. The bottle cap rolled away to find its casual freedom, leaving me to decay, alone, in the dark.

Jamie, Amy, Nicole, someone, anyone. The janitor, a passerby, a Good Samaritan. My parents, my 3rd grade teacher, my first kiss Benjamin, my first boyfriend Carter. Please, please, please, help me. Please, God, someone help me. Find me, rescue me, pull him off me. Now before the rest of me is gone, before I can no longer function, before I'm no longer me.

Tri-Delta had twenty pledges that year. Our graduating class had forty-five members. The Greek system on campus consisted of ten sororities and twelve fraternities.

No one heard my screams.

Chapter 14
Sarah Law
Date: February 1st, 2003, 8:02 p.m.

S hit, the library was locked. Again. I'd double-checked the hours online and would swear on a stack of bibles that the time said nine p.m. Straight ahead, written in italics on the double doors, in big white letters, my error was showcased. Closed at eight p.m. on Saturdays, the stencil correct, proving my memory was flawed.

No surprise there.

My dad always said I'd lose my head if it wasn't attached, and sometimes after a couple of beers, he'd say it was a wonder I'd survived natural selection.

He's an asshole, sure, but it didn't mean he's wrong.

"Shit," I said out loud, the weight of my bookbag burning into my shoulder blade. How many times could a person forget a detail? I wanted to maim myself for my mistake, to take all my iniquities onto my body, to cut long, jagged lines into my flesh, a permanent punishment for all my disappointments. If I carved a reminder into my skin, at least I couldn't lose it.

It's unlikely I'd be able to execute whatever punishment I'd prepared. I'd lose my preferred blade, the razor knocked underneath the bathroom counter, the sharp knife discarded in a sink full of unwashed dishes. I couldn't be trusted because chances are I'd forget my plan before I could enact it.

I peered past the dark double doors, stomping my feet in frustration. It was immature, but it relieved some of the pent-up tension. Nothing flickered inside the library, the staff having packed up and left an hour ago, my study plans disintegrated to dust.

Behind me, something rustled. I turned, figuring I'd find another sad student who got the time wrong, too. At least I wasn't alone in my ineptitude. A companion did little help with my physiology test tomorrow, or the wasted thirty minutes I'd spent hiking across campus to get here.

Another student was looming next to me, standing much too close, a true space invader. He donned a gray collared V-neck, the bulk of him almost tall enough to reach the library doorframe. With shoulders hunched, he looked too serious to be a scatterbrain. His face was shadowed, swallowed by the darkness. The wind picked up, whistling around us, breaking the silence of the night.

"Whoa," I said, backing up against the door, wondering what kind of monster had landed on the library stoop.

He smiled and gestured. A light had come down the hallway of the library. He cocked his head, and I began to breathe again, until my bad habit caught up to me.

Since grade school, I fended off awkward pauses and stilted conversations with bad jokes. All forms of social anxiety caused me to make conversation, often of the sarcastic and careless variety. It resulted in grimaces and rolled eyes so many times, and yet I couldn't help it. The words escaped out of my mouth before I could edit them, another symptom of that damn impulsivity, the foot-in-the-mouth syndrome, that I'd battled my whole life.

ADD or ADHD, whatever you wanted to call it, I had it. Focusing, concentration, executive functioning, poor attention: I checked all the distracted symptom boxes. And I should've taken meds for it, but I couldn't bring myself to ask for a pharmaceutical push.

That would entail testing, paired with scaled scores and percentile ranks, evidence of memory deficits in Excel charts. The proof was already splayed out, in all the forgotten assignments and the twenty-point deductions that came with tardy work. My faulty memory needed no confirmation. My lifetime was spent in copious uncertainty, facts reduced to best guesses. It created a life spent looking in the rearview mirror because I'd missed something crucial, if only I could remember what it was. The shame of it was more than I could bear most days. I could understand physics and write a term paper, but I couldn't remember where I put my pen.

"Yo, tall dude," I joked. "You get the time wrong, too? Epic fail for us suckas." I shrugged, like it didn't matter, though my neck flushed lipstick pink.

I had nowhere else to go. I couldn't go back to my room, since my roommate Talia was hooking up with Brian, made obvious by the sock-on-the-door routine. I wanted to be sensitive to her right to get some nooky, but I needed a quiet place to review my notes, and their moans wouldn't cut it. Plus, I'd be such a creeper, reviewing my PowerPoint slides like a sad, nerdy noob, while they enjoyed each other beneath the twin bedsheets.

No way. I possessed too much dignity to study in the hallway, to quarantine outside, ever the lonely loser. I didn't want their permission to let me back in, their sheepish grins paired with spit and sweat. That's why I'd sought refuge here, only to meet another dead end.

The other student nodded, briefly, his eyes roaming my body. He acted like he knew me, the way he smiled and stepped closer. True, everyone looked tall to me since I clocked in at five foot one if I stretched. This guy resembled a manmade Gumby, straight out of a fairytale, too lanky to be healthy, with his bones extended and mismatched. He licked his lips, and that was my cue to leave.

"Okay, well. Have a good one," I added, turning to trek toward campus. "Creeper."

I muttered my last retort before booking it to the campus coffee shop.

I generally devoted multiple hours per week to studying and cramming, but my parents had come into town, throwing off my routine. Instead of highlighting and making notecards, I gorged on pricey meals, happy to eat food that wasn't fried and battered. I let them hug me tight, while I sluffed all responsibilities in favor of some quality time. Now I regretted letting my guard down and allowing myself to relax. My brain buzzed with everything I hadn't memorized, the slump in my shoulders matching my growing pessimism.

I heard the student clear his throat, and a cheery chirp escaped.

I hadn't realized he'd followed me.

"Ha, well, if that's all you have to say."

"Excuse me?" I asked, uncertain of how to respond.

"Well, now. You're Sarah, right? I know you."

I squinted at him, still two paces ahead. I wasn't great at matching names to faces, the details jumbling together until Kim became Karen and Ben turned into Brent.

"I don't think so. I don't think I know you."

His steps quickened, closing the gap between us.

"You're sure?" He crept an inch forward, his arm dangling within reach.

"Uh, yeah. I'm sure, and that's my cue to leave."

I dashed down the street, putting long strides between myself and the weirdo. Without slowing, I glanced over my shoulder, clocking the distance I'd traveled. The giant was still watching me, his eyes tracking my retreating figure but not giving chase. I continued to run, the books in my bookbag jostling into my back. The encounter felt icky, his stare similar to how my brother pursued deer, with the same engrossment, mindful of every movement.

I'd never mastered that kind of focus. I was envious of my brother Toby's perfect silence, his easy effort of concentration. Envy was a villain, so different than its fraternal twin jealousy. At first I wished I could conjure Toby's attention. Then I dreamed of taking it, replacing my train-tracked broken brain with his brand new one. Envy told me if I couldn't have it, neither should he. It wasn't fair my life held all the chaos and messy rooms. Our family tree should have spread it out a bit.

I counted to ten and checked again. The stranger was gone,

evaporated into the night, and my heartbeat resumed a normal pace.

I'd avoided the stalker, but my mood declined further, the late night and wasted energy sinking me further into despair. The coffee shop remained blocks away, and my feet ached from my sudden sprint. I pivoted back to my dorm hallway, admitting defeat. The cacophony of sounds created a distracting soundtrack, combined with clomping shower shoes and laughter.

I balanced my textbook on my lap, flipping through the pages, trying not to look at the clock and calculate all my lost time. The curved wall bit into my lower back, and I lost feeling in my legs, the tingling sensation like needle pricks on my thighs. Worst of all, I'd was still roomie roadkill in the hallway.

It was after midnight when Boyfriend Brian slinked away, and by then both my motivation and good humor had dried up. I slammed our door and climbed into bed with my clothes on, exhausted but with little to show for it. Talia had the good sense to keep quiet, completing her bedtime routine by lamp light. I sighed twice, itching to pick a fight, before trading my anger for sleep.

As predicted, the late night didn't translate into a good test score. My mind was shaky, and I almost ran out of time, putting my pencil down at the last possible second. Two more tests nipped at my heels, ready for highlighters and low level self-hatred.

The rest of the day was devoted to library work. I'd burrow into physio and Latin since midterms chomped closer each day, my binders full of barely legible notes I had to squint to read.

I hustled through the day, parking myself in front of the

library at four p.m. I scanned my surroundings for last night's lurker, but he'd vacated with the daylight. I sighed in relief, releasing tension I hadn't realized I was holding.

I picked the first wooden table near the door, spreading my stack of books forcefully, daring anyone to sit beside me. I pulled out my chair, reaching for the highlighter in my front jacket pocket. It wasn't there. I tapped again, shaking my head, searching for something to write with. Nothing.

The front library desk was acres away, and I debated whether it was necessary to take notes. But it was best to begin with all my materials, since pencils rolled away from my grasp, with pens forgotten, my possessions strewn everywhere inconvenient.

The thump of the book-return slot startled me. The library was quiet, no hushing octogenarian required. The rest of my university brethren had different pursuits, snuggling new lovers or playing frisbee golf in the quad. Most of NCC could rest in their laurels. I was the outlier who couldn't take my foot off the academic gas pedal, always scrambling to make up for lost time. I scuttled to the desk, embarrassed, but Ms. Cross predicted my need, reaching for an extra writing utensil.

"You, again? What'd you forget this time?" She peered at me over her bifocals, her voice radiating scorn, the uptick at the end conveying how little she thought of me.

"Pen or pencil. A highlighter. Anything really." I didn't even try to lie.

"Look at you. My mom used to say you're running around like a chicken with your head cut off." She clucked at me. "Every single week you're here, running in harried, with half your stuff missing. It's a wonder you can make it through the day." She shook her head, her lips releasing a torrent of humiliation.

I shrugged, but inside a surge of familiar shame ignited. If my forgetfulness was easily explained, I would've fixed it by now. I was used to the snide looks from teachers, my deficiency labeled as lazy or worse. Even my family dismissed me, assessing my capability as below average from birth. Toby never had these problems, never knew what it was like to be second place. The best I could do was not disappoint them further.

She found a pencil and passed it to me, offering me a smile, a soft consolation prize. I waited for the familiar, "Oh, Sarah," refrain, the chorus of discontent wrestling in my head. The people that knew me kept their expectations low, and now I could add the librarian to the ever-growing list of people I'd let down.

"Hold on a minute, it's not sharp." She inspected it, rubbing the lead point between her fingers. She located the manual sharpener amongst the treasure trove of paperclips and erasers. I watched her twist the pencil, the muscle movements lulling me into the quiet place in my mind, where daydreams lived.

I could spend all day there, alone with my private thoughts, pondering my priorities. My most recent fashion purchase took center stage, the backless red dress pairing perfectly with my new Sam Edelman heels. I pictured it hanging in my closet, looking polished and ready to wear. If only life were as easy as matching textures and colors, the blend perfect and unexpected.

"Hey, isn't that your stuff down there?" she interrupted, my attention far from the borrowed pencil.

We both peered at my stack of books, yards from the front desk. A tall man with dark hair rifled through my things, his knees boring into the back of my chair, his hands resting on my textbook.

"Hey!" I yelled, forgetting I was in the library. "That's mine," I clarified, certain that my irritation would stop the voyeur pronto.

He turned, made eye contact, and hurried out the front door. I couldn't be sure, but he resembled the student from last night, the angle of his face noticeably sharp. His pace was fast and jaunty, his escape blurring the rest of his features.

Ms. Cross and I watched him go. I debated trying to sprint and catch him, my feet pulling into a runner's stance. But a gentle caress stopped me. A hand, slicked with lotion, grasped mine, rounded with water spots and deep lifelines.

"Let him go," Ms. Cross said. "We get strange types in here all the time, like you wouldn't believe. Best to ignore him; he's scared off now. Keep your things tidy and closer next time."

And there it was, the admonishment. Even though I'd done nothing wrong, it still was my fault for leaving my things unattended. For my disappearing pencil, for being distracted, the loop complete, a full cycle of all that's wrong with me played on repeat.

I nodded because it was easier than arguing. I debated lecturing Ms. Cross about my stressors, about my roommate and the workload, and how college was harder than I predicted. My lack of focus tapped insistent circles around my good intentions and checklists, causing me to question my self-worth. Maybe then she'd understand the degrading umbrella I lived under, the unrelenting difficulty that came with completing everyday tasks.

I bit the inside of my cheek. That would only result in another misunderstanding. Authority figures sniffed at my excuses. Hell, they'd use my explanations as evidence of how wrong I was, how irresponsible, how unmotivated. My whole life was one long synonym for deficit, and I knew it. I embraced it, took on the mantle of disorganization and made it my own.

I hesitated to sit back down. I debated moving closer to the library station, though I'd had enough of Ms. Cross' convictions. I'd packed up my work to relocate when I saw a circled address.

My dorm and room number were underlined. I'd left my room assignment paired with the other papers I needed for class. I'd forgotten to remove it, and my personal information beamed at me, out in the open for purveyors or identity thieves.

A live wire of worry initiated. This was another blunder, a shining example of why I should've settled for an associate degree or headed straight into the workforce. My parents warned me, their voices strained with elevated concern, sounding both genuine and offensive simultaneously. They cautioned that my university classes would be difficult, even with tutoring, and in their doubts I heard everything they didn't say. I saw their secret glances at each other, the whispered snippets about how much I could really understand, with words like plateau and assistance coming out like curses.

It wasn't some secret. I was used to their repeated directions, their alarm when I backed out of the driveway. I was formed by the words they ate, the looks they gave me when I was incorrect, their pleas for me to check one more time. *Be careful, stay alert, are you sure, could you be mistaken?*

Toby tried a different tactic. He sat down beside me on the front stoop, his knees knocking against my own. He told me he was proud of all that I achieved, that I didn't need to prove myself to anyone. Underneath his pseudo compliments lay the hurtful truth. He didn't believe college was worth a try. He plied me with compliments, so I'd foreclose, save my tuition money for his advanced degree.

"Some people aren't built for higher ed, and that's okay, Sis. It's not a competition. We each have our strengths, and yours comes in a different form, right?"

Their lectures kept me stunted and insecure. I struggled to stay focused, every decision a roadblock.

I should give up. I'd never belong in this space, with the studious, elbow-patched majority, the teacher's pets, the golden, gilded ones.

The outside sun burned my eyes, momentarily blinding me to the milieu of students tumbling into the quad. There was safety in numbers, and I wanted to join in, to relax and sun myself with a beach towel and a brew, to soak up the rays and highlight my hair with lemon juice.

But the pressure reached a fever pitch, removed of all flippancy. My reality was deadlines and percentages, syllabuses and office hours, no extra time allotted for the student with her head in the clouds.

Luckily, Talia made herself scarce, having vacated our room from last night's lingering tantrum. The quiet made me sleepy, but I fought the temptation to nap. I'd reject my bed and the rumpled covers, ignore the midday doze of sleep so sweet. I eyed my alarm clock, negotiating with myself. I could rest for an hour, then wake up energized. But when my eyes closed, I sank into the dark, the pillow cold against my cheek, my blankets high over my head.

When I awoke, it was evening. The stress must've possessed me, sleeping too hard for too long. A crick in my neck confirmed my suspicions. I yawned, registering that my roommate hadn't returned.

I stretched, moving my legs left to right, drumming up some energy. I'd need it since I'd spent sacrificed precious study time for sleep. I dangled my feet off the edge of the bed, and my stomach rumbled. I debated ignoring it, to push away hunger for note review. But I couldn't skip lunch and dinner, with no fuel left in reserves for a night devoted to learning.

First, sustenance. I'd browse the cafeteria before it became packed with the dinner crowd. I'd eat fast, grab a Coke, and dash back upstairs to my locked door and sound machine. Then it was a date with my textbook and no interruptions.

The buzz of the cafeteria, and the lengthy line, kept me occupied. I grabbed a salad, slurped some soda, and ate like it was a competition. I focused on packing my stomach to capacity, and when I left, my jeans felt tight, my belt a boa constrictor.

I grabbed more caffeine for study support and headed back upstairs. I looked over my shoulder twice, then sprinted to my room before I could change my mind.

My door was unlocked. I knew I'd locked it before I left, my key dangling from my wrist bracelet. I angled to the left so I could see inside without entering the room. Nothing moved. I took another step forward. I saw my bed, covers still frumpy, and my nightstand with my journal beside my lamp. I stepped inside, surveying the scene. Nothing was out of order, though I was certain I'd kept the door closed.

My desk was scattered with stray paper. I walked closer, noticing a breathing lump on my roommate's bed.

"Hey," mumbled Talia, from underneath her covers. She

poked her head out, her lipstick smudged, and she shot me a smile, with hesitancy behind it.

"So, listen," she initiated, "I hate to do this to you, but Brian's here. He went to get me some water. But, um, he's coming back."

I waited, my blood bubbling before she finished her sentence.

"What the hell, Talia?"

"Listen, Sarah, take a chill pill. I know you're frustrated, but there's, like, literally nowhere else for us to go," she pleaded. "And it's my room, too, by the way."

I reached for my purse on the nightstand, not trusting myself to speak, fearing what I'd lead with would be violent. My mind tried to formulate words that sounded less harsh, but all I produced was a string of screamed expletives. I tampered it down to a low boil.

"This is so beyond selfish of you. I get you want to hook up, but you are being so bitchy about it. It's your choice to be slutty, but I wish it didn't impact me as much."

She sputtered again, trying to explain her self-centeredness, but came up short, intoning that his frat was boys only, no sleepovers allowed.

"I can't believe you," I hissed, cutting my eyes at her.

Brian re-entered, waddling by our door, moving from foot to foot.

"Whatever! Just, ugh, whatever, Talia." I couldn't even form a rebuttal. I flung my pencils and pens across the bedspread, shoving them deep into my bookbag.

They stared, without the decency to act chagrined. I shut the door, resting my head for a moment on the doorframe, overhearing Talia's giggle. I wanted to barge back in, every inch a dangerous dragon, letting my lips find fire or worse.

Instead, I hiked down the stairs to desperately search for another place to study.

The student union wasn't far, and it offered free sodas if you hit the Coke machine twice on the left side, a trick Talia taught me before she went boy crazy. The tables next to the girls bathroom were usually vacant, with space enough to spread out.

My rage urged me to climb the hill fast, my pace quickening into a jog. The night was cool, and the crickets chirped a happy rhythm that only made my vexation worse. I trampled the pavement, certain I'd already forgotten something important, fired up at how lusty and lame my roommate was becoming.

Behind me came a flutter of footsteps, the clomp of Clydesdale hooves. I half turned to see the student from the library, his coat barreling behind him like Batman's cape. He was running double speed, catching the corner of my backpack. His momentum clotheslined me, waylaying my balance.

I fell to my knees, skinning them in the process. The student union was housed by a gaggle of oak trees, the protected land providing a wooded area reserved for hacky-sack tournaments and hammocks. It was a popular lounge spot when the weather was nice and the workload was manageable. Wannabe musicians strummed guitars while tie-dyed onlookers swayed to the beat.

This time of night, it was deserted.

I scrambled to stay upright. He tackled me, our legs colliding, my shoe connecting with his shin. He grimaced but held firm, his hands gripping my right leg.

"Get off me!" I shouted, squirming to rid myself of my backpack and escape.

He held tight and circled my waist, his meaty arms a forcefield.

I pressed against him and screamed, my words lost to the wind.

He dragged me toward the trees. I clawed at his arms, scratching and drawing blood.

"HELP!" My voice was wispy amongst the forest sounds of frogs and cicadas. My sharp fingernails dug into his skin, and I could feel him wince.

"Not again," he shushed in my ear, "not one more sound, Sarah." He reached into his back pocket, securing my wrists with one arm, distracting me with a blade shimmering in the moonlight.

"Now then," he whispered, "do what I say, and this will all be okay." He touched his nose to my neck, making me squeal.

We were alone in a circle of trees, the ground beneath us damp. His tongue melted into my ear, the slurping sound a soundtrack to my fear. I flinched. One of his hands encircled my wrists. The other tapped the knife against the base of my throat, to prohibit me from writhing. A drop of spittle wetted my earlobe. I heaved, my dinner threatening an escape.

"Get on the ground now." He pointed to a bed of pine needles and mimed for me to lay on my stomach. I hesitated, surveying the woods, searching for a makeshift weapon.

"I said, get down," he commanded. The tip of his knife slashed a pinky-sized gash on my neck. The nick brought a sliver of pain, encouraging me to comply.

The pine needles scratched my cheek, the sap sticking to my hair. I steeled myself, certain this was a precursor to rape.

A scratchy rope secured my wrists, the itchiness cutting sharp into my skin like it was curated from splinters.

I lay still, waiting for him to progress. My feet were still untied, and when he undressed, I could leap and make a run for it. My body was galvanic, each particle ready to make a move when he stripped me.

He rested his knees against my spine. I felt him run the knife blade against the curves of my back, poking little circles in my flesh, drawing pinpricks of blood.

"Turn over," he instructed, his voice pillow-talk soft, reserved for story time and children half asleep. "Turn over," he asked again, a cradle song of syllables.

I moved, my head encircled by leaves, and I stared at the sky, wishing I'd learned the constellations. The moonlight was spotlight bright, encouraging me to study my captor. His face was smooth, except for a smattering of acne across his chin. His inky hair grazed his shoulders, and momentarily he looked kind, a solitary Boy Scout camping alone.

He balanced on his knees with me in between them, my hands restrained by my head. He cupped his head next to my chin, caressing my jaw the way a lover would.

I turned away, not wanting to allow him access to my body, to pretend this was free will. I waited for the torment to begin, certain that after he abused me, he'd let me go.

He giggled, clownish, into the dark.

"There's nothing to be afraid of, Sarah. It's me and you. Here, together." His eyes flashed, recounting a future only he could see.

I whimpered, seeing myself in his reflection, my eyes bulging in horror.

"Please," I begged, "Let me go. Please, I won't say a word to anyone. You don't need to do this."

"Shhhh. It's all right," he soothed me while he traced imaginary scribbles with the knife up and down my arm, equations only he could solve.

I closed my eyes, my head dizzy with fear. I could buck him off me, catch him off guard, let the additional adrenaline take control.

"Look at me," he growled, his good mood vanished, and I saw his face change, his mannerisms morph into anguish. "Look at me, *now!*" he demanded, my eyes following the blade, the serrations connecting with my stomach.

The anguish seared my insides, surgical and blunt, and I howled. I used my voice to fill up the sky, to tell the earth exactly what injustice was occurring. I heard my scream wobble and waver and imagined the trees crying after a heavy rain. He stabbed me again, this time lower, and I vomited, a rush of wetness soaking my grass-stained shirt. I saw the knife with my blood on it, watched Jason lick the tip.

A brown leaf drifted onto my forehead. I felt a shriek die in my throat, shriveling too fast. My head lolled to the side, delivering me elsewhere, into a secret place—numb, taciturn, and safe.

A crack to my sternum held the strength of an earthquake. I imagined the forest responding in kind, shaking up dirt, using the roots to tangle my attacker, burying him until he was rotten, his teeth mixed in with boulders and sticks, his pearly bones strangled under thorns and bristles.

That's my fate, not his, I realized, my fingers flush against the mud, the first of my bones connecting with air, the sting of a severed tendon. Fear poured from every surface, my body radiating horror, and I could do nothing to make it stop.

One tear for Toby, one tear for Talia. I counted the droplets, tracking their progress from my eyes to my cheeks, down my chin, and my neck. Two for my parents, and the rest reserved for me.

I cried for all the things I'd never become: a college graduate, a wife, an A student, someone to be proud of. I sobbed and ached for the achievements I'd never earn, my life forever paused. The purpose of me was never clarified, because my adult life had only just begun.

The dirt rose to carry me, a muddy brown caravan from this world to the next, fueled by the rattling of my teeth, a road slicked with regret.

Chapter 15
Timmy Richardson
Date: September 10th, 2001, 3 p.m.

I returned from the disgusting dorm restroom to find an ogre leaning against my bed, flipping through my personal items, his spindly fingers stoking my new Clinique face soap, digits deep into my toiletry bag.

"Whoa, dude. Stop. Boundaries, man," I said, while he turned, providing a full view of this horror show. My karma was a shit show to get saddled with this monster as a college roommate. As sophomores at NCC, we'd chosen to try out our luck in the dorm lottery system, a choice I now regretted.

One look at him, and I was already dissatisfied, my dreams of being a campus Lothario dried up into fantasy dust. There's no overcoming him, his height making him crouch, a gargoyle with hunched shoulders and secondhand clothes. The golem straightened, growing large against the low dorm ceilings. He stood next to the twin bed, with a crown of limp, shoulder-length black hair, evoking a young Herman Munster with poor eyesight. His glasses were two seasons out of style, ill fitting, with no croakies to secure designer lens. No way this dude had heard of Ray-Bans; he didn't even belong in this century, since he was rocking pressed pants and a too-tight polo.

He was an ugly six foot two at least, his shoulders curved evoking some Quasimodo flair. If he couldn't make use of the best thing about him, which was his height, then there was no saving this Shrek wannabe. I knew men that would kill for that kind of wingspan, who spent their lives lying about being six feet tall, an ocean of envious five-foot-seven shorties in subtly heeled loafers. Instead, he kept himself curled, his posture a lumpy hill.

I positioned my leather satchel on the floor, continuing to stare, making no attempt to conceal my disappointment. My mouth opened, and I let it fall, surprised that hillbillies like this were admitted to North Carolina Central. Holy Hell, it was like that movie *Deliverance*, with the violins and rotten teeth. This dude was from the mountains, sure as shit, and now he was stuck with me.

I knew I should've roomed with Ricky Lee. He was annoying in high school, and he interrupted me every other second, but at least he didn't have crater-size acne or Ozzy Osbourne hair. I would totally trade this oaf for Ricky's chattiness and his home-made protein shakes. Yes, he reeked of fish oil and discounted kale, but there's a solid chance this dude might smother me in my sleep.

I could probably beg at the registrar's office for a last-minute switch. Maybe they stayed open late on moving day to address mishaps like this. I couldn't be the only asshole who drew the short stick in the round two roommate lottery. I grabbed my bag from the floor, eager to find a campus map and set things straight. I scanned the room for my wallet, which had drifted between the unpacked clothes and broken boxes. I patted my jeans while taking a quick self-inventory. My Abercrombie shirt had withstood most of the moving-in wrinkles, and my blond tips were still spikey underneath my trucker hat.

This would be fine; I could work this out.

My new roommate frowned at me, his expression dismissive. He stared at me, his lumbering arms crossed, waiting for me to speak. These state schools had mandated quotas to fill and diversity numbers to meet. My dad had warned me about this when I'd chosen NCC over Cullowhee. I could picture my dad, smirking, his cigar pointing at me, a laser of self-righteousness.

I hated that he was right. My freshmen year roommate was a similar dud, an exchange student who lacked English and basic hygiene skills. Our relationship was dead on arrival. I assumed, like lightening, a bad roommate couldn't strike twice. The only positive was that my parents weren't here to witness this travesty.

Mr. No-Name continued to gawk, making no moves to introduce himself or unpack. I'd already begged my parents to back off, certain they'd lessen my social status if they entered the dorm. They'd already completed their debut move-in duties last year. This year, they wobbled to the car, granting me my sophomore dorm independence. My back's gonna ache tonight, all to impress the Hunchback of Notre Dame, straight from the dungeon, flinching in the sunlight.

I sighed, my discontent palatable. I'd let him know this wasn't gonna work, put him down like he's rabid. With looks like that, he's gotta be used to rejection. I'm another passerby in this dude's long line of letdowns.

I stalled over my suitcase, wondering if I should even unpack.

"I'm Jason, Jason LeDown," he finally muttered, avoiding eye contact. He stood stiffly, his high-pitched voice doubling the awkward encounter. He sounded like puberty had surpassed him for superior options.

"Right, I'm Timmy Richardson," I replied, my voice thick with sarcasm. He responded with a quick eye flick. Apparently, I needed to be blunt. No time for niceties when my rep's on the line.

"Not sure you should unpack, man. Don't mean to state the obvious but no way this is gonna work." I puffed my chest, thankful I'd spent the summer lifting with my cousin Tim in his tricked-out basement. I flashed him a taut muscle, my bicep flexed and on point.

Jason ignored me, plopping his withered gym bag onto the other twin bed. He began to unload, removing a flurry of identical collared shirts, acting as if I hadn't said a damn word.

I moved closer, aggravated that he wasn't comprehending the problem.

"Yo, idiot, did I stutter?" I asked, my voice awash with irritation, ramping my frustration up further. "I mean, not to be um, mean, but I worked my ass off to get in here. And I don't think me plus your whole emo vibe is going to click. It's sketchy." I clipped my words, making my critiques land harder.

He must realize his height was no match for my muscle mass. As a freshman, I was scrawnier, a four-eyed nerd who spent Saturday nights studying or watching laugh-track sitcoms in the dorm lobby. Over the summer, I'd rebranded, earning my spot amongst the other hot co-eds. My plan was to join Lambda Chi, not be linked with a loser in Wal-Mart threads.

I waited for his rebuttal, but he remained silent. He continued to fold his clothes neatly into the closest dresser. It was strange he didn't respond to a direct insult. Maybe this was some kind of disability thing? My nana was deaf in one ear but went through life smiling, not wanting to admit she couldn't hear. If this was charity related, that could work in my favor. I fiddled with my suitcase zipper, debating overenunciating or scooting closer.

"We both got in, didn't we?" he uttered, his voice polished but creaky. He kept his hands busy, unpacking a stack of pleated black pants. I glanced at their tapered legs and almost gagged.

"Yeah, but I mean… the roommate thing is random. You shouldn't take it personal. There's others peeps out there, ones that may suit your style… better." He didn't ask me to explain, but I kept looking at him, wondering exactly what he didn't get. "No harm if we call it today. We're sophomores, we know the drill. They'll let us switch if we let them know. No need to wait another year."

He didn't refuse or come out swinging. Instead, Jason reached for another duffle bag, this one stuffed with socks and yellowed boxer briefs. Tension dominated the room, his lack of response a passive-aggressive whiplash.

Well, time to plead to the higher-ups. My family wasn't drowning in riches like the Chapel Hill preps down the road. But we weren't scraping the bottle of the broke barrel, either. Hands could always be greased; meetings could appear on schedules. If I buttered up Dad and admitted defeat, he'd funnel some cash my way. I could increase the drama, with knees on the floor, hands clasped, set to bring the humble house down. Anything to get out of this room assignment.

"Well." Jason paused, interrupting my thoughts. "Here's how I see it. We both hope to graduate from this college. We can leave each other alone and focus on our studies. Seems to me like there's a way to make this work." He continued to smooth his clothing, his long fingers patting the creases, his touch the only iron needed. A subconscious shiver did jumping jacks on my spine. Jason's movements appeared mundane, but underneath was a sinister riptide, urging me to flee.

I ignored it and upped the ante.

"As I said," I remarked, "you're already bothering me. I don't know how to make it clearer, but this whole thing," I added, gesturing to his general area, "is not working for me. As in *currently*."

He stopped unpacking and turned slowly, his fists clenched, his pockmarked jaw made of concrete with eyes interlocking mine.

"It's time that *you* listen to *me*," he growled, a fierceness punctuating his words. He squared his shoulders, climbing to his full height.

"You think you have some authority here, but that's not the case. I tried to keep it civil, but I am beginning to become… annoyed." He sneered, my words a pest best suited for swatting.

I could challenge him, throw a punch, start a modern-day duel in the hallway. He was tall but waifish, the opposite of an experienced fighter. But the way he kept himself poised, already anticipating a punch, made me hesitate. I'd get this situation resolved, but I needed more intel first.

"Whatever, dude," I acquiesced. "I'm going to the cafeteria. Take your time. I expect you to be gone by the time I get back. If not, then you'll take your chances."

He shook his head forcefully, but I let the door slam speak for me, making it crack for good measure. The bustle of happier students saturated the hallway, the squeals of laughter and Green Day's guitar solo crowding my deliberations. My mood soured, the unfairness avalanching against my abdomen. A dash of dizziness reminded me to not make major decisions on an empty stomach.

The campus cafeteria provided a pick-me-up in the form of Greek grilled chicken salad. I drank down a Sprite and reformulated the plan. I'd give Jason some space, and when I returned, he'd be agreeable. We both needed to release the bravado, and my leaving allowed him to keep his pride. That's my contribution, and tomorrow we'd make our dissolution official. I tossed my trash, happily acknowledging I'd beat the swarming dinner crowd with lines as long as Disney World.

I took a self-imposed walking tour around campus, trekking a mile, then two. It felt good to move, my optimism rising with every step. By the time I jogged up the dorm steps, taking them two at a time, I was certain that my good luck had returned to Richmond Dorm.

Jason's massive bright-white tennis shoes greeted me, along with his books scattered across the floor. He languished on his bed, an open novel at his navel, his legs angled across basic checkered bedsheets. Jason leaned back, a skyscraper smirk on his face, with one arm entangling his greasy hair.

"What the hell, dude?" I asked, my face becoming redder by the minute.

He continued to grin and let out a girlish titter, a strange sort of taunt.

I gaped at him. I'd given him time to reflect, I'd threatened him, and still, he wouldn't disappear. It was time to switch tactics, to offer up a consolation prize.

"Okay," I wagered, my voice dipping. "Look, I've got some friends on campus. You probably do, too. We can make a trade, no harm, no foul. My buddy can take your place, and you can crash with whoever. We'll get it settled before school begins." I stood next to my bed with palms outstretched, the universal sign of peace and goodwill.

"Or better yet," I continued, "you can keep this room. It's a good location, and you've already unpacked. I'll head to my friend's place, bunk with him until we get this worked out. If you brainstorm some names, we can clear it with administration."

I offered him a helpful nod, using my body language to seal the deal.

Instead of replying, Jason flicked off his bedside light, and the room tumbled into darkness.

"Hey!" I squeaked. "It's barely eight p.m." The evening sky had only begun to swerve to black. I heard the creak of Jason's bed, his back against the wall, huddled in the dark like the night creature he was.

I felt my way in the dark, twice rattling against the unfamiliar dresser. I'd planned for this night to include Ugg-boot-wearing blondes, drowning in a river of Bud Light and red Solo cups, the opposite of turning in early with a weirdo breathing heavy in the corner. In the prime window spot, too, sequestering me with the florescent hallway lights and the revolving door of co-eds. I wasn't in tears, but if I closed my eyes tight enough, I was certain they'd come.

I gave in to the exhaustion, the increased stress leading to fatigue. My mind flitted onto a highway of hurt, until it all became too much. I shucked off my shoes, escaping into a dream where problems didn't exist. I covered myself with my softest blanket, the smell of home soothing me to sleep.

I awoke to the sound of panting and a wet sensation on my chest. I sat up, reaching to push the animal off me. My hands groped at my bedsheets, which were soaked straight through, liquid covering my clothes and face.

The ammonia smell was overpowering, my bed a public urinal. I touched my pants, wondering if I'd wet the bed.

"It's not your pee, it's mine." His voice tickled my earlobe. The bastard had peed on my face, my pajamas immersed in his waste. I moved to stand, but my arms and legs were clasped together. I glanced down, the glint of a rope reflecting in the dark. His hair danced on my forehead, while Jason nestled his mouth against my right ear.

"Wakey-wakey," he said in his high voice of helium balloons. "I told you, I need this to work. Now, you will listen to me. If you behave, it will be like I'm not even here. I will study, I will leave you be. But if you pull any more stunts like the one you did today, well, then, this is only the beginning."

He raised his finger, stroking it against my rib cage. A jagged hangnail sliced my skin, scratching a zip-zag line down low. He grabbed the side of my face, cupping it, an unwanted lover's embrace.

The splat of his tongue wormed into my ear, a fat slug slick with spit. I yanked my head away, disgust rising in my chest, my wrists cutting against the restraints. He pushed my head down into the covers, muffling me in case I screamed.

He continued to writhe his tongue in my ear, pushing too far as if trying to lick my brain. Jason's cackle echoed, its intimacy unsettlingly close. Tears leeched from my eyes, while I continued to squirm, desperate to put space between us.

He allowed me to move, his tongue releasing my ear with a satisfied smack. I sucked in air, careful not to pass out. Jason stayed by my bedside, tracing patterns on my sheets with an unsheathed dagger, the blade threatening in the moonlight.

My buddy Hess worked at the stockyards, and he used to brag about the kind of knives they sold there, those with ten-inch blades and ivory handles, taken from the tusks of elephants. He boasted about machetes and other weapons of war, until I tired of his nonstop bluster. This one didn't look as fancy as what Hess described, but this knife was formidable, the length of it longer than a ruler.

I thought about my death. My obituary would read that I was stabbed to death by my psychotic roommate, the result of the university's momentous mistake. I prayed my parents sued the shit out of them. I moved down the bed, reciting the Lord's Prayer, my liturgies overpowered by Jason's laughter.

Jason held his knife aloft, keeping it steady.

He leaned into me, the blade even with my stomach, letting me acknowledge the weight of it.

"Do you like that?" he goaded, the cold metal creating goose bumps on my skin.

I wasn't sure how much time passed. I kept still, not wanting the blade to tip or slide into my belly button.

Jason grabbed my wrists, cradling them in his over-sized hands. He traced tiny circles in my palm. I flinched, waiting for whatever horror came next. I squeezed my eyes shut, preferring to not see the next act.

He released the binds, the tension in my hands alleviated, though they tingled from being locked in place. Jason freed my shins before sending a whistle my way, the childlike sound at odds with my rapid heartbeat.

Another puddle of ammonia spread across my crotch. My urine mixed with his, the smell furrowing my nose, the shame of it burrowing into my skin.

He laughed from across the room, his shoulders heaving with frivolity. He continued, a carnival clown boast, while I gripped the bedpost to keep from shaking.

"Shower," I muttered, grabbing a towel and whatever clothes were within arm's reach, my heart threatening to leave my body.

I wasn't sure he'd let me leave. He could stop me, force me to soak in our combined liquid until morning, his knife ready to chop me to pieces.

I waited, my hesitation a way to ask his permission. A minute passed, and I ran, my hastily grabbed belongings clutched to my chest.

I sprinted into the hallway, careening with a student heading in the opposite direction.

"Hey!" he screeched, but I didn't stop, not until my feet found the blue of the bathroom tile.

I threw my belongings into the sink, barely making it to the nearest toilet. I vomited my early dinner and fear and dry-heaved the rest for what felt like hours. Bits of lettuce clung to the basin, my stomach continuing to purge my panic. I wiped my mouth against my contaminated shirt, then pulled it off, eager to trash the evidence of my humiliation. The bathroom was vacant, the only sound the repetitive drip of a leaky faucet.

I staggered to the shower, my towel dragging behind me, a traumatized version of Linus from *Charlie Brown*.

I let the heat do its work, the shower pressure covering my suntanned shoulders. I would never see Jason again. Discarded toiletries left for communal shower use saved me while I prayed, scrubbed, and sobbed. Soap suds washed away the grime, but there was no going back. I'd never be able to rest in that room or in his presence. My fingers scraped my scalp, and I wondered if I'd ever feel clean again. I rinsed my ear under the water, on repeat. Nothing could erase the memory of his slippery tongue. I stayed until the water turned frigid, until the quiet of the bathroom increased my nervousness. I drip-dried, letting the water rinse my back, down my legs, and into the cold puddle at my feet.

I would switch schools or move back in with my parents. I'd take a gap year or stand outside the dean's house until he granted me a meeting. I'd leave every one of my possessions inside that room before I'd see Jason again.

A plan formed. I'd get dressed, find Ricky Lee, then I'd lie, cheat, or steal to get off campus. A dash of logic reminded me of the textbooks, backpack, and closet full of clothes that my parents had charged on their Visa. I couldn't show up to class empty-handed, devoid of even a pencil or my student ID. I'd need my wallet, especially since I planned to head to the admin's office at first light.

I pushed the door open, anticipating an assault. Jason sat hunched in his corner, his gigantic feet tapping against the floor. I felt his eyes on me as I packed, stuffing everything into trash bags at record speed. I didn't take the time to organize or find my suitcases. Instead, I swooped all my toiletries into one large clump, not even bothering to see if the lids were secure. I crammed my clothes, still on the hangers, into another bag, then jammed the rest of my books into my bookbag.

"I see you've decided to leave. That's acceptable, too. I'm better on my own," he chuckled.

I zipped on, piling my things into a makeshift mountain.

"Aren't you forgetting something?" he asked, pointing to the top of his dresser. The lone picture of my parents smiled from his side of the room, my mother in her blue cashmere, my father's bald head shining.

I gulped and nodded. Quickly, I moved to snag it, ready to grab it and go.

"Nuh-uh. Not so fast. This picture, this one, I keep." He smiled at me, wider than necessary, and twice as deadly. "Just in case you get any grandiose ideas. Call it an insurance policy, perhaps. Or maybe I like the way they look. So wholesome." He raised his eyebrows, the nonverbal equivalent of a guillotine.

I backed up, mentally throwing mea culpas to my parents for

leaving them with this lunatic. But it wasn't worth the Polaroid, or the fight that would happen, if I tried to remove it by force.

I walked backward, clearing my throat, weighing myself down with everything I could carry and almost toppling over my belongings. I wrapped my soiled sheets to my chest, a urine-soaked toga, and swung my backpack onto my shoulder. I headed down the stairs, carefully balancing my possessions, while trying not to cry in the stairwell. I didn't stop until I got three blocks away from that room, huddling against a brick building with everything I owned.

I wandered around campus until breakfast, reorganizing my personals so I could carry them better. I spied a payphone, dialed my parents, and spun an ocean's worth of lies in two minutes. I fibbed that my roommate didn't speak English and that he'd pleasured himself in front of me, providing enough details to make my mother gasp. My father's deep baritone promised he'd get a hold of this, and he instructed me to head to the headmaster's office. He stated he could make the two-hour drive in record time if they left immediately, and I leaned against the payphone window, weak with relief. They'd bought my story, and that was enough.

"No need to make the drive, Dad. Just wanted to update you. I'll head to the admin office now. I'm sure they'll be able to help."

I found the front office and waited until they opened. No one was surprised to see a student carrying bedsheets and trash bags full of clothes, which both shocked and settled me at the same time. A friendly, middle-aged woman reassigned me to a New Residence single, and I had to stop myself from kissing her hand.

"Now, don't thank me yet. It's at the other end of the campus. Far away from where you were."

"It doesn't matter, ma'am. It's perfect. It is." I laid it on thick, scared that she'd take it away if I was anything less than effusive.

She gave me a look like she thought I was on drugs but also slid over the key, along with a campus map, her acrylic nails click-clacking against the desk.

My buckling knees had reached their max limit. I stuffed her offerings in my pockets, allowing her a furtive glance.

"You okay?" she queried gently, blowing her bangs from her forehead.

All I could manage was a nod.

She shrugged, turning her attention back to the paperwork, the tap of her home keys loud in the too-warm office.

As soon as the moving-in was complete, for the second time, I locked my door. I'd go to the store later to find a deadbolt, once my parents arrived with the car, but first I allowed myself a second's rest on my bed. The room was tiny, no bigger than a broom closet, but I didn't mind.

My mind reviewed what I'd experienced, and I let myself cry, relieving the knife, the ropes, and the threats. I could wail all I wanted here, so I did.

I made the decision to stay on campus, though partially it was because I wasn't sure where else I could go. I had planned to do all the typical college-kid shenanigans, the staying out late, sneaking in flasks to football games, participating in fraternity rush week.

I stopped participating in most social events. Jason's actions spooked me and made me hesitant to go to the library at night. My fraternity dreams evaporated, along with late nights and crowded keggers. I was certain he was hiding in the shadows, a malevolent scarecrow lurking in dark alleyways.

I was terrified I'd see him on campus. Someone with dark hair, leaning over a textbook, would cause my heart to race. A student drinking the remains of a Sprite in a neon-white polo caused a minor panic attack. The drop of a book, the sound of running water, all caused chronic nightmares for weeks.

I didn't tell anyone what had happened, afraid that if I did he'd know, and he'd find me, or stick his blade into my parents. He'd soak me in his piss and threaten me or complete his script with a twist of his knife.

I lost weight, and motivation, and had to be reassessed by the campus doctor twice. I waited outside for hours to secure my room assignment for next semester, since I couldn't take the chance of messing with my housing. My asthma guaranteed my single room, and I gathered all the necessary documentation in a laminated folder.

The registrar filed my continuance. I could have skipped out of the office, my mood hopscotch light, a shade of my old enthusiasm.

It confused me, then, that back in the safety of my room, a wave of emotion rushed through me, ending in buckets of snot and tears. The shock of what happened could overtake me, even months afterward, causing unpredictable mood swings.

Really nothing could make me feel safe. I could plan, and I did. I bought a Louisville Slugger that I kept upright next to my door. I scanned every new class twice, double-checked every class-room roster, and always sat in the back. But even with all my precautions, the sense of Jason lingered, dancing on the edge of my consciousness.

I told myself he had better things to do with his time than antagonize me. Then I recalled the wetness in my ear, seared into my brain like a brand, his giggle my tortured soundtrack.

I found safety in repetition, the click of a deadbolted door, the buzz of a nearby taser. I slept with a nightlight, with pepper spray nearby on my nightstand. I locked my door and turned off the light, washed my face, and combed my hair. Then I rested against the wall, my back secure against the hard brick, the covers pulled up to my chin, the gesture meant to keep all monsters away. Before I closed my eyes, one grateful refrain settled by soul.

Another day spent far away from the evil Jason LeDown.

Chapter 16
Tina Adams
Date: June 26th, 2001, 4:32 p.m.

I t'd been more than a year since Betty died, but my hometown of Hickory, North Carolina, refused to relinquish the collective grief of losing Hickory High's best and brightest. Flowers languished by the roadside memorial, with handwritten letters left to wither, Betty's name an embodiment of gone but not forgotten.

The local gossips swore she was killed by a drifter, who flitted in and out of our zip code under the cloak of nightfall. Busybodies whispered behind homespun curtains, debating conspiracy theories paired with pitchers of sweet tea. Since no criminal was ever caught, everyone became a suspect, turning local bridge games into murder clubs.

There was no going back to the old ways of unlocked doors and garages left open, with lawn mowers and weed eaters lying adrift and fresh for the taking. The town circled the wagons and kept everything in sight, fearing the discovery of another body half-buried in the woods.

My parents weren't immune to the city-wide paranoia. They instituted a curfew that was non-negotiable, their arms crossed in concrete, daring me to protest. I took the lashes without complaint, same as every other teenager in town. Our parents were firmly toeing the line, a consensus decided in a phone tree standoff, each preaching that the antidote to trauma was to lock us in tight. Homicide was immune to deadbolts and nightfall, or at least that was what our parents promised. Even my neighbor Mindy peeled her cherry-red Jeep Wrangler into the driveway at seven thirty p.m., the last notes of the pop radio terminating before the sun went down.

I hadn't known Betty, but my older sister Kathy swore they were tight and would gather some crocodile tears to prove it. I'd never seen them together, but Kathy swore they'd shared a cafeteria table, the black streaks of mascara bleeding down her face like parallel train tracks. She'd look around quick to see if anyone clocked her despair before reaching for a wet wipe. Kathy couldn't elaborate on any of Betty's other characteristics, keeping the script centered upon her academic accolades, like the whole of her was reflected in her report card.

It made me sad, that lazy oration, the focus on the grades, not the girl. But I didn't argue with Kathy since she'd respond with hysterics and slamming doors, Betty's death a euphemism for feeling misunderstood. Kathy also used bereavement as an excuse for her poor math grades and low ACT scores. I shot my parents skeptical looks, but they drank in the drama, leaving her to her grief. I'd seen firsthand the remnants of Kathy's sadness, which included a hastily buttoned blouse, smeared lipstick, and clothing that reeked of her boyfriend's CK One cologne. Mourning, my ass. She'd used her faux friend as the fall guy for late nights with Brandon.

But Kathy wasn't the only one hell-bent on keeping her clothing black.

The *folie à deux* extended to Lowes, which made bank on selling deadbolts and portable door locks. Conversation flowed in strangled groups of twos and threes, pressed into a tight circle, coffee in hand, their collective worry a functioning generator to keep families warm all winter.

Shadows crossed on my parents' faces, their silhouettes anxiously skimming the newspaper with pursed lips, never finishing their breakfast. That's the gist of Betty's legacy, her name a warning, her heritage boiled down to bogeymen and hissed parental threats, turning a real person into folklore.

I was tired of my city's exaggerated sorrow, ready to kick the town and its heartbreak to the curb. My grades weren't good enough for college, but I'd secured an internship with an upstart marketing company two hours south. Fall would bring not a new semester, but an innovative opportunity. The pay was minimal, but the job included training in digital marketing and a discounted two-bedroom intern apartment. None of the other details mattered if I could escape from Hickory, a town devoted to reliving its worst day.

I was counting down the months until my new life began. I'd seen firsthand the trap of those who stayed here, trying to carve a life out of nothing. My coworkers at Betty's Boxcar were proof of those who'd traded the life they wanted for the pennies they could get. The head waitress Nancy had been filling orders since she was my age, and her knuckles paid the price of all that overtime, swelling up like chestnuts by the end of her shift. I watched her hands curl into tight ovals, the arthritis carved into her skin, the curse she'd earned from nursing paltry tips in sudsy water. Watching her move in tiny increments, a hobbled ghost of Christmas yet to come, reminded me to never settle.

The days at the diner ticked by, a veritable Groundhog Day of customer complaints and rushed writing on lined paper, of notices to turn off the open sign and empty the trash. I had no time to complain about Betty's Boxcar, as double shifts refilling ketchup bottles left me short on friends and free time.

Most of my graduating class had already left for school, their cars weighed down with new clothes, bedspreads, and high aspirations. Downtown felt deserted, and my days were spent eyeing the clock, my hands sticky from pouring lemonade. The sameness of it all threatened to tip me over the edge, but the finish line was in sight, mere weeks before I'd earn my freedom and the open road.

My tips were a farce on top of a paltry paycheck, but I remained diligent with deposits to my BB & T savings account. Sometimes I stared at my balance, and my pulse would quicken, the readout so minimal compared to my needs. Independence was a pricey mistress, and I worried about additional expenses. Ten dollars here, a twenty there, and suddenly I was grabbing onto the side of the bank building so I wouldn't collapse. The numbers on the ATM receipt swam, my eyes no longer seeing individual digits, only a flashfire of failure.

I focused on my breath to steady myself against the grainy brick, shoving off the pessimism so I wouldn't drown in it.

Back in my Toyota Camry, I blared Destiny's Child, my neck against my headrest, flatlined by my anxiety. After two songs, I could push the gear into drive without shaky fingers.

The next day was a duplicate, juggling coffee mugs and pushing dessert menus into calloused hands. The customers were a stream of steady regulars who'd been coming since the restaurant opened in 1984. They'd known the original Betty, then her daughter Susan, who'd retired to Florida and left the restaurant to her daughter Mia, a spunky blonde currently barking orders at the cook.

Each patron had their favorite booth, and they always inquired about the daily special, though they knew the menu by heart. There's comfort to be found in the twinkling diner bell and the motor memory of fixing sweet tea. On bad days, I'd call it mundane, but a certain security remained in the hum of the lunch crowd and the promise of a favorite meal.

Today, I was in thundercloud mode, my irritation rising against the dreaded lunch crunch, my voice nonexistent over the clanking silverware and order-ups.

"What can I get you?" I yelled at table two to a long-haired patron, my voice coming out harsh amidst the bustling four-tops.

Two tables down, I spied Ms. Calero, her mouth already downturned, her famous frown waiting to ruin my day. No matter how I performed, she complained that her order was wrong, or the service was slow, one criticism away from addressing my manager. And while this job was temporary, I still needed the money for future groceries and utilities not covered by my lease. I kept my paycheck in the front of my mind, as a security deposit against telling Ms. Calero to go to hell, though sometimes the words tasted so sweet in my mouth I wanted to unleash them. I hated that old lady and her striped leather purse, her gray hair styled to the sky like Betty's diner was the height of sophistication. I watched her tap her fingers against the laminated menu, each movement associated with another grievance.

"Um, I'm not sure yet," the man stalled, studying the menu like he'd be tested on it later. He loomed over the booth table, his dark hair greasy, with bits of white dandruff glinting against his scalp. He took his sweet time perusing the options, mouthing each word like it was inscribed in French. Betty's offered standard lunch fare, with the typical BLTs and Reubens, paired with fries or chips. We didn't even have different kinds of mayo. Just a one-stop shop, and a busy one. He kept at it, scanning every offering, his eyes never leaving the menu.

I sighed. "It's not rocket science," I quipped, staring down at him, hands on my hips, pencil in hand, one hundred percent in a huff. "Take your pick. Sandwiches, soups, salads, and that's about it. Nothing to it."

"I said I'm not ready," he grumbled, his voice edgy.

I watched him closely. He wasn't much older than me. His face was unlined, with his unwashed hair tucked behind his left ear, one arm cradled around his concave stomach.

I tapped my foot, loudly and on purpose. No response.

"Suit yourself. I'll be back." I stomped off, bracing myself for a younger version of Ms. Calero, ready to wreck the rest of my shift.

After refilling some waters, I came back, still fully annoyed. It wasn't this guy's fault that the restaurant was understaffed, but I couldn't shake my sour mood, not with the counter bell signaling another row of ready lunches.

"You decide?" I clicked my pen, attempting to offer service with a smile.

He looked up at me, his face a mask. His features were flat, and I couldn't tell if he wanted to yell at me or ask me out, because he gave nothing away. *Quite a poker face*, I mused. I kept quiet, summoning the last of my patience.

He continued to stare at me, moving his eyes to my name tag, muttering my name under his breath.

"Hmmm. Well, I'll take a ham and cheese sandwich. Water, no ice. Fries, no ketchup."

His squeaky voice relayed an average order, no substitutions to be found.

"See, that wasn't so hard, was it?" I said, jotting down his order, but it came out rougher than I intended, aiming for jokey but landing harsh. I grabbed his menu, keeping it locked under my armpit. Before I could clear the corner, he reached for my wrist, his movement so fast it was blurry.

"Tina. That's your name," he began, putting pressure against my skin. "Well, Tina, you're not a good waitress. I'd say you're impolite." His tone was professorial, but his grip was hard. "You should learn better manners." He dropped my hand but continued to scowl at me, my eyes darting to his tattered, long-sleeve shirt and the chemistry textbook open on his table.

"Got a complaint? Get in line!" I roared, narrowing my eyes and leaning closer to his booth. "And don't ever touch me again, you jerk, or I'll have you thrown out of here."

I clomped away, two seconds from hanging up my apron. I blasted through the sweltering kitchen and out the back door. Damn the orders, I needed some fresh air. I sat on the stoop, regulating my breath like I did at the bank. I couldn't throw a tantrum, not with a dozen hamburgers cooling under heat lamps. I wiped the sweat from my brow, pushed my frustration aside, and vowed to get to the end of this disaster day.

I put in his order and delivered it to his table with a fake grin, trying to assuage my angriest customer.

"Bon appetite," I joked, aiming for apologetic. I laid his meal down gently, but he harumphed anyway. "It looks good, and hey, I remembered, no ketchup." He didn't reply and laid his napkin in his lap without comment.

I shrugged, knowing this tip was lost. Between this dude and Ms. Calero, there was no pleasing to be had on this Tuesday.

"Get you anything else?" I attempted one last time, the effort of all this bogus pleasantry making my voice tremor.

He shook his head. I left him to his lunch, writing the meal off as another financial bungle.

The backend of the lunch hour was a mix of rushed orders, spilled soda, and feet that swelled under aching soles. I forgot I'd promised to work both shifts for LeAnn, who left to go on a date with her dream crush. I cursed myself for agreeing but gritted my teeth and wiped down more tables. I cleared the unhappy man's booth and seated the Smith family without even registering how his meal had been.

As expected, he'd stiffed me, taking the coward's way out. I stuffed his receipt in my pocket. The diner was busy enough that I could make up what was lost if I hustled.

At close, I stank like I'd run a marathon. The insides of my armpits were soaked, my uniform was crumpled, and I had ketchup dollops on the backs of my hands. I flipped the door sign to close, leaning on the mop to keep me steady.

I closed my eyes, dead on my feet, letting the silence of the restaurant comfort me, the absence of noise a welcome friend.

"I'll close up, Lendon," I called to the adolescent busboy, who was loading the dishwasher. "There's no salvaging this day, might as well take the brunt of it for us both."

"You sure, Tina? You look exhausted." He smiled at me but had already removed his apron, placing it on the hook above his station.

"Nah, it's fine, you go on. I got nowhere else to be."

He shrugged, threw a quick thank you my way, and tossed the diner keys onto the counter. The jangle of the doorbells confirmed his departure, his lanky frame scurrying to the only other car in the parking lot.

Nothing moved inside the restaurant, and I allowed myself another reprieve, soothed by the lack of harried orders and squeaking seats. I took my time scrubbing the laminate tables and stocking the salt-and-pepper shakers. Stacking up the stray chairs made my arms ache, my muscles urging me to call it a day. My checklist complete, I finally closed up shop on another dead-end day.

The night air felt luxurious on my skin, cooling me off in all the right places. I reached into my pocket for the car keys, my fingers brushing against the crumpled receipt in my apron pocket. I removed it, easing myself slowly into my leather seats and smoothing out the folds under blinking car light.

My handwriting shown through the wrinkled paper, but I saw he'd replied, his penmanship a pinched scrawl.

BITCHY TINA
DON'T END UP LIKE BETTY

I shivered, the chills sneaking up my spine, quick with a rapid look over my shoulder. The rush of suspicion came quickly. But nothing creaked or moved in my backseat, no whisper of laughter or glint of a knife. I cranked up my engine, eased by the satisfying click of the crankshaft.

I read the note again, then tore it up, sprinkling it like confetti out the window. I flipped on my headlights, and an owl hooted close by, breaking the night's silence.

The parking lot was empty, except for flickering streetlights flashing a burned-out morse code. I looked at my watch; it blinked 10:55. I rolled down my window to let in the cool air, one blistered foot on the brake pedal.

A whistle cut through the darkness. It sounded manmade, the kind hunters used to attract birds, the language of pheasants and quail. The rhythm started again, two short rifts, then a long warbling one. It was a signal; I was sure of it.

I flashed my brights, but nothing flickered in their glare, no shadowy figures, no disgruntled enemy with a rifle.

But then again, nearer now, came the same three-note message. The restaurant was right off the highway, surrounded by gravel and engines, not tree-lined woods. I was used to the roar of diesel engines and snippets of conversation, not turkey calls late at night.

There was no reason I should hear that sound.

This was how all urban legends began, a girl alone in the dark, a man bursting with bad intentions, the big bad wolf, but on two legs, the kind that butchered and maimed. With Betty on my mind, and the warning nestled in the dirt outside, I floored the gas, not wanting to find out how the horror story ended.

My mind zoomed to the boy who was so angry with me, and I wondered if this was his way of paying me back to my lunchtime slight. If so, it was overkill. He'd already made his point by stiffing and threatening me; no need to scare me, too. Only a madman would go to this extent, and I didn't want to push him further.

I let the engine tumble and pushed the gearshift into drive. No figures bounced in my peripheral vision, but I reversed fast anyway, spinning my wheels and kicking up pebbles, giving the whistler a warning in the form of fast tires.

My drive home was uneventful. The radio played bad '80s love songs, dedications to midnight listeners for the queen of late-night radio, Delilah. I took every turn at Indy 500 speeds, testing the limits of my tires. My house was close, and I could see the glow of the porch lights left on for me. They twinkled, high-lighting the dusty welcome mat, the homemade quirks I normally took for granted. I locked my car and heard only cicadas in my quick dash to unlock the front door.

Quietness greeted me, safe and sound, the snores of my family, the soft glow of all things safe.

My bedroom was down the hall and to the left. The bathroom I used was upstairs, but I was too exhausted to spelunk them in the dark. I decided to forgo a shower; the most self-care I could muster was removing my ponytail holder and shoes before climbing under the covers. I wore the day on my body and teeth, but I was too tired to care.

I dozed poorly, tossing and turning, the adrenaline whirling, while my body yearned for rest. The push-pull between weariness and the whistling kept me suspended in a sleepy no-man's-land. The morning sun came too soon, along with my parents in the kitchen, their clanking of mugs and pans a too-early alarm clock.

I groaned, realizing I'd agreed to first shift again. With a spit shower, and a quick see-ya to my parents, I finger-combed my hair, grabbed a piece of dry toast, and braced for another bustling morning.

The radio in my car blared something too poppy for my tired head, so I took my commute in silence, mentally prepping for another chaotic shift.

I swung into the parking lot earlier than normal, but that was preferrable. I visualized myself making the coffee, letting the savory sting of caffeine enrich my veins. I could take my time prepping, get into the groove and a good headspace. If I could garner a bit of peace, maybe the day wouldn't be unruly.

I jammed the gear into park and squinted. The dew of the grass made everything shiny, with tiny cobwebs stuck to the pebbles and grass. It was almost beautiful, but I hurried on, restaurant keys in hand.

LeeAnn owed me a long gossip session about her date, given the day from hell that was yesterday. Thankfully, I'd hear about it before breakfast, her wide grin enlightening me on the swoon-worthy moments. We'd gotten close, with shoulder bumps conveying collegial empathy, a friendship formed slinging orders to hungry customers. We were the same age but hadn't hung out in high school. She was a cheerleader who pepped and stepped her way to the upper rings of popularity, while I remained reserved, content to sit in the bleachers and fly under every radar. But her good nature spread across the diner, worming her enthusiasm past all my introverted walls.

I cradled the keys in my right hand, pausing at the restaurant door stoop. A mish mash of fur, the size of a house cat, huddled on the mat with tuffs of hair splaying all around. It was too big to be a possum, and a trickle of crimson blood came from its head, the wound still fresh.

I stepped back, hand to mouth, registering the slice across the animal's belly, a gutted line from head to tail. There were no tire marks; this was not an accident. It was placed for maximum impact, its white, crumbling intestines pulled out into a gory snapshot. The animal sported a disorganized smile, its row of crooked teeth barely visible in the desecrated mouth.

I stumbled backward, putting space between me and the vermin, struggling to stay standing.

I glanced around, my vision wild, but I was alone. Just me, the eviscerated creature, the spotlight dew, and my fast-paced pulse. I tripped, my palms slamming into the gravel, piercing my skin with speckled wounds. Over my lumbering breath, I heard the spooky soundtrack of that familiar whistle, way too close for comfort.

"Help!" I screamed to the vacant parking lot, officially scared and sweating.

I stood, ready to sprint to my car, when a dark blue pickup careened into the parking lot. LeeAnn, sporting her aviator sunglasses and a wad of bubble gum, parked beside my Camry, her radio up and window down. I hobbled to her truck, my feet unsure against the pavement, and grabbed her passenger door like it was a life raft.

"LeeAnn! There's a dead animal, and it's, like, gutted! It's on the steps and I don't know what to do!"

I crawled into her seat, not bothering to remove the stray McDonalds bag and straw wrappers. The words tumbled out, LeeAnn providing her hand to hold.

"I was here early, after a helluva day yesterday, I gotta tell you."

I reached over and locked the door, my pockmarked hands speckling drops of blood onto the window. LeeAnn's eyes widened, and she mimicked my movements, locking her door and handing me a napkin. I scooted closer to her, our shoulders touching, both of us eyeing the windshield window like an intruder.

"I was closing last night, and I felt like I was being watched. I'd received this creepy note from a customer." I pressed the napkin into my torn hands, grateful for the makeshift tourniquet. "Then I heard this sound, I would show you, but I can't whistle. It was like a bird call, or something hunters do. I heard it twice yesterday, and when I came here this morning and saw the thing on the steps, I heard the same whistle again."

I stopped to catch my breath, wishing I'd kept the note instead of shredding it. But it seemed like a stretch to link a bad tipper to animal dismemberment.

"You think it's some kind of signal?"

She stared at me, her blue eyes alight with concern.

"I'm not sure, but it creeped me out. It seemed like a warning."

"Well, I'll tell you what we're gonna do. We're calling Lendon right now, and Mia, too. We aren't dealing with any of this shit alone." She grabbed her Motorola Razr, her fingers racing to the numbers she needed, escalating the concerns with quick and focused summaries.

When Lendon didn't answer, Sherri dialed her date Jack, because he was a boy with a shovel, and because she'd see him again. I was too shocked to analyze her motives. I wanted someone else to take the lead, and it was Mia's husband Renaldo who finally answered our phone call roulette. His deep baritone voice sounded none too happy at our interruption. LeeAnn switched on her soothing voice, peppering her sentences with copious yes sirs.

"He didn't take it well," she explained, her chipped fingernail pressing end, her voice calmer now that she'd sounded the alarm. "He wants to check it out and implied that this was an excuse for wanting the morning off. Or recovering from a long night out." She picked at her cuticle. "I told him this wasn't a prank, that he'd better hurry 'cause something was dead on the doorstep." She bit her pinky nail, making the end jagged. "Anyway, he's on his way. All of them are."

LeeAnn was interrupted by a maroon Toyota skidding into the lot. Jack was quick to offer reinforcements, saddling up to her window with a shovel resting on his shoulder. He looked capable, a SOS prince in jeans and sweatshirt, his forehead covered with messy brown curls. LeeAnn stared at him, a capable conquering hero. He gave her a wink and started toward the restaurant, volunteering to remove the carcass if it would impress her.

Slowly, LeeAnn and I stepped out of the truck, keeping a football field's length between ourselves and Jack's body disposal services.

A small breakfast crowd gathered and watched him work, with snippets too soft to make out individual words.

Renaldo ushered to the front, using the diner's door as a backdrop for his stump speech.

"This is nothing, nothing at all. Please come in. We've removed the unfortunate vermin. No need to fret. There's breakfast and coffee inside." He gestured, his arms directing into a line, his fingers snapping at me and LeeAnn, urging the hired help to hop to it.

"What kind of animal was it?" asked one of the onlookers, but Renaldo shook his head and shot him a look that said there'd be no further questions.

My head was in the clouds, half set on refilling mugs, half flashing back to the animal's grin and stony eyes. I spilled coffee on two tables and tipped over a toddler's sippy cup, my fingers doused with apple juice. Renaldo and LeeAnn kept tabs on me, and by lunchtime it was decided I'd be sent home.

"Take the day off," Renaldo relented, his voice all confidential. "It's fine. That would have ruffled up anyone. Jack said it was some kind of badger that had been turned inside out." He winced. "Also, LeeAnn said you thought you heard something—some kind of warning whistle?"

My first instinct was to deny it, to shrug off the sound and the scribbled threat on the discarded receipt. But I'd already been honest with LeeAnn, so I might as well come clean with him, too.

"I had a bad shift yesterday. It was busy. There were some customers that were displeased."

He glared at me, all sympathy removed. He and his wife took umbrage to any negative thought about their precious

Betty's Boxcar, since it was the only generational wealth they possessed.

"I mean, it was nothing, a student who didn't tip."

He exhaled, his shoulders releasing. Loss of income for me wasn't high on his concerned list.

"Okay, well as a waitress, that happens. Go on," Renaldo encouraged, quick to write me off and get back to work.

"Anyway, I closed up, and I thought I heard a whistle; it was distinctive. I heard it when I was locking up last night and then I heard it again this morning when I discovered—well, you know." I glanced at him, looking for assurance.

"A whistle?" he asked, a seed of doubt in his voice. He'd expected a gunshot, something tangible and criminal. I shrugged, unsure of what else I had to offer.

"Yeah, a whistle. It made a combination of long and short sounds, and it was the same each time I heard it."

"Well, that could've been anything. I wouldn't worry too much about that." He tied his apron tighter behind him. "Listen, we'll see you bright and early tomorrow. This will all get sorted out," he added, dismissing me by turning into the kitchen.

I unhooked my apron and nameplate before the crowded tables made him change his mind. Between the bad night's sleep and the decayed animal, I'd had a boatload of drama before I ingested my morning caffeine. The adrenaline had turned into full-time fatigue, and time away from the restaurant could cure it.

LeeAnn pulled me in for a quick hug goodbye before hurrying to cover my tables. I debated pulling her into a longer conversation but instead let her go, her shoes squeaking in the other direction.

The parking lot was full, no evidence of the animal's impact on those wanting pancakes and eggs. I sat in the front seat, pondering my next move. I thought of my bed and down comforter, until I considered the time. It was still early on a Saturday, and my parents would question me about my sudden arrival. I didn't want to discuss the whistle again, since Renaldo had deemed it a non-starter. It wasn't worth igniting their anxiety over something so subtle.

I decided instead to explore the new greenway trail. It was our town's pride and joy, a bustling walking path with benches dedicated to bookish grandmas who'd earned their golden remembrance plaque. My mom had urged me to see the million-dollar update, complete with a center statue dedicated to Betty's memory. It wasn't muggy yet, and I could use a walk to clear my head before my parents' grand inquisition.

I looked down at my tennis shoes and started the car, with nothing to dissuade me from enjoying nature.

I dodged the hungry pedestrians making their way up the café steps and turned onto the two-lane road. The greenway was less than a mile away, but I kept the radio off, preferring the peace to the jumble of the morning DJs and traffic alerts.

The park wasn't crowded. The after-lunch visitors would begin walking off their calories in the afternoon. In the morning, the pathways were bare, empty of power walkers and marathon trainers. That suited me just fine. I longed for space to examine the morning's events. The day had been a manic muddle, and I needed time to set things right.

The benches were unoccupied. My waitressing attire consisted of shorts and a tank top, under the uniformed apron I'd left behind. The sun warmed my shoulders while I placed my keys under my front tire, an admittedly lackluster hiding place. Carrying them while walking was such a drag since they jangled like a tambourine, and the Camry wasn't prime thieving material. I'd welcome getting rid of it, but it was firmly in the camp of being too shitty to steal.

The path ahead jaunted into two pristine lanes, no pigeon poop or discarded Coke bottles in sight. My mom was right. The landscape was lovely, all winding curves, with flowerbeds of orange and yellow marigolds. They'd spared no expense, lining the stone path with sweet-smelling azalea bushes. I quickened my pace, eager for the burn in my legs that signaled my blood was flowing.

Half a mile later, I stepped into a cul-de-sac that created a tree-lined alcove. An empty bench provided a bit of shade, perfect for watching the dandelions blow. I breathed, urging my body and mind to slow. I leaned against the back of the bench, the sun beaming against my eyelids, forcing them to close.

I'd shook myself loose, gearing up for the walk back, when I heard the whistle, within earshot, right behind my shoulder. My hands clutched the bench's armrests. Without holding on to them, I might've tumbled off my seat in surprise. The molten lava metal seared my fingers, but I held on tight, trying to locate the sound.

I heard it again, the same three note rhythm, piercing through the trees behind me. It came from a small, wooded section, about seven feet from the bench. I squinted but only registered a tangle of trees and bushes. Nothing moved. There were no rapid footsteps or leaves crunching beneath anxious feet, waiting to lure me into places unknown.

My brain reached for a logical place to land. Maybe it was a bird trying to attract a mate, an innocuous ritual I'd pathologized. That was a better explanation than being stalked in broad daylight, followed to this bench dedicated to Ms. Karen Struble and her reading prowess. My muscles relaxed an inch.

I glanced again at the tree line, peering into the shadows. A dash of movement, quick as a photo flash, darted through the underbrush. I blinked and it was gone, fading into the background of the forest.

I hesitated, unsure of myself and my next move. But when I heard the whistle again, my body reacted, and I leaped. Anger pulsed through my body, my feet fast and bold against the concrete. It was one thing to try to scare me at work, quite another to taunt me. The trees blurred into a muddy smudge, but I ran in search of the sound, eager to get an answer.

I waded further into the forest, just in time to see someone duck behind a statuesque oak tree.

"I can see you!" I boasted, like I'd won a game of hide-and-seek. The pale peach flesh of an arm burned bright amongst the muted brown landscape. I'd caught him in the act, and now I wouldn't relent.

I sprinted full speed in the direction of the stalker. A stray tree root connected with my ankle, turning it sideways, the pain spreading through my leg. I collapsed, the sting of the injury catching me off guard. I scrambled to push my knee into an engagement pose, taking a moment to access the scraped skin mixed with a swath of mud. Time froze while I inventoried my injury.

Until someone cleared their throat, relinquishing their secret position.

The student from the restaurant stood tall, still with his tattered clothes and disheveled hair, missing his chemistry textbook but wearing the same resentful frown. He wore thick ski gloves and black sweatpants, both too hot for this heat. His height merged with the towering pines, surprising me since I'd only seen him seated in the booth. His skin was opaque and slick with sweat, the equivalent of a vampire taking a daytime stroll.

"What in the hell are you doing?" I lobbed at him, but my voice was withered, the opposite of putting him in his place.

He crept closer, his lean body swaying, with arms brawny and straight. I was no athlete, but the waitressing had made my legs stronger from all the hours spent on my feet. He was bigger than me, true, but not by much, and my anger fueled me forward. I got to my feet, planting them into the soft undergrowth, ready to take him to task.

"You did it, didn't you? You put that nasty badger on the steps, just because I was rude to you? And you wrote that crazy note! What kind of psycho does that? You need to… You need to get a life!"

A spew of words, with a life of their own, came out in a rush. This lunatic was in the wrong—his crimes of animal cruelty and stalking were far worse than my rudeness.

I stood up straight, angling my chin upward, my hands resting on my hips. He hadn't answered me, though I wasn't sure I had asked a question.

"Explain yourself!" I demanded, thumping my good foot for emphasis.

Instead, he stepped closer, finding his balance as he went. He lengthened his arms and pushed at my chest, harder than I expected. The force of the shove knocked me backward, and I fell to the ground, my back pushed against broken sticks.

Before I could regroup, he pounced, putting the whole of his weight against me, pinning me onto my back.

The back of my head connected with the ground, stunning me temporarily. His heaviness surprised me, the whole of his body covering mine. I squirmed, trying for a kick, but he held firm. I was a squished pancake of a girl underneath his girth. But he stayed silent, unsure of what to do other than keeping me contained.

I wiggled, letting out a good yell in the process.

"Let me go! Help!" I cried. "What are you doing?!" I screamed, the bulk of my words connecting with his right ear.

He reached his gloved fingers into my mouth, squashing my voice, his face crumpled in concentration.

"Shh…" he said, his green eyes full of pleasure. I gagged against his thick gloves, his fingers blocking my airflow.

Critical ideas flashed, including the idiocy of antagonizing a crazy person. Dread twisted my intestines, clenching them together, a tight, painful coil. My tongue rammed against his fingers, and I tried to clamp my teeth together. I watched him hold my shoulders down firmly, his hands simulating steel boulders. I turned and tried to shift my weight. I could almost lean onto my right side, finding a gap in his grip.

I darted, curling my body into itself, and his hands released. My hands clawed at the dirt and roots, desperate for a seated position.

A whack and lightning crack blurred my vision, sending a jarring constellation of discomfort that converged at my temple. My forehead tingled, and gravel chipped near my eyelashes, pieces of rock fluttering against my nose.

I toppled, my woozy mind centering on a discarded crimson rock near my ear. I watched his fingers cradle it as he raised it higher, and I braced for impact. The weight of it cut through my cheek bone, slicing deep into my jaw. The sky seemed covered in plastic-wrap, made of funhouse mirrors, everything distorted and illogical.

He continued to breathe heavily from exertion, his breath a spurting car engine on the fritz. Blood pooled in my mouth, too much of it, the thickness of it strange and lukewarm. I tried to open my mouth, to pour out the contents, but my lips sealed tight. The effort of moving my head caused a jolt of torment so severe the Earth wobbled on its axis.

He looked amused, his face full of wonder. His eyebrows were bushy, just inches from my eyelashes. I urged my fingers to find a weapon, but they wouldn't respond.

He breathed deep, careful not to touch me. I thought of my internship and the future I'd never know. The friendly roommate, the nights we'd spend on the kitchen floor, tipsy on cheap beer and cold pizza, laughing about the boys we met at the bar. There'd be rushed mornings where I'd breeze in, with a head full of unfamiliar terms, drunk on my own ambition. There'd be karaoke and trivia nights spent in smoky haunts with newfound colleagues turned friends. The money would've ballooned my bank account, providing the funds needed for a nicer car and maybe a better life.

Instead, I was just a girl, on her back, the chirp of the woods fading in and out, my throat unable to swallow. A noise gurgled, and I realized it was me. A future turned fantasy, with a much simpler reality. I was dying, the shaking of my leg my only connection to the ground, the sky, the world.

He never stopped watching me, his golden pupils narrowing, closing the only window left to me now. I saw the ghost of a smile on his mouth, the upturned crook of it, until the final shade of black.

Misery washed away every other sensation, the roar of immense torment, devoid of anything but hurt. My head exploded, firing off messages I could no longer understand. I thought I heard a whistle, but it could've been the drumbeat of my heart, a final thump, the soundtrack to all my dying dreams.

Chapter 17
Betty Allen
Date: April 2nd, 2000, 01:45 p.m.

The new kid was one of them, the backward-hat boys, full of stupid questions and cockiness. They enunciated each word, asking how many items were on the exam, like that data was crucial for acing the test. Some boys—no, most of them—just loved their own voice, even during the cracking and breaking of puberty, and the shrill squeak of their Adam's apple. I coveted that confidence, the way they sauntered in their baggy jeans, two sizes too big, ready to accept their trophy just for living.

My friends and I only spoke freely on ICQ Messenger. In class, we'd learned to work with our heads down, taciturn and thoughtful, while the boys waltzed everywhere with their hands outstretched. Gimme this, and then some more. And the system continued to function the way it was meant to.

I could play the *Tragic Kingdom* CD as loud as I wanted, singing along with Gwen about how what I'd succumbed to was making me numb. Y2K changed nothing, the truth still apparent in modern rap lyrics. The new millennium would be another re-do, another decade of keeping my mouth shut, reducing my gender to thong songs and video vixens.

I slipped out an eye roll, not even bothering to conceal it. The male bravado was worse in the math and science classes, with teachers embracing the lie that XY minds were built for greatness. The boys never questioned their status, drunk on their own distinction. Cindy sniggered at my annoyance and palmed me some lip gloss in the process.

I beamed a reply. She was my best friend, another forgotten feminist stuck in a script we didn't write. Both of us hated when the boys blasted Smash Mouth and cackled at Eminem humping a sex doll, their lupine mouths thrown back into a laugh. Cindy stifled a whisper behind her hand, her fingertips fresh with pastel polish. She sprayed a wall of Bath & Body Works Plumeria, the scent a fortress that could separate us from them. It was a temporary barrier, but the scent spoke of another long weekend spent at Cindy's house. We'd rewatch *Clueless* and cruise Myspace on her bed, dreaming of a better life.

The new kid rounded out his inane questions, proving himself to be another lemming in the line of dudes who assume they're smarter than me. Doubtful. There was only one who'd been up for the competition of valedictorian, a repeated challenger in all things scholastic. Jason LeDown and I had been locked in a dead sprint since I learned to sound out syllables with shaky crayon penmanship. I still remembered him from kindergarten, sitting tall two seats in front of me. I'd had to crane over my miniature desk to glance at his work, falling out of my seat in the process, my legs splayed across the tiled floor. I wasn't embarrassed about tumbling. I righted myself, tiny forehead creased, watching his tight penmanship, the way the letters looped and swooped. Watching him made me ashamed, the splattering of freckles on my cheeks heating up while I compared our handwriting samples. That was the moment he became my academic adversary, and our rivalry continued ever since.

At Hickory High, our war for top honors had reached a fever pitch, and the fast-approaching finals week promised one last showdown. Graduation was chomping at our heels, and both of us evenly matched. I'd give up a kidney to win or forfeit all the money on *Who Wants to be a Millionaire* if I could beat him when it really counted.

My college-bound heart was set on the Ivys, but I knew no one in our Appalachian town was Harvard bound. In rural Hickory, North Carolina, we'd be lucky to escape the boundaries of our own zip code. The town was founded on furniture and manufacturing, and most students were still encouraged to stay, safe in the trade of their family tree. The majority of local students headed to Appalachian or NC State, with the wealthy set slated for Chapel Hill or Duke. But no one I knew had crossed the Mason-Dixon line, their hopes of bigger and better limited by instate tuition.

Despite my grades, and a diary drunk on dreams for Brown or Stanford, I knew finances were a limitation. My dad worked at a garage, and my mom taught middle school math part time. Those kinds of universities weren't funded by paltry teacher salaries and state-funded health insurance. I couldn't blame my parents for their menial jobs, not when my father fell asleep in front of the television, the ink of motor oil still stretched across his hands. My mother also lacked any free time, between doctor visits for Jonathan, my brother with Down syndrome. He required transportation to physical and speech therapy, which limited her income generating hours. What he lacked in motor skills, he made up for in love. I'd never resent Jonathan, he was my constant cheerleader, saving his biggest smile for when I came home.

I learned to compromise, to accept that being valedictorian would allow admission to any state school of my choice. I'd scrimp and save money, load up on work study offerings, and make the most of my free college education. But all that was predicated on receiving my reward, doused in tassels, my speech already secured in my desk drawer.

Jason was the outlier in my plan. He was naturally bright, never one to study or use a calculator yet still broke the grading curve in most of our classes. He broadcasted his laziness, his arms a hard desk pillow, preferring to sleep through most of our AP classes. His stained hoodie covered his greasy black hair and served to hide his headphones, which connected to the secret CD player in his desk. The intro notes of Linkin Park blared in his ears, his attention to the teacher terminated.

That was why I hated him. The way he shrugged yet scribbled down every right answer on the pop quiz made me sick with jealousy. Sometimes dark thoughts churned in my brain about ways to sabotage him, to create an accusation that would tip the scales in my favor. Cindy warned me to cool it, parroting her mother's triteness about comparison being the thief of joy. But I couldn't stand how Jason plucked down A's like cherry-red tree apples, while I studied and cursed behind him.

The bell rang, releasing me from my cares into the crowded hallway, my mood remaining bitter. I hunched my shoulders, books at my chest, my mind a million miles away.

"Why do you do this to yourself?" Cindy asked, calling me out on my piss-poor temperament before I'd even sighed. "I can't even! I know you're thinking about the end of the school year again. Chillax. LeDown is, like, *sooo* on the outskirts of everything. You act like he's extra. But you've won in every way that matters. Everybody thinks so. They aren't going to let Jerk-Off Jason represent our class."

Cindy chomped on her Hubba Bubba bubblegum tape, squinting at herself in the miniature locker mirror, which was scrunched amid countless Coldplay posters. She handed me a piece of gum, securing a new twin pink wad into her cheek, sticking the discarded piece onto the wall of her locker.

"I know, I know. You're right. I'm not trying to be a Debbie Downer. It's just so close, and I want it to be over."

She closed her locker, leaning casually against it, her high ponytail threatening to get caught in the locker slats.

"What you should be focused on is the party at Calvin's. Or we can skip and just hang, whatever. But, like, this mood or whatever needs to peace out." Cindy was lecture ready, her Limited sweater displaying her crossed arms.

"We don't have much time left, and I'd prefer to hang with my BFF instead of focusing on the skeezy boys at school. You're the one that matters to me. Now, are you going to spend the weekend studying, or are you going to take those new Steve Madden boots out for a spin? Seriously, Bets, just don't go there, 'kay?"

She popped a bubble, giving me her patented girl-boss smile, her head cocked in my direction.

"Oh, and FYI, there's a Leonardo DiCaprio marathon this weekend. I'm talking prime Leo like *Basketball Diaries* and *Romeo + Juliet*, which I know you cannot resist. Even Jonathan loves that movie. I gotta bounce, but call me later on my phone line? Thank God my parents totally caved, and this way Mom can't listen in anymore. Peace out!"

Cindy sashayed down the hall, leaving a wake of glitter and body splash, and I was tempted to follow. But even a river of Red Bull wouldn't be enough to salvage my senior year. I'd traded Zimas for energy drinks, slurping down the sugar to cram in extra study hours after school. I'd maxed out my volunteer hours candy striping at the Frye Regional Hospital but still sacrificed sleep and my social life for more textbook time. Twice this week, I'd woken up with my fingers twisted around a highlighter, an angry crease pockmarking my face, the result of sleeping on my science textbook.

The problem was physics, or more specifically, rotational motion and dynamics. I'd stayed in the study hall every day, the ticking clock and Dr. Brown's tapping foot providing a distracting soundtrack. So much of that class seemed made-up, undeserving of its inclusion in the science department. This was not biology, with its vertebrae and fossils, the tangible taxonomies laid out in classic straight lines. Physics was la-la land, packaged with gravity and reciprocal force, which for me only created a blooming headache and sense of despair. I dutifully packed my marbled notebook with indecipherable notes. The tsunami of frustration kept me anxious, while I copied from the chalkboard words and charts that looked like pictographs.

There was no one at home that could help me. My mom was too busy attending to Jonathan, forever fearful he may choke or experience another mild seizure. Between her late-night work grading papers and her full-time caregiving duties, Mom was more of a ghost than a parent, barely keeping it all together. She never complained about my brother or the toll his illness took on her life, but sometimes her eyes would get misty for no reason, and I'd see all the stress piled upon her, thick as Jenga blocks. There was no way I'd add even an ounce of worry onto her hearty back, especially since I feared my problems would collapse her, drowning Mom for good in all she juggled. She was too important to sacrifice for my troubles, and anyway she'd majored in finance, eons away from gravity, Newton, and apple trees.

My dad was all blue collar, working the long hours demanded of a car mechanic, with grease-stained fingers, hard calluses, and sweat that bled through his uniform. He belonged at the garage, where everything had a place, no sickness or medical bills found amongst the wrenches and tires. He probably had good spatial reasoning skills, since he'd eyeball a bad carburetor from miles away or diagnose a fledging engine by its rattles. But Dad kept his words and his location locked up tight, barely home before the owls squawked a hello. It was too loud to work at the car shop, with the squeals of tires and roars of engines providing a thunderous soundtrack. The shop kept him gone, and that left me hunched over my homework, doodling in the margins, on the stiff-backed chair at our nicked dining room table.

My notebook was full of half-done equations, and the more I looked at them, the less I understood. As a latch-key kid, the loneliness felt palatable. I was hyper responsible and alone, solving my own problems by default.

I laid my head on the table. I had a B average in Dr. Brown's class, which was going to sink my GPA. With only the wooden oak grooves at my witness, the truth was clear, written in equations I didn't understand. I'd lose all I'd worked for because of this class. I chewed on my pencil eraser to keep from crying. I was frantic for a lifeline, something or someone concrete to stabilize the world of movement and stability.

My fingers shook, my brain soaking in pessimistic thoughts, right at the finish line. Jason would sail ahead, his tree-branch fingers gripping the final prize, his eyes boring straight into mine, a smug smile framing his gawky features.

It was undeserved, and worse, it was unfair. Jason never stayed afterward for physics and was the first to turn in every test. I knew it impressed Dr. Brown, the way his proud smile spread across his mustached mouth when Jason brandished his paper. Dr. Brown didn't even remove his red pen. Instead, he'd grade Jason's paper on the spot, nodding and never uncapping anything because no mistakes were made. Perfect score, every time, while I pushed back frustrated tears to begin question five.

I could fuel a power grid with how much hatred I felt for Jason LeDown and his easy intelligence. In a semester, I'd gone from star pupil to second string, the proof found in Dr. Brown's downcast eyes fixated on his wristwatch, his glasses fogged with disappointment.

Jason was the only person who could help me, and the most

likely to say no. For such a bitter rivalry, Jason and I never spoke directly to each other. I had no idea where he lived, and I'd checked ICQ for an online presence but found none. My account name, BookishBets, flashed down a list of accessible friends, but Jason was sketchy, so it tracked that he wasn't on the web.

The details about Jason were sparse. He had a younger sister, but the age gap was lengthy, so I'd never met her. Rumors began early about him, a modern-day Boo Radley, since he skipped every football game, quick to reject the school spirit. He kept to himself, which only perpetuated the gossip, as did the poor hygiene and formal clothes meant for a homeschooler. No one I knew would converse with Jason unless they had to, content instead to label him a nerd, his long arms swinging too fast, his used Jansport bookbag wedged too high on his shoulders. Cindy swore she spied him smoking cowboy killer cigarettes and glaring at the swinging bridge next to Alleghany Park.

"Bets, the click of his lighter was the only sound for miles, and OMG, I got out of there so fast. I used to be like whatever to all those rumors, but now I dunno. He's loner weird, you know what I mean? So trench-coat mafia."

That was about a month ago, but he could've created a hide-out, some insidious lair where he could suck on sweet nicotine and complement his recluse routine.

Either way, it was settled. The time had come for a hat-in-hand conversation, and Cindy had gifted me the treasure map of his whereabouts. I resolved to find him on Monday and air my vulnerabilities aloud, the only avenue for aid I had left.

I let Dr. Brown know he was off the hook for tutoring. He couldn't hide his relief, his cheeks alight in pink, before he muttered an "Are you sure?" just 'cause he felt bad for me. I promised to address the problems solo, and he didn't even muster a rebuttal. Instead, he packed his briefcase at a breakneck pace, fumbling with a pencil that fell to the floor, his forehead scattered with sweat. He grabbed his notepad, glancing at me like I'd change my mind and saddle him with another study session. It made me feel worse, my teacher's mad dash to the door, and all my unanswered questions died inside my mouth, drowning in shame. Dr. Brown couldn't get away from me fast enough, and that added another layer of defeat onto my sinking shoulders.

The hunt was on. Jason's locker was near the gym since they were assigned in alphabetical order. I found him with his knees on the floor, his back curled catlike, adjusting his mountainous height to adapt to the lower locker. His threadbare backpack slumped next to his tower of textbooks, with crumpled papers peeking out from his half-zipped sack.

I swayed from foot to foot, hating myself yet eating my pride, the scent of desperation wafting off me. If it meant I'd win, I'd chomp through buckets of humiliation to get what I wanted. I just had to keep my eyes centered on the prize and do whatever it took to secure it.

"Hey, Jason," I said nonchalantly, leaning against the locker, going for cavalier. He began transplanting the books one by one into his backpack, his spacing quick and compact. He didn't make eye contact or react to my greeting.

I cleared my throat and tried again. "So… umm."

"What is it? What do you want?" His frustrated tone was barely audible in the crowded hallway, his eyes and posture content to ignore me.

"Listen. I… Well, I wanted to ask you…" I stalled, willing the words to come out. "The truth is…" I took a deep breath and thought, *Oh to hell with it, tell the truth.* He'd pity me, but I could use that and rustle up some tears. "Well, I'm struggling in physics. Maybe you knew that already. I've tried, and I'm not able to figure it out, even after studying with Dr. Brown every day. I thought that you could explain it to me. Or to teach me the way you do it. Since I, uh, know you know what you're doing."

He paused, his shoulders smacking into his locker, enough to steady him or provide strength to continue the conversation. He heaved a heavy sigh and looked up; his eyes zeroed onto mine. They were green, the color of emeralds and twice as intense. Almost pretty, with lengthy eyelashes outstretched, amidst caterpillar thick eyebrows. I'd never been this close to Jason before, never noticed any of his features, like the dash of freckles across his upturned nose.

"You need *my* help?" he stated, disbelief making his voice rise an octave.

"I do." I slumped down, wishing I could fast forward into the future. I felt dizzy with humiliation, the heat of my emotions searing onto my skin, a personal brand of mortification.

"Wait, say it again… *You* need *my* help?"

I bowed my head, in that moment acquiescing to his greater skill and despising him for it. That smug dash in his syllables, the sneer, it all made me want to call this off. But I needed him, and that was the very worst part. I couldn't afford for him to say no.

"Well," he considered. "No. That's not gonna happen." He slammed his locker with a satisfied smack and swung his backpack, almost pelting me in the process.

"Umm! Ouch! Excuse you!" I stepped back, surprised he could move so quick.

He shook his head to reject me again before jogging to the double doors that led outside.

"What is your deal?" I skittered close to him, attempting to block his way. I'd imagined I'd have to work for his help, but I didn't think he'd flatly refuse, with no negotiation offered. We were colleagues, both of us Hickory High School's top pupils, who'd shared classes since before we could read.

"No, just… no." He cut in front of me with a swift stride, no longer interested in debating.

I trailed him, confused. He'd shot me down, strangling my air of politeness with one conversational punch.

"Wait, stop!" I ran, panting to match his pace. "Oh, come on, Jason! You're being ridiculous!" I yelled to his back, his silhouette disappearing around the side of the brick building. I was left in his shadow, my hands empty and trembling, mortified at his swift public rejection.

I walked home, my feet kicking the gravel, embarrassed and angry at Jason's callousness, the conversation loop on repeat. I slammed the door to an empty house, a scribbled Post-it Note directing me to the casserole in the freezer. I debated kicking the table, discouraged at another night of baffling equations and a meal so sodium laced I could barely choke it down.

I didn't want to look over my homework. Even my bookbag made me frown, a reminder of the pointlessness of it all. Instead, I went outside, trusting that my backyard would energize me or provide me with my next good idea.

A lone soccer ball rested next to our shed. I kicked it so hard it almost jumped the fence, the smack of it against the wood proof of my fury. I fumed and kicked it again, my mind reeling with the iniquity of Jason's lack of respect for the competition we'd shared for so long. My foot ached, and the anger bled into sadness, my temper transformed into a puddle of unruly sobs.

"Stupid Jason LeDown!" I shouted, kicking the fence with my tennis shoe, burrowing it deep into the wood. I continued to rage against the fence until my emotions leaked onto the grass. My eyesight got blurry, and I stumbled inside, the house silent and waiting. I grabbed my physics textbook, the very symbol of my incompetence, and tossed it onto the kitchen floor. I debated burning it but instead left it discarded in favor of curling up on the couch. I cried out my frustration amid my brother's backup crutches and the decorative pillows smelling of Febreze. The tears dried up, in time with my mom's car in the driveway, and I tucked my emotions tight.

The next day, after discharging all my feelings and snot onto our secondhand couch, I woke up re-energized. Maybe Jason valued perseverance, yearned for validation and extended effort. I'd seek him out, and this time, I'd demand to be heard. I deserved that much, since I was his equal, or I had been until I admitted my stupidity. He owed me a conversation, and this time I'd be sure to get one.

When the last bell of the day rang, I sprinted to his locker, almost flatlining a freshman in the process. But Jason was absent, perhaps anticipating another awkward encounter. I observed a swath of gelled black hair and tight pale shoulders ahead of the burgeoning crowd. He was dodging me, but I could catch up if I broke into a full-on run.

My shoes tapped hard against the concrete, my staccato breath coming out in shattered spurts.

"Hey, wait!" I cried, sprinting to him. "Come on, dude. Just, like, wait."

I collapsed when we were shoulder to shoulder, my air coming out in little puffs. I pressed on, letting my resentment energize me, while Jason eyed me warily. I tried to smooth my irritation into a pleasantry, but the torrent of my dislike for Jason was housed in my soul. This was definitely a fake-it-till-you-make-it situation.

"Okay, so here I am again," I began, winded from the sprint, my words spotty. "I know that I asked you yesterday for help, and you said no. But I'm here, and I can make tutoring worthwhile for you." I squeaked out the last bit of it and hated how it sounded, like I was begging, or worse, willing to trade something for his tutelage.

"I mean, I can pay you. I have a little money saved up, if that would change your mind," I clarified, eager to set the terms of the agreement. "Or if you could just tell me what you want, then I can try to make that happen, too. Look," I stopped, planting my feet down firm, "this isn't easy for me, asking for help. But I am willing to do what it takes; I promise you that." My chin met my chest. "Just tell me what I need to do."

He slowed, his body slanting sideways, his face full of impending refusal.

"I *told* you no yesterday. I meant it. It's ludicrous to think I'd change my mind for you, Betty. Or do you friends call you Bets? Whatever. I just don't care." He said my name like it was synonymous with trash, the syllables drawn out in disgust, appropriate only to discard. He marched on, his pace a conversational dead end.

"But why?"

"Because I just. don't. want. to, Betty." My name was his favorite curse, all niceties removed. He cut his eyes at me, hatred jumbling his features until they obscured.

My hands warped into a fist, a tirade of my own on deck.

"You're a loser, Jason LeDown. I might not know physics, and I'll admit that," I uttered, lacing every word with my wrath. "But you're a weird son of a bitch with no friends, a nasty ugly scarecrow with a big brain but that's all. And that is something without a fix. There's no cure for what you are sick with, psycho."

I glared at him, certain I'd wounded his ego.

"I'll find a way to correct my physics grade, you can bet on that. But what is wrong with you is permanent." I aimed the last phrase like a dagger, bursting his over-the-top confidence.

He was subdued, registering my outburst. He didn't move or glare, didn't offer a witty comeback. Instead, he stared at me, his face frozen, with unblinking eyes, like a trance had overtaken him. I lengthened my posture, daring him to contradict me, but instead he did nothing at all. I watched him regain consciousness in parts, the swift tightening of his jaw, the squeak of his loafers, a quick turn of his head, leaving me on the sidewalk.

That night I cried myself to sleep. I felt low down, my soul heavy with the meanness I'd flung at Jason because I'd been turned down. It wasn't his fault that I was struggling, and he didn't owe me anything. We weren't friends, barely even acquaintances. Instead, I hung every hard thing on his skinny shoulders instead of taking ownership for my dilemma. It wasn't right, and my regret produced tangled sheets and insomnia. I promised to atone, my apology drafted in sleepy sentences that I hoped I'd remember tomorrow.

I left my last class early, getting outside the front double doors before the throng of upperclassmen descended into the parking lot. This time I'd catch Jason before he sprinted away or got lost in the zombie herd of lumbering students. I hung left by the outdoor awning, watching the doors spread wide amidst the crowd. Jason's gangly frame made him noticeable, bouncing in an arrhythmic rhythm, the opposite of gliding, with jerky mismatched steps. He walked like Ichabod Crane, and another flash of remorse swirled in my stomach. His social awkwardness made him easy prey, and I'd pounced, ready to spread vitriol over all his appendages.

I can do hard things, I reasoned, while keeping a wide berth between us. My parents raised me right, to be the kind of person to own my mistakes and learn from them. Jason already knew the worst thing about me, that I couldn't outsmart or outstudy him this time. I'd take my punishment, let his snideness fall heavy on my shoulders, because I deserved it. Appropriately chagrined, I'd head to Cindy's house to sink in my sorrows. This way, I'd grad-uate salutatorian, but I'd still have my character.

I stalked Jason, his frame sauntering up Allagash Road, before he ducked behind a gaggle of trees next to Allegany Park, where Cindy had spotted him before. I hadn't been here since middle school. This park was close to our school zone but remained deserted, not big enough to attract families, not small enough to demolish. It sat abandoned on the outskirts of a tiny forest, the path obscured by bushes and brambles. I waited for Jason to tread deeper into the tree line before following him. Best to address him on his turf, appropriate to the level of deference required.

It was quiet, no birdsong twitter or snatch of laughter, no chatter other than a solitary chirp and a quick rustle in the woods. The trees provided shade and shadows, the makings of a gloomy fairytale. I crept closer, watching Jason push through the undergrowth, a man on a mission to the creek bed. He didn't dawdle but careened forward, no stroll found in his footsteps.

He wasn't aware he had a visitor. I kept low to the ground, my knees locked together, away from the main trail. He stopped next to a dank embankment, the musty smell of the creek tickling my nose. It wasn't a rushing river, but the flowing water tinkled a refrain, and Jason leaned back, his face skyward, as tranquil as our forest surroundings.

I spied a white lawn chair tilted on its side. Beside it was a midsize cooler, with discarded Coke cans scattered on the ground beside it. The chair made indentions in the silt, and Jason settled into his makeshift hideout. He righted the chair, dusting off the dirty armrests. I glanced around for a fishing pole but saw only pebbles and sediment.

So this was where he went after school. A smile played on my lips, the ho-hum hideout providing solitude from our bustling school. All those audacious rumors about him drinking bat blood and murmuring incantations seemed silly when paired with this wannabe Johnny Appleseed. He spent his days communing with nature, not drawing pentagrams on his hands. The pariah of the school was a hippie, content to rest in the solitude of the trees and his private babbling brook. My mood declined further, since I hadn't just insulted him, I'd misjudged him.

Jason collapsed into the chair, his lengthy legs outstretched, and let out a contented sigh, all very *honey I'm home*. He didn't take off his shoes but scooted his feet next to the water's edge. He closed his eyes, the very image of taking a load off, before opening the cooler lid. I expected crackers or Doritos, or wriggling earthworms, and I stood to speak before I stole any more of his free time.

I stopped when I saw him cradle a gigantic brown bullfrog. It moved, trying to twist from his grasp, the toad's foot stuck in Jason's palm. He held onto it tight, one hand griping the slick warty belly, while it continued to kick and try to weasel from his grasp.

I crouched back to my knees, wary of what was happening.

With his left hand, he reached into his back pocket and removed a switchblade. The gleam of it caught the sunlight, sending shards of light into the woods. It was not a Boy Scout knife, not used for opening bottles or releasing packages. It was intimidating with a curved dagger and thick handle, the sheath bulky, wrapping the knife like a gift.

Jason moved the blade slowly, savoring it with languid movements. He admired it, outstretched in his left hand, his right hand devoted to securing the toad. His shoulders curved closer, his breathing turning into a pant. I watched him balance the knife, hovering over the toad's rib cage.

I squinted, unsure of what I was witnessing, until with snake-strike quickness, Jason jammed the knife into the toad's stomach, severing its spine. It didn't squeal, it wasn't a cat, but it writhed, the pain evident in its desperate attempt to escape, the trail of green slime oozing from the wound.

It was Jason that moaned when the neon-yellow fat entrails released in his hand. He squished the insides in and out of his fingers like the intestines were Play-Doh, emitting another grunt of pleasure. The gutted toad continued to writhe, its leg movements slowing into a spasm. Jason twirled the intestines around his fingers, like he was gripping his lover's hair, dropping the knife onto the creek bed. He used his left hand to undo his belt buckle, unzipping his pants, his right hand still covered in the dying animal.

"Stop that!" I screeched, blowing my cover, barreling from behind the trees. He had to stop; I couldn't witness another moment of his sick arousal.

He toppled from his chair, surprised at being interrupted. His eyes blazed with fire from pleasure thwarted. He stumbled to his feet, the discarded frog thrown to the ground, with bits of its guts smeared on his belt buckle and hands. He wiped his hands nervously on his jeans, staining them with blood and entrails.

"You followed me," he stated, his inflection serious. "And now, again, you think you can tell me what to do." He angled himself in my direction, his arms dangling at his sides.

I recentered, arms crossed, waiting for him to continue, to attempt some explanation for the horror I'd witnessed. Instead, he seemed unconcerned with my presence, his posture full of shrugs. His simple statements paired with his forced serenity felt dangerous. I was in his territory, and yet he was unperturbed, though I'd witnessed his sexual proclivities, the toad guts resting on the space next to his crotch. The gossipers would have a field day when they learned Jason masturbated to frog guts. I'd found my leverage and it was triumphant.

I stepped closer, ready to negotiate. My fingertips ground against my hip bones, ready and willing to initiate a bribe. I stalled, noticing the frog's body deflating like a balloon, which made my stomach churn, the slashed-out belly continuing to leak fluid. Jason shrugged and sat back down, waiting me out.

I strode to the chair, angling my knees against the back of it, secure in the many options that lay ahead. I opened my mouth to begin, but he tipped himself back, using all his weight to collapse the chair. The sudden movement buckled my knees, and I slid backward, onto the slope of the hill. He aimed a kick at my side, and I toppled, the back of my head colliding against a large rock. The sky above me bent, saturated with small, intertwined circles. Jason leaned over me, so tall he looked otherworldly, an ogre with an iridescent glower.

I tried to sit up, the wet ground making a ring in my low-rise khakis. I wasn't fast enough. Jason tackled me with a linebacker block, the bulk of him connecting hard against my chest. The full force of his body weight slammed my head against the boulder again. My brain bounced, the impact creating a loud crack against the lower part of my cranium. I screamed, as an earthquake splintered by brain, dividing it in half. A warm ooze dripped down my neck, connecting with the collar of my shirt.

The occipital lobe, I rehearsed, the words on my lips. The back of the head, reserved for motor movement, not a place you'd want to take any damage. A bullet of pain signaled trouble. The tangy smell of blood soaked my brown hair, the trickle turning substantial, and I reached my hand back to find it soaking red.

"Jason," I murmured. "I'm hurt." It was obvious now an ambulance was needed, and I tried not stare at my blood-covered palm. A jagged force, much worse than a migraine, slashed against my head, the sensation akin to a lobotomy, cleaving my brain down the middle.

Or the corpus callosum, I remembered, my anatomy class once again bubbling up to the surface, providing a backdrop of alarm.

"Just an accident, though," I wheezed. "No, no one's fault. But need help. P-p-please." I gasped, the brief conversation pocketing all my energy, the mental equivalent of running a seven-minute mile.

"It's wrong," I said, but my words slurred. I couldn't make them sound right. "I hurt, feel bad, b-b-bad." It felt like I was speaking through cotton, my throat congealed, with a tongue twice its normal size.

Jason scooted to my right side, his face resting on his head, mimicking the pose of *The Thinker*. I wondered if I was the new frog, and dread drummed through my body. I urged myself to sit up, but my legs disobeyed, my toes refusing to comply.

I instructed my hands to rise, but the searing whoosh of agony in my head claimed all my attention. I gagged, a reaction to the train barreling through my mind. I ordered my pinkie finger to lift, but it betrayed me. My eyesight began to falter, with blinks of Jason's face, a View-Master toy.

"Jas—Jason," I whispered, no longer trusting my voice to function. My heart pounded heavily, and static obscured my vision.

Jason watched me, his face studious, my death a sequence to memorize. His gaze lingered, his face close to my neck without touching me, his eyes wide, watching the blood soak through my shirt. He was inches from my face, his mouth moving, but I couldn't register any sound.

I wanted to twist away from him, to shake my head, to howl, but my spine stayed immobile, my wounds pulsing into the dirt.

"Help-hh-h-h," I murmured, my back stiff, straining against my last word, with eyes that bounced uncontrollably. My head pounded, my lungs full of copper, of blood, smothering my nostrils, the taste rusty and vile in my mouth. I pictured my teeth tinged in red, with molars jagged and broken, my injuries too numerous to count.

There's too much blood, I knew, my eyesight disappearing in swatches, my final location swimming. For a moment, there was nothing, the blankness of a page, and then Jason's face re-appeared.

He cocked his head, observing me, his upturned nose sequestering my vision.

The look on his face was not fear or regret. It was curiosity. The blood dripping from my skull was just alchemy, my wounds molecules, this scene a lab, the rock an instrument. A smile, crescent-moon–shaped, formed, the green of his electric eyes squinting. My wounds were fascinating to him, passion sparkling over his features, my wilting becoming his attraction.

He licked his lips, and it looked like love.

My bee-stung tongue failed me; my heart creaked its last. A montage of Jonathan began, his first steps into my arms, the awareness he wouldn't understand what happened to me, would never know how my heart cracked and healed at his arrival. The police at the door, my parents wailing, the commotion this would cause.

I'm not here for your enjoyment, I wanted to howl, my furor enough to disrupt the whole town. The absence of a first kiss, the graduation tassels left hanging in my closet. Cindy, curled in a ball on her bed, refusing to leave her bedroom.

A rancid taste pooled at the back of my throat, made of mold and bleu cheese, the strain of swallowing too big a bite. No words escaped. Fireworks of suffering roared their release, but my body remained unresponsive, a sculpture stuck in burning torment.

The last thing I saw were the gold centers of his green eyes, his irises honey colored. He wasn't beautiful, but his eyes were lovely, freeze framed for eternity, close enough to touch. They were my universe, until another smile.

Small, dainty almost, like he'd discovered something new, satisfied down to his translucent skin.

This was his dissertation, my death a gift, my last memory a snapshot of his face, imprinted with joy, engraved forever on the canvas of my mind.

Epilogue

They hardly needed to vote, so sure were they on the outcome. It was unanimous, their wrath unspoken, running wild beneath their blue-black veins. They had re-lived their last moments, through gritted teeth and buckling knees, through bruises, shrieks, and endless wails. All died two deaths, but this time together.

Betty, Tina, Sarah, Leslie, Chrissy, Sheena, Sherry, Lena, Debbie, and Ashley.

They chanted their names, just to hear them, just to remember, even if the world forgot.

They'd been through a war, and Jason LeDown was their collective adversary, his name hissed with indignation, with hate.

Maybe some would judge them and preach forgiveness, a righting of earthly wrongs. But the time for mercy had long passed, their collective minds set to a righteous fury.

A jumble of hands grasped the lever, fingernails clashing and *digits interlocking, pulling down hard. No one hesitated. Jason screamed when the portal opened, and they watched with unrepentant eyes. A tentacled dark creature seared his skin with a touch. He capitulated with an inhuman howl, his body dragged into the open hole. The darkness swallowed up the rest of his anguish.*

Closed-mouth smiles volleyed around the room.

No regret was found, not a teaspoon, not a drop. Regular Hell wasn't enough punishment for the likes of Jason LeDown.

Long may he rot.

They nodded, their hands clasped together in a semi-circle.

Their decision yielded no internal peace, no vindication. Fairness would've been that they'd been spared or overlooked, not victims of his bloodlust and need. It was finished, and it was satisfactory, but don't call it right.

This was an honest verdict, not a happy one, a solution rendered, but justice wasn't served.

There's no closure for complicated grief.

That's what others couldn't understand. The damnation of Jason LeDown would not erase his evil deeds and offered no comfort to those he harmed. There were no toothy grins, no high fives, just the solemn bond of those who wished their lives ended differently.

Even in death, there was no freedom from him, the worst of his deeds already a memory, of lives extinguished before the living was through.

THE END

Acknowledgments

First, I'm thankful for my husband, Bruce Baker, for encouraging me to follow my literary dreams, and taking the children out of the house so I could have the space and energy to write. I love you so very much.

I'm also wildly thankful for the staff at Genius Books & Media, especially Leya and Steven Booth. Your belief in me and my writing has been life changing and I am so happy to bring this novel to fruition. Thank you for supporting me and providing a treasure trove of book wisdom. Thank you for your edits, and your attention to detail.

Thank you to Igor Andrich for the beautiful cover design and for his patience with me while crafting it.

I remain in the debt of the staff at the Sharon Forks Library, especially my friend and editor Alicia Cavitt for all her wonderful ideas and her love of novels.

To my best friends, Hayley Trimble, Katie Jackson, and Mackenzie Crigger, for being there when the bottom fell out and staying to make sure we were all going to be okay.

I'm also so blessed to have two of the best kiddos in the world, Addy and Julian Baker. You are much too young to read this book, but I hope you can enjoy it when you're older. Your creativity is a wonder to behold!

Finally, thank you to the readers. Before I was a published author, I was (and remain) an avid reader, and I am continually thankful for anyone who prioritizes books, creativity, literature, and a love of words. You truly make the world go round, and I've never met a reader I didn't like.